Empowering Workers and Clients for Organizational Change

Also available from Lyceum Books, Inc.

Advisory Editor: Thomas M. Meenaghan, *New York University*

SOCIAL WORK AND SOCIAL DEVELOPMENT: PERSPECTIVES FROM INDIA AND
THE UNITED STATES
Edited by Shweta Singh

SOCIAL SERVICE WORKPLACE BULLYING: A BETRAYAL OF GOOD INTENTIONS
By Kathryn Brohl

NAVIGATING HUMAN SERVICE ORGANIZATIONS, THIRD EDITION
By Rich Furman and Margaret Gibelman

THE RECOVERY PHILOSOPHY AND DIRECT SOCIAL WORK PRACTICE
By Joseph Walsh

BEST PRACTICES IN COMMUNITY MENTAL HEALTH: A POCKET GUIDE
Edited by Vikki L. Vandiver

CHILD AND FAMILY PRACTICE: A RELATIONAL APPROACH
By Shelly Cohen Konrad

SOCIAL WORK PRACTICE WITH FAMILIES: A RESILIENCY-BASED APPROACH,
SECOND EDITION
By Mary Patricia Van Hook

GETTING YOUR MSW: HOW TO SURVIVE AND THRIVE IN A SOCIAL WORK
PROGRAM
By Karen M. Sowers and Bruce A. Thyer

SOCIAL WORK WITH HIV AND AIDS: A CASE-BASED GUIDE
By Diana Rowan and Contributors

CIVIC YOUTH WORK: COCREATING DEMOCRATIC YOUTH SPACES
Edited by Ross VeLure Roholt, Michael Baizerman, and R. W. Hildreth

Empowering Workers and Clients for Organizational Change

Marcia B. Cohen
University of New England

Cheryl A. Hyde
Temple University

LYCEUM
BOOKS, INC.

Chicago, Illinois

© 2014 by Lyceum Books, Inc.

Published by
  LYCEUM BOOKS, INC.
  5758 S. Blackstone Avenue
  Chicago, Illinois 60637
  773-643-1903 fax
  773-643-1902 phone
  lyceum@lyceumbooks.com
  www.lyceumbooks.com

6 5 4 3 2 1 14 15 16 17 18

ISBN 978-1-935871-34-7

Cover image by © Pakmor | Dreamstime.com

Printed in the United States of America.

Library of Congress Cataloging-in-Publication Data

  Empowering workers and clients for organizational change / [edited by] Marcia B. Cohen, University of New England, Cheryl A. Hyde, Temple University, Chicago, Illinois.
    pages cm
  Includes index.
  ISBN 978-1-935871-34-7 (pbk. : alk. paper)
  1. Social work administration. 2. Social service. 3. Organizational change.
I. Cohen, Marcia B., 1950– II. Hyde, Cheryl A.
  HV40.E466   2014
  361.0068'4—dc23
                                         2013009839

Chapter 11 was previously published as Cohen, M. B. (1994). Overcoming organizational obstacles to forming empowerment groups: A consumer advisory board for homeless clients. *Social Work*, *39*(6), 742–749. Reprinted with permission from the publisher.

We dedicate this book to the memories of Shirley Cohen (1925–1972) and Philip Hyde (1928–2010), and to our students, the social change agents of the future.

Contents

Figures and Tables

Figures

Tables

Foreword

During the 1960s, social work began to attend to possibilities of social change we had only dreamed about in prior decades. Stimulated by a wave of progressive legislation that provided public resources to support programs aimed at eliminating juvenile delinquency, hunger, substandard housing, and poverty, the literature of social work began to focus attention on change—broad-scale, societal change. Our literature in practice, specifically group work, community organizing, program development, and social policy, became preoccupied with issues of *change*. As that era and its associated public resources passed, a new focus of change practice began to emerge. We began to turn our attention to a much narrower but quite important change focus: organizational change.

Those of us writing about organizational change practice characterized these interventions as efforts initiated from the service delivery level of the human service organization to modify organizational policy, procedures, or operations to more effectively serve the needs of the organization's clients or to expand services to a wider client group. The practice was predicated on the notion that those who operate at the service delivery level are most in touch with client need and most aware of possible unintended negative consequences of the organization's operations in the lives of its clients. The challenge that such practice poses, of course, is that although lower-level workers may be particularly aware of what needs to be changed, they have neither the authority nor the power to directly execute such change. This literature focused attention on a practice in which relatively low-power workers developed a broad range of effective means of working through others to accomplish organizational change designed to advance the interests of their clients. Organizational change literature matured in the 1980s and early 1990s and instruction in the practice of organizational change became increasingly popular in the curricula of schools of social work. However, by the end of the century we were failing to sustain the literature of organizational change. As we enter the second decade of the twenty-first century, the need for a contemporary text in organizational change practice has become increasingly apparent.

This work by Cohen and Hyde is clearly overdue and will be welcomed by many. The thrust of the work is responsive to the classroom: that is, it is designed for use as a text to teach students in social work about organizational change practice from below. The first part of the volume offers three chapters written by the editors and a fourth coauthored by Brett Seabury and the editors that together summarize and build upon the primary arguments for and insights associated with the original literature of organizational change. Part II presents chapters by guest authors whose case stories provide lively examples of organizational change theory and practice. These seven chapters are written by social work academics and practitioners who are clearly steeped in the teaching and practice of organizational change practice. The chapters are rich with illustrations of change practice and insights into how change can be effected by students and line workers in a wide range of practice settings. Part III of this volume is unique. It consists of three papers written by social work students who describe change projects executed as part of their master's education. Students using this text are certain to find these exemplars useful.

For quite a few years, there has been a consensus within the social work education community for the need to update and advance our literature on organizational change. Thanks to Marcia Cohen and Cheryl Hyde, we now have a very strong contribution to this effort.

Stephen Holloway
Dean Emeritus, Barry University School of Social Work
Miami, Florida
December 2012

Preface

Organizational change is a critical area of social work practice. Our text is a response to the need for all social work students to learn the knowledge and skills necessary to bring about change in their agencies in order to create environments more conducive to addressing the concerns of clients or constituents, as well as being supportive of staff at all levels. Unlike many books about organizational practice, the emphasis in this book is on change from below—in other words, change brought about by low-power actors.

Low-power actors include direct, community, or line staff; volunteers; students; and clients and constituents—groups that have the least formal power or authority in human service agencies. Low-power social workers typically have the greatest amount of contact with clients and constituents. They are frequently the best informed about areas in which client or constituent needs are being inadequately met or not met at all, which can then be the impetus for organizational change. Clients and constituents are change agents when, for example, they initiate (or help initiate) demands for more-responsive programs and services, worker behavior, or agency procedures.

Social workers, however, often lack the training and skills necessary to bring about change in their organizations. We believe that it is the responsibility of all social workers, in all practice settings, to intervene at the organizational level on behalf of client or constituent needs. This can mean working for changes within the worker's agency as well as being aware of and responsive to the larger community of organizations that the agency is embedded in. Thus, it is critically important that social work students learn the theory and practice of organizational change. The purpose of this text is to prepare students to engage in organizational change practice from below.

Change from below is distinguished from change initiated at the top of the organizational hierarchy; the skills involved in the former are very different from those that agency managers or leaders usually employ. Having less-formal authority in the agency, low-power staff need to discover and mobilize resources and sources of power that will help them to bring about change. They also need to consider how to collaborate or partner with the clients and constituents in ways that empower everyone. Unlike individual interventions, organizational interventions have the potential to benefit a large number of clients or constituents. Social workers have a professional, ethical obligation to their clients and the communities that clients come from to seek remedies for and prevention of inadequate responses to client needs. This text will provide students with a practice methodology geared toward enabling social workers with less-formal power to influence those with more-formal power. It is through this type of influence that change from below comes about. We recognize that social workers generally gain organizational power over the course of their careers, and believe that lessons learned as low-power actors can inform their approach to future change efforts at subsequent points in their organizational tenure.

ORGANIZATION

This text is organized into three parts. In part I, we provide the theoretical and conceptual underpinnings as well as the practice methodology employed in organizational change from below, including characteristics of human service organizations and organizational culture, empowerment, and the uses of power and force field analysis as an assessment methodology for change. We examine tactics and countertactics used in organizational change, and discuss the differences between the ethics of client change and the ethics of organizational and community change. Part II consists of seven guest-authored chapters, each providing an example of real-life organizational change. The authors include social worker practitioners and educators. Part II is rich in illustrations of organizational change practice across diverse settings, such as a homeless shelter, a settlement house, and child protective services. Part III consists of three organizational change papers written by master's social work students in response to a course assignment; it includes an introduction outlining that assignment and its purpose.

We believe that the chapters in parts II and III, providing application of the more conceptual material in part I, will make organizational change practice come alive for readers. Together, these three parts provide the necessary tools for practitioners to bring about organizational change within human service organizations. This approach to organizational practice is critically important. As suggested by the title of this book, workers, including volunteers, and clients, including constituent groups, can become truly empowered through the process of agency change.

Marcia B. Cohen
Cheryl A. Hyde

Acknowledgments

We offer our most sincere thanks to our contributors—academics, practitioners, and students—without whose hard work this book would not have been possible. We also want to express our gratitude to David Follmer, publisher, and Catherine Dixon, editorial associate, of Lyceum Books, for their generous guidance throughout the process of writing and editing this text. We are grateful to David Wagner, professor of sociology and social work at the University of Southern Maine (and Marcia's spouse) who read parts of this book, offered helpful suggestions, and supplied the title. Alex Gitterman offered consistent support and consultation from the book's conception all the way through to its birth. We shared some of the chapters in draft form with our students, who provided instant feedback regarding how informative and palatable these readings were. On a more personal note, Cheryl greatly appreciated the support provided by friends and family, and the patience and amusing diversions of her daughter, Linnia.

We are deeply indebted to George Brager and Stephen Holloway, whose pioneering work on organizational change practice served as the inspiration for this book. Another significant intellectual debt is to Mayer Zald, whose groundbreaking work on social movement organizations, specifically the dynamics of transformation and the strategic repertoires of change agents, provided us with a critical conceptual framework. Our work rests on their shoulders and we hope we have done them justice.

Part I

Key Concepts and Frameworks

The four chapters that comprise part I lay out the theoretical and conceptual constructs that underpin our approach to organizational change from below, and present the assessment methodology geared toward organizational change from below. Chapter 1 describes the salient characteristics, structures, and processes of human service organizations within the framework of organizational culture, and explains the relevance of organizational culture to assessment for change. It indicates why an understanding of an organization's culture is essential in bringing about change, and illustrates this through a concrete example of agency change from below. Chapter 1 also describes a range of agency ideologies and the role that an understanding of these ideologies can play in organizational change efforts.

Chapter 2 describes the relationship among power, authority, and organizational change. Because organizational change involves use of power throughout the agency bureaucracy, the chapter focuses on sources of power in human service organizations. Chapter 2 addresses organizational structure and decision making and examines organizational hierarchy and leadership. It discusses the role of organizational characteristics such as complexity and formalization in influencing change. This chapter introduces the concept of the low-power actor and discusses ways in which students and line social workers can be empowered by engaging in effective change from below, enabling social workers and social work students who have less-formal organizational power to influence agency personnel who have more-formal power. A case example is used to show these key points.

Chapter 3 provides a step-by-step description of force field analysis, the assessment methodology best suited for organizational change from below. This chapter includes identifying a problem for change, framing a change goal, determining participating actors in the change process, and analyzing the forces promoting or inhibiting the accomplishment of the change goal. Brief examples from students' change efforts highlight and clarify important points in organizational change practice. Chapter 3 introduces the range of

1

tactics available to the change agent, and the principle of least contest as a means of assisting change agents in determining which strategies to employ and under what circumstances. This chapter concludes with a discussion of how to evaluate the outcomes of organizational change efforts.

Chapter 4 addresses the ethical principles underlying organizational change practice, particularly where change agents are social workers in low-power positions. The chapter distinguishes between the ethics of micro and macro social work practice. It describes some of the basic strategies, tactics, and countertactics of organizational change from below and explores the ethical implications surrounding the use of more-adversarial change tactics. These points are illustrated in a detailed case example.

1

Characteristics and Culture of Human Service Organizations

Cheryl A. Hyde and Marcia B. Cohen

Key topics of this chapter:

- Defining the human service organization
- Classifying human service organizations
- Characteristics of human service organizations
- Components of organizational culture

INTRODUCTION

It is difficult to imagine our lives without human service organizations. Hospitals and medical clinics, self-help and recovery groups, neighborhood associations and recreational centers, welfare offices and immigration services, job training and child care, hospice programs and grief support associations, family counseling centers and mental health clinics are all examples of human service organizations. Through thousands of organizations, the human service sector provides for our health, education, and well-being literally from cradle to grave. Social workers are perhaps the single largest group of professionals within the human services, providing the knowledge and skills needed to operate, and if necessary change, these organizations.

Since the focus of this book is on change in human service organizations, we begin by clarifying what we mean by this type of organization. The literature contains many definitions of human service organizations. One of the clearest and most useful for our purposes comes from Barker's *The Social Work Dictionary,* which describes the human service organization as "a social agency that delivers social services and is usually staffed by human service personnel (including professional social workers, members of other professions, paraprofessionals, clerical personnel, and sometimes indigenous workers). It provides a specific range of social services for members of a population group that has (been) or is vulnerable to a specific social problem. The agency may be funded by combinations of philanthropic contributions and privately solicited donations, by governments, by fees paid by those served, or by third-party payment" (Barker, 2003, p. 202).

This definition suggests that human service agencies encompass a wide range of organizations in terms of issues addressed and services provided. The small neighborhood-based violence prevention program, the mid-size family counseling center, and a large public welfare institution are all examples of human service agencies.

CLASSIFYING HUMAN SERVICE ORGANIZATIONS

Given the breadth of human service organizations, there are several ways of classifying agencies in order to better understand their diverse forms and functions. Next, we summarize some of the more commonly used categorizations.

Agency Auspices

Human service organizations operate under public (governmental), nonprofit, or for-profit auspices. Public organizations are those social agencies that are directly run by governmental agencies. Examples include federal government agencies such as the U.S. Department of Veterans Affairs, state-run agencies such as state departments of human services, and locally administered services such as public welfare departments and public homeless shelters.

Nonprofit organizations include agencies that may (or may not) receive substantial public funding but that are privately run and under the direction of a board of directors with day-to-day management by a director. This group includes counseling services, family service agencies, child welfare agencies, agencies serving homeless people, agencies serving victims of domestic violence, and many others. Any profits accruing to these organizations either go back into the agency's budget or are returned to the funding source.

For-profit human service agencies provide many of the same services as nonprofits, but they are privately owned and operated companies and their goals include generating profits. These agencies are generally managed by a chief executive officer (CEO). The for-profit sector has been steadily growing since the late 1960s, in part because of the availability of public funding (Gibelman & Furman, 2008) and third-party (health insurance) reimbursements. This is true in many areas of practice, but is especially true in the health and mental health fields.

As Gibelman and Furman (2008) note, the distinction among these three types of agencies can be confusing. The public financing of private services and similarities in structure between private nonprofit and private for-profit agencies have led to boundary blurring. Language from the corporate world has crept into some nonprofit settings, where the director is referred to as the CEO and the agency as the company. Nevertheless, in assessing an agency for the purposes of bringing about change, it is useful to identify the agency auspice.

The Nature of Services

There are numerous reasons why people make use of the programs and services offered by human service agencies. Some human service organizations, counseling centers and rape crisis hotlines as examples, provide voluntary services, whereas others, including correctional facilities and child protective services, provide mandated (nonvoluntary) services. Some organizations, such as psychiatric hospitals where some patients voluntarily seek services while others are mandated through commitment procedures, provide a combination of the two. How services are provided often influences staff and clients interactions, decision-making processes, staffing requirements, and relations with environmental actors. For example, clients in a nonvoluntary setting may resist assistance because they are mandated to be in the agency's program. Such settings also are likely to have work processes designed to control client behavior and hire staff with that criterion in mind. In contrast, clients who are voluntary may have more influence on the agency's offerings and procedures, in part because they choose (or do not choose) to access these services. Such organizations often have formal ways in which clients can participate in agency planning and governance, most often through positions on the board of directors or advisory committees.

Human service organizations also vary as to whether they are primary service sites or units situated in what are known as host agencies, which include hospitals, schools, correctional settings, and other large institutional settings whose primary mission is other than the provision of human services. In host settings, individuals from disciplines other than social work (e.g., medicine, education, and criminal justice) are responsible for organizational leadership and decision making. This is in contrast to settings such as family service agencies and community centers where social work is the primary discipline and more likely to hold significant organizational status and power.

Finally, some human service organizations include explicit social change activities such as lobbying, advocacy, and organizing in their programmatic repertoire. Moreover, the services that they provide typically are guided by clear political ideologies. These organizations may be termed "social movement agencies" because they combine the provision of services, usually in innovative and nontraditional ways, with change strategies (Hyde,

1992; Minkoff, 2002). Many feminist or gay and lesbian health centers would be examples of this type of human service organization. Such agencies provide health-related services in concert with political engagement activities.

Faith-based or Nonsectarian

In recent years, primarily because of federal-level policy initiatives, there has been increased attention to human service organizations sponsored by religious denominations (Gibelman & Furman, 2008). Faith-based organizations, however, have existed in the United States for more than two hundred years, offering immigration assistance, poverty relief, family support, and substance abuse counseling. While many of these efforts originally were targeted to meet the needs of members of those denominations (e.g., Jewish family and children service agencies that originally served Jewish immigrants and orphans), today most faith-based organizations serve a much wider population.

Faith-based human service organizations adhere to the principles or guidelines of their respective religious affiliations, in addition to the rules and requirements that apply to nonsectarian (nonreligious) human service organizations. For example, Catholic social service agencies follow the church's position on reproductive issues, including birth control. In contrast, nonsectarian (nonreligious) human service agencies are guided by their specific missions and may hold membership in broader-sector associations that could promote particular regulations or guidelines.

CHARACTERISTICS OF HUMAN SERVICE ORGANIZATIONS

In comparison with other kinds of organizations, such as manufacturing plants or financial institutions, human service agencies possess distinct characteristics (Hasenfeld, 2010). These attributes stem from the broad purpose that human service agencies address the human condition, which is accomplished through the provision of programs and services to individuals, families, groups, or communities (Gibelman & Furman, 2008). Usually, the mission of a human service organization embodies altruistic values and its goals focus on enhancement of the human condition. The characteristics of human service organizations can be clustered in micro, mezzo, and macro levels of analysis.

Beginning at the micro level, Hasenfeld (2010) suggests that the fundamental distinguishing feature of human service organizations is that people are the raw material. In order to function, all organizations require input (raw material) that is then transformed into its product. The auto industry, for example, uses the raw materials of steel, rubber, and glass and alters them through the production process into a car. In human service agencies, individuals who seek assistance are changed (hopefully for the better) through the organization's activities. Thus, humans are the input or raw material in human service organizations.

Yet unlike steel or glass, humans are not inanimate. They react to what is being done with or to them, and those reactions can be positive or negative. They may defy labeling or engage in the process, resist treatment or demand different programs or services, passively participate or mobilize for change. Thus, the raw material of human services is somewhat unpredictable, which creates variability in the work that agency staff does and uncertainty in the measurement of outcomes.

Not surprisingly, client–worker relations are another distinguishing characteristic of human service organizations, and this signifies a mezzo level of analysis. This relationship is a primary means for carrying out human service work. Within this relationship, staff engages in what is termed "moral" work, meaning that they use the values of the agency to guide or assess client eligibility, performance, compliance, and outcomes—in brief, the worthiness of the client to qualify and receive services. Hasenfeld (2010) notes that vulnerable or disenfranchised clients tend to experience "moral devaluation" by workers (p. 13), which in turn perpetuates a cycle of self-blame and disengagement.

This moral dimension underscores the emotional nature of human service work. Emotions are used to frame and guide client–worker communications and other interactions that can range from respectful to manipulative. Clients and workers also emotionally attach or invest, to varying degrees, to one another and to the organization. Thus, a client's commitment to a program or a worker's dedication to ameliorating a certain problem can be understood as emotional work.

Thus far, the unique characteristics of human service organizations have focused on internal (micro and mezzo) factors, specifically work processes. External or environmental attributes also shape human service organizations; this represents a macro level of analysis. Primary among these attributes is organizational legitimacy, which is determined by the institutional environment. A human service organization gains legitimacy when it successfully negotiates the demands of the state, regulators, resource providers, relevant professional associations, and public opinion. Yet securing and maintaining legitimacy can be difficult because the institutional environment is constantly changing. New or different licensure requirements, funder criteria, and policy regulations have an impact on organizational priorities and functioning. While human service organizations may go through periods of stability, such periods are relatively short. In order to survive, human service organizations need to be adept in responding to the crises and chaos of the environment. Yet in coping with the environmental demands, organizations may turn away from their core values and mission.

Human service organizations exist within a complex environment. Most critical of these to organizational change are two highly interrelated societal forces—the economy and politics. When times are lean and human service budgets shrink, a conservative political climate is created or reinforced, leading to a retrenchment in spending on human services by governmental and private sources. The former are particularly vulnerable to changes in the economy. Public sector budget cuts, in response to economic crises, directly impact agency revenues. Because many private sources of agency funding derive their funds from the government, private funds also decrease during a lean economy. A strong economy can influence political ideology in more liberal directions, often increasing social services expenditures. Public and private funding streams expand, with political pressures and demands impacting the nature of the expansion. The availability of monies for new programs or other costly changes increases the likelihood of organizational change.

Reduced funding generally results in constrictions and reductions in agency services. However, budget cuts can open the door to creative change efforts that save money without negatively impacting services to clients; in fact, such cuts can even improve services. For example, an agency providing outreach and day program services to elderly clients found itself seriously understaffed, a result of major cuts to its budget, which included both public (state) and private funds. A staff social worker who had previously been unsuccessful in persuading the agency administration to expand its pool of volunteers found the director to be much more receptive to this idea than she had previously been. This social worker was successful in reorganizing and expanding the agency's volunteer program, increasing and enhancing services to clients.

The impact of the economy and politics depends on the nature of the change. Increased accountability mechanisms are frequently introduced into agency settings during periods of retrenchment; some of these measures benefit agency clients, while others, including those that place efficiency over effectiveness, can be harmful to clients. Organizations are most likely to change when available funds shrink or increase. Change can be most difficult during periods of financial stability. In the absence of budgetary pressures or the availability of increased funding, the organization is most likely to preserve the status quo in agency programming (Brager & Holloway, 1978).

Public opinion, which is a reflection of political ideology, can have a negative impact on the delivery of social services to stigmatized populations. This is particularly evident in services for poor people. As Gitterman and Germain (2008) point out,

> the historical ideological distinction between worthy and unworthy poor, as well as the current public reaction to the tax burden, have led to stigmatizing and stereotyping recipients. Financial aid is provided in a punitive, demeaning manner, demonstrated by inadequate allowances, time limits, deteriorated and uncomfortable physical facilities, long waiting

lines, and negative attitudes and behavior of some personnel in many welfare offices. Such conditions attest to the impact of social policy on service delivery, particularly budget stringencies that are supported by societal values and norms. Political and economic pressures place significant constraints on human service organizations, compromising their ability to fulfill social mandates. (pp. 476–477)

Negative public opinion is often exacerbated for political gains; for example, conservatives often blame poor people for various societal problems (i.e., the economic downturn) because of their reliance on public assistance. Some may indiscriminately and detrimentally apply such views to all human service organizations (Bloom & Farragher, 2010).

These macro factors, alone and as they affect the micro and mezzo levels of the organization, suggest a complex and volatile environment for human service work. The adept practitioner needs to successfully negotiate this terrain, as well as organizational policies and procedures, in order to provide needed programs and services. Understanding these factors begins with the kind of relationship that is developed between social worker and client. Yet the relationship does not exist in a vacuum. The client comes from a community, with assets and challenges, and that community is influenced by prevailing political, social, and economic trends. Similarly, the organization is situated in a community, which may be the same as that of the client. And, as detailed above, the organization is subjected to various macro forces. A skilled practitioner takes all of these factors into account, learns to maneuver around them, brokers relationships across them, and facilitates the acquisition of resources for and skills by the client. In essence, social work is a transactional enterprise with the organization serving as the practice context as well as the conduit for micro, mezzo, and macro factors (Meenaghan & Gibbons, 2000; O'Connor & Netting, 2009).

While the change agent may not be able to influence the various forces we have been discussing, it is imperative that she or he assess these, and plan the timing or nature of the change goal accordingly. In sum, human service organizations are unique because of their unpredictability. The moral and emotional work embedded in the primary worker–client relationship generates degrees of instability. The turbulent institutional environment adds to this instability. The result is an organization that may have little control over its internal functioning and external context. This unpredictability also influences the ability to frame and pursue organizational change.

ORGANIZATIONAL CULTURE

There are a number of different approaches to understanding organizational dynamics. The framework we will use is organizational culture, which is a holistic and change-oriented paradigm. Culture can be understood as a "pattern of basic assumptions—invented, discovered, or developed by a given group as it learns to cope with its problems of external adaptation and internal integration—that has worked well enough to be considered valid and, therefore, to be taught to new members as the correct way to perceive, think and feel in relation to those problems" (Schein, 2004, p. 17).

There are several key assumptions that inform this definition. First, culture is made by humans, and therefore can be changed by humans. Second, culture develops and solidifies because it is critical to the survival of a group. And third, culture is transmitted over time to new members so that they can be functional members of the group. Culture, then, is not a static but rather a dynamic construct.

Organizational culture is manifested on three levels (Schein, 2004), as illustrated in figure 1.1. The most obvious level is *artifacts and creations*, including all objects, behaviors, and processes that transmit an organization's beliefs, values, technologies, and ways of doing things. Examples of artifacts and creations are

- art and symbols, such as a program's brochure, organization's logo, or posters on waiting room walls;
- norms and rituals, such as a preferred treatment method, meetings with clients in a private office, or a graduation ceremony celebrating the completion of a job training program; and
- language that is specific to an agency's program, such as use of medical terminology or diagnostic labels.

FIGURE 1.1. Levels of Organizational Culture

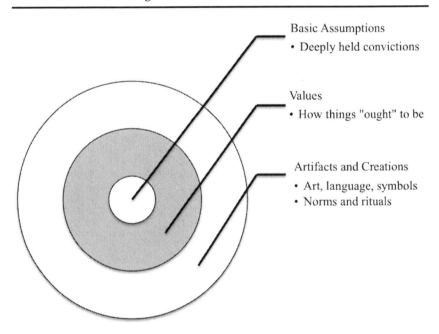

Basic Assumptions
• Deeply held convictions

Values
• How things "ought" to be

Artifacts and Creations
• Art, language, symbols
• Norms and rituals

The next level of culture is slightly more abstract. *Values* indicate a sense or understanding of what ought to be. Values are often codified in an organization's mission or goals statements, as in, "We believe that hunger can be eliminated" or "All women should be safe from violence."

Finally, there are *basic assumptions*, which is the most difficult level to ascertain because they are deeply embedded in the cultural system. Examples include convictions concerning

- time and space, such as being oriented to the future, the norm of beginning an event promptly, or level of comfort with physical closeness;
- human nature, such as whether people are essentially good or evil; or
- our relationship to nature, such as destroying or preserving the environment.

Inferring an organization's basic assumptions is accomplished through careful, systematic observation and analysis.

EXAMPLE: ORGANIZATIONAL VISION, MISSION, AND VALUES

Project HOME was founded in 1998 in Philadelphia in response to the growing street population in the city. Currently, it offers comprehensive employment, education, health, mental health, and housing programs to homeless individuals and families. With the motto "None of us are home until all of us are home," the organization's About Us webpage provides an example of how an agency's culture is conveyed through its vision, mission, and values.

The Vision of Project HOME

None of us are home until all of us are home.

The Mission of Project HOME

The mission of the Project HOME community is to empower adults, children, and families to break the cycle of homelessness and poverty, to alleviate the underlying causes of poverty, and to enable all of us to attain our fullest potential as individuals and as members of the broader society. We strive to create a safe and respectful environment where we support each other in our struggles for self-esteem, recovery, and the confidence to move toward self-actualization.

Project HOME achieves its mission through a continuum of care comprised of street outreach, a range of supportive housing, and comprehensive services. We address the root causes of homelessness through neighborhood-based affordable housing, economic development, and environmental enhancement programs, as well as through providing access to employment opportunities; adult and youth education; and health care.

Project HOME is committed to social and political advocacy. An integral part of our work is education about the realities of homelessness and poverty and vigorous advocacy on behalf of and with homeless and low-income persons for more just and humane public policies.

Project HOME is committed to nurturing a spirit of community among persons from all walks of life, all of whom have a role to play in making this a more just and compassionate society.

The Values of Project HOME

- The work of Project HOME is rooted in our strong spiritual conviction of the dignity of each person.
- We believe that all persons are entitled to decent, affordable housing and access to quality education, employment, and health care.
- We believe in the transformational power of building relationships and community as the ultimate answer to the degradation of homelessness and poverty.
- We believe that working to end homelessness and poverty enhances the quality of life for everyone in our community.
- We believe that the critical resources entrusted to us to achieve our mission must be managed honorably and professionally. (www.projecthome.org/about/)

An agency's vision, mission, and values are core elements in an organization's ideology and goals. Consequently, we want to provide more in-depth discussion of ideology and goals, and how these organizational components affect change.

Ideology

Brager and Holloway (1978) define ideology as "a commonly shared coherent and intensely held set of beliefs and commitments [which] is a potent social lever" (p. 57). Ideology influences individual and organizational behavior and can come to define an organization. As a force, ideology can facilitate or inhibit change efforts and can be harnessed in the service of a change goal. Brager and Holloway (1978) describe four broad ideological systems that characterize human service organizations: campaign, client service, process, and venerational:

- *Campaign ideology* characterizes organizations growing out of political or social movements. These organizations reflect commitment to specific social missions and generally have external social change goals. Examples include mental health consumer advocacy groups, organizations for poor people, and organizations for battered women.

- *Client service ideology* revolves around a commitment to providing services to a specific client population, such as children, and adults who are elderly, homeless, and developmentally disabled. There can be some overlap with campaign ideology agencies as some agencies with client service ideologies have grown out of social movement–focused organizations, for example, organizations providing services to women who have been abused. However, organizations with client service ideologies are primarily committed to providing direct services rather than engaging in more politically oriented reform efforts.

- *Process ideology* describes agencies that are committed to a particular process or practice methodology—community organizing, legislative advocacy, solution-oriented brief treatment, or psychodynamic psychotherapy. The emphasis in process ideology–focused organizations is on the particular methodology employed rather than on social causes or client populations.

- *Venerational ideology* characterizes agencies that are highly invested in their own traditions, past history, quality of services, and leadership in the field. Such organizations are likely to perceive themselves as pioneers in the field. Such agencies place great importance on upholding their status and reputation. They emphasize the unique identity of the organization rather than a cause, a specific client population, or practice methodology. Venerational ideologies tend to be found among older, more-established institutions.

Campaign and client service–oriented agencies may be most receptive to change. Campaign-oriented organizations are inherently predisposed to reform and change in the wider environment and therefore potentially are more open to internal change (O'Connor & Netting, 2009). Client service–oriented agencies are seen as being more receptive to change than are process or venerational organizations because of their greater dependence on the environment and their vulnerability to external forces such as changes in the client population. Settings least open to change are likely to be those characterized by venerational ideologies that are well established, stable, and rooted in tradition. However, it must be noted that there are additional factors that influence an organization's predisposition to change. Organizations vary in the intensity of their ideological commitment. A strong ideological stance can be harnessed in favor of a change effort whereas a weak stance may be of little influence. Also, the ideological beliefs of organizations can change over time and often are not uniform across all of the organization's units (Brager & Holloway, 1978).

It is important that the change agent identify the existing ideological orientation(s) and its (their) intensity. One type of agency is not always easier to change than another but its typology can be very useful for assessing the organization and determining how to frame the problem for change. In order to gain the legitimacy necessary to bring about change, the change agent must speak the agency's language and echo its ideology. A change agent seeking change in a small, campaign-focused, grassroots organization will frame the problem for change very differently from how a change agent in a large, prestigious psychiatric clinic will frame it. The change agent in a campaign agency might express the sentiment, "We are undermining the power of those we seek to help." In a venerational agency, the appeal might be expressed as, "We aren't being true to our great reputation." Once identified, the organization's ideology can provide a potent force when harnessed in the service of the change goal.

Goals

The formal purposes or goals of an organization generally reflect its ideology and are most often expressed in broad terms in its mission statement (Gibelman & Furman, 2008). Neugeboren (1991) speaks to the importance of social workers being able to visualize organizational goals and appreciate the importance of those goals. Identifying agency goals that support a proposed change can greatly enhance a change effort and suggest how it might be framed. The greater the extent to which the problem for change is framed in terms of agency goals, the more likely it is that the organization will be receptive to the proposed change. Some organizational goals are more likely to predispose an organization to change than others. Thus, an agency whose mission emphasizes client empowerment as a goal may be more open to the proposed inclusion of clients on the board of directors than an agency that simply emphasizes the goal of servicing clients (Cohen, 1994). Moreover, to the extent that the goal of empowerment reflects an agency's values of inclusion and egalitarianism, it may be more open, in general, to input from low-power actors.

Brager and Holloway (1978) describe goals as functioning as contracts between the organization's funding source(s) and the agency's administration. These, in turn, determine what services will be provided, to whom, and (often) for what social benefit. They draw an important distinction between manifest and latent goals or purposes. Manifest purposes are explicitly stated by the organization, whereas latent purposes are implicit and unstated. There can be discrepancies between these—for example, a city homeless shelter with the manifest goal of improving the social welfare of undomiciled individuals may also have a latent function of removing the homeless from the public eye with a minimal expenditure of funds. A member of the shelter staff seeking to have the city provide more-permanent housing for its homeless population is not likely to succeed, particularly if the latent purpose is being successfully served. It can be difficult to determine an organization's latent purposes as they are, by definition, unstated. However, it is important to organizational change efforts that the change agent identify them because they can pose serious obstacles to the desired change, particularly if they remain undetected. The reason these purposes have gone unstated should also be identified. Hidden purposes, such as ridding the streets of visible homelessness, may be at odds with stated purposes, such as improving the social welfare of homeless people.

Multiple funding sources can create multiple organizational goals. These goals can be mutually reinforcing, creating a high level of stability and limiting which changes are likely to be successful. For example, a home health agency providing social work, nursing, occupational therapy, and physical therapy may include specific goals for each discipline along with a shared goal of providing high-quality primary patient care. A proposal to offer public health education to the community might be seen by several of its disciplines as redirecting agency resources away from the services they provide. The change agent proposing this educational program would be well advised to frame the proposal as enhancing patient care and involving the input of all of the agency's units. This possible competition for resources among the agency's various disciplines can be reframed by the change agent as an incentive to work together. In a larger bureaucratic organization (e.g., a hospital), the units made up of various health-care disciplines may be insulated from each other, leading to reduced competition among disciplines. This scenario can potentially reduce the number of decision makers whose support for the proposed change is needed. Thus, the existence of multiple organizational goals can either increase or decrease organizational receptivity to change, depending on organizational size and structure.

Transmission of Organizational Culture

Every organization has its own unique culture (Ott, 1989) that results from the intersection of several internal and external factors. The internal factors are the assumptions and beliefs of the founder and, if a different individual, the vision of the current leader. The external factors are the norms and values of the general culture (e.g., American, German, or Canadian) and, if appropriate, of specific subculture (e.g., African American), and the sector(s) in which it operates (e.g., nonprofit or child welfare). Figure 1.2 is a general illustration of the factors that shape an organization's unique culture.

Of particular concern within the organizational culture framework is the transmission of culture to new organizational members, including staff and clients. Organizations develop structures and processes that teach and reinforce cultural values and norms (Ott, 1989). These operations encompass (1) recruitment and selection of members, (2) orientations and initial socialization activities, (3) reinforcement of appropriate behaviors and punishment

FIGURE 1.2. Factors that Shape an Organization's Unique Culture

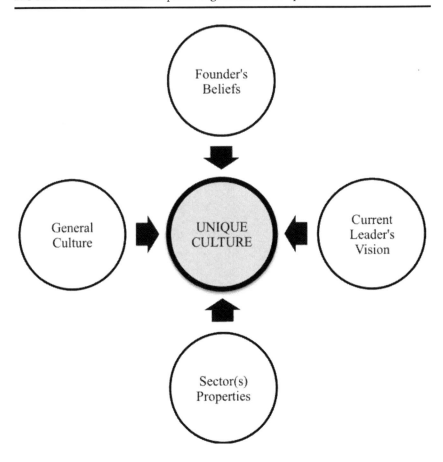

for unacceptable behavior, (4) removal of deviant members in ways that emphasize cultural expectations for remaining members, and (5) use of various forms of communications (i.e., newsletters, memos, gossip networks) that further support the organization's culture.

EXAMPLE: THE TRANSMISSION OF ORGANIZATIONAL CULTURE

The Sexual Assault Crisis Center (SACC) provides a variety of support services for men, women, and children who have been victimized by sexual violence, including a crisis hotline, group counseling, medical advocacy, and court appearance support. As with many nonprofit organizations, SACC relies on a large pool of volunteers to meet the demands for its services. SACC's comprehensive volunteer training program, which emphasizes the organization's focus on professionalism, illustrates how a human service agency transmits its culture to new members.

- Recruitment and selection: All prospective volunteers must apply to be considered for a volunteer position in any victim service program. The application includes an essay that asks for comment on SACC's mission, criminal background checks, and three references. A board and staff committee reviews these applications; successful applicants are invited in for a screening interview. The interviews cover reasons for wanting to volunteer, attitudes regarding sexual violence, and other issues germane to the organization. Those individuals who make it through this process are accepted as volunteers.

- Orientations and initial socialization: All volunteers must complete a forty-hour training program that addresses the mission and vision of SACC and the antiviolence movement, crisis counseling techniques, court and hospital protocols when accompanying victims, self-care, and practice role plays. Volunteers are evaluated throughout the training period, and some individuals may be dismissed.

- Reinforcement of behaviors: Once a volunteer has successfully completed the training program, he or she is paired with a seasoned volunteer for a three-month period. The seasoned volunteer is there to guide, provide feedback to, and evaluate the new volunteer, and needs to report any concerns to the volunteer coordinator. At the end of this three-month period, the successful volunteer is scheduled into a hotline shift and other victim service activities. Volunteers are expected to give eight to ten hours each month.

- Removal of deviant members: Determination of whether an individual is appropriate for a victim services volunteer starts from the moment of application and continues through the three-month post-training period. Once that period has ended and the volunteer is working solo, there are regularly scheduled evaluations and refresher trainings. The organization expects that volunteers will remain committed to professional performance. If at any time it is determined that a volunteer is not meeting that expectation, the volunteer coordinator can ask him or her to leave. When that happens, other volunteers are informed (in a general way) of what happened and why, in memos or meetings.

- Use of communications: SACC relies on a constant flow of information to keep volunteers abreast of any organizational developments, opportunities, and events. There is a dedicated website for volunteers, as well as a LISTSERV® (both of which are managed by the volunteer coordinator). Periodic meetings are held to discuss issues that pertain to volunteering. There is an annual appreciation banquet that acknowledges the work of the volunteers.

Using organizational culture as a framework to understand human service agencies allows us to take into account essential properties and processes within the organization, as well as key environmental factors. Organizational culture helps focus attention on underlying dynamics, for example the commitment to the founder's vision or impact of sector politics, which often shape agency function and effectiveness. Organizational members must understand all these factors for a change effort to be successful.

A change agent needs to decipher, and use strategically, the rituals and routines that have informed prior organizational change. The change agent also needs to understand the relationship between the organization's cultural assumptions and the proposed change. Not only does the change agent need to work with those cultural artifacts and values that support change, but she or he also needs to identify and understand culturally situated barriers to change. Some questions to consider include the following:

- How do organizational members view change? Is it considered to be a learning opportunity, a threat, an annoyance, or another pipedream? What is the overall receptivity of the organization's culture to change?

- Does change need to be initiated, sponsored, or facilitated by the organizational leader(s) in order to be successful, or can it come from anyone within the organization?

- Does the proposed change support or threaten basic organizational values? Even if the change agent believes that the change is supportive, is it possible that others might perceive it as a threat?

CONCLUSION

Within the organizational culture paradigm, the change agent usually is the leader. This makes sense, since the leader has a significant impact on the organization's culture. Yet our focus is on the low-power actor as change agent; consequently, the understanding of culture becomes even more important. This is because organizational culture includes those rituals, protocols, and practices that inform rewards or sanctions for innovation and risk taking that are necessary for change. Therefore, a critical aspect of organizational culture is formal and informal structures that shape power and authority within an agency. We turn to these dynamics of organizational life in the next chapter.

DISCUSSION QUESTIONS

1. What are some reasons that people seek services from human service agencies?
2. Give an example of a public human service organization, a nonprofit agency, and a for-profit organization. How do they differ? How are they similar?
3. In an organizational setting familiar to you, ask the members what they think the key values of the organization are. Do these values resonate with the organization's activities?
4. What are the organization's goals and mission? Are the values you identified in question 3 reflected in the mission and goals? Are there any conflicting goals?
5. Think about the setting you are in. What are some of its norms and rituals? What functions do these norms and rituals have for the organization?
6. How are elements of the organizational culture in your setting transmitted to new members?

REFERENCES

Barker, R. (2003). *The social work dictionary* (5th ed.). Washington, DC: National Association of Social Workers.

Bloom, S., & Farragher, B. (2010). *Destroying sanctuary: The crisis in human service delivery systems.* New York: Oxford University Press.

Brager, G., & Holloway, S. (1978). *Changing human service organizations: Politics and practice.* New York: Free Press.

Cohen, M. B. (1994). Who wants to chair the meeting? Group development and leadership patterns in a community action group of homeless people. *Social Work with Groups, 17*(1/2), 81–87.

Gibelman, M., & Furman, R. (2008). *Navigating human service organizations* (2nd ed.). Chicago: Lyceum Books.

Gitterman, A., & Germain, C. (2008). *The life model of social work practice* (3rd ed.). New York: Columbia University Press.

Hasenfeld, Y. (2010). The attributes of human service organizations. In Y. Hasenfeld (Ed.), *Human services as complex organizations* (2nd ed., pp. 9–31). Los Angeles: Sage Publications.

Hyde, C. (1992). The ideational system of social movement agencies: An examination of feminist health centers. In Y. Hasenfeld (Ed.), *Human services as complex organizations* (pp. 121–144). Newbury Park, CA: Sage Publications.

Meenaghan, T., & Gibbons, W. (2000). *Generalist practice in larger settings: Knowledge and skills concepts.* Chicago: Lyceum Books.

Minkoff, D. (2002). The emergence of hybrid organizational forms: Combining identity-based service provision and political action. *Nonprofit and Voluntary Sector Quarterly, 31*(3), 377–401.

Neugeboren, B. (1991). *Organization, policy and practice in the human services.* Binghamton, NY: Haworth Press.

O'Connor, M., & Netting, F. (2009). *Organization practice: A Guide to understanding human service organizations.* Hoboken, NJ: John Wiley & Sons.

Ott, J. (1989). *The organizational culture perspective.* Chicago: Dorsey Press.

Schein, E. (2004). *Organizational culture and leadership* (3rd ed.). San Francisco: John Wiley & Sons.

2

Power and Empowerment in Human Service Organizations

Cheryl A. Hyde and Marcia B. Cohen

Key topics of this chapter:

- Power and authority
- Organizational structure
- Structure and decision making
- Organizational leadership
- Low-power actors
- Empowerment in organizations

INTRODUCTION

A common lament from many students and more than a few practitioners is that they do not like engaging in organizational practice because of all the politics and power plays. Human service organizations can be political minefields and power does get abused. Agencies also can be arenas of empowerment for staff, clients, and constituents. It is naïve at best to think that one can be a social worker and not contend with the dynamics of agency power.

In chapter 1, we identified and discussed the importance of organizational culture, with particular attention to goals, values, and ideologies. In this chapter, we first discuss the manifestation of organizational power and power discrepancies in organizations. We draw on the work of sociologist Max Weber (as cited by Roth & Wittich, 1978) to aid our understanding of different types of organizational structure, and thus to refine our earlier

20

discussion. We conclude with a discussion of empowerment as an essential component of healthy organizations and organizational change practice.

POWER AS AUTHORITY

Power can be defined as "the possession of resources that enable an individual to do something independently or to exercise influence and control over others" (Gibelman & Furman, 2008, p. 200). Power comes in many forms and is based on a number of characteristics—personality, expertise, relationship, or position. Within the organizational context, there are several sources of power:

- Legitimate power: based on title and position
- Reward power: based on ability to provide incentives
- Coercive power: based on the ability to force others to do something, usually by withholding rewards
- Referent power: based on interactions and mutual obligations
- Expert power: based on specific knowledge, skills, or education/training (French & Raven, 1960; Lunenburg, 2012)

Certain individuals or groups in an organization are able to have influence over others because they have access to one or more forms of power.

The work of Max Weber (as cited by Roth & Wittich, 1978) serves as a foundation for most understandings of organizational power. Weber focused attention on authority, which is *legitimate power*, and delineated four types:

1. Traditional: authority based on long-standing customs and structures (e.g., a monarchy)
2. Charismatic: authority based on the extraordinary inspirational qualities of the leader such that the followers feel compelled to act as directed (e.g., social movements or cults)
3. Legal-rational: authority derived from formal rules, laws, and protocols (e.g., bureaucracies)
4. Value-rational: authority that is based in the group, as a whole, rather than held by an individual (e.g., Quaker meetings that use consensus)

Most human service organizations fit the pattern of a bureaucracy, including a top-down hierarchical decision-making structure. This structure is frequently depicted in organizational charts. Small campaign ideology organizations may have flatter structures than other agencies, but few organizations are totally without bureaucratic elements. Weber (as cited by Roth & Wittich, 1978) elaborated a series of principles that characterize a bureaucracy:

1. There is a formal, hierarchical division of labor in which each organizational level controls the one below it and is controlled by the one above it. These hierarchical relationships are codified on organizational charts and other written documents.

2. Management of staff is accomplished by the consistent application of rules, which allows decisions made at high levels to be executed consistently by all lower levels.

3. Formality, impersonality, and objectivity are paramount. Employees and clients are to be treated equally without regard for individual differences.

4. Employment is based on technical qualifications and expertise. Jobs are specified with detailed rights, responsibilities, and scope of authority.

5. Organization is by functional specialty. Work is to be done by specialists, and people are organized into units based on the type of work they do or the skills they have.

6. There is extensive use of written documents and a complex system of record keeping and standardized communication.

7. There is an assumption of total loyalty toward the organization.

Weber described a pure bureaucracy. In practice, human service organizations vary in the extent to which they exhibit these characteristics. It is also worth noting that while some of these principles of bureaucracy (e.g., a hierarchical structure, management through rules, and loyalty to the organization) can sharply limit workers' organizational freedom, others (e.g., objectivity and employment based on expertise) can enhance workers' organizational life.

While not often seen, there are examples of human service organizations employing value-rational authority. Such an organization is a collective and is marked by

1. little or no stratification;

2. the group as a whole making decisions;

3. little or no division of labor, with tasks rotated among members;

4. a high degree of participation, interaction, and engagement by members;

5. relatively simplistic documentation, including record-keeping; and

6. personal relationships critical to the organization's functioning.

Collectives typically are small in size and often are part of a broader social movement or social change effort. Examples include feminist health clinics, worker cooperatives, and women's centers (Hyde, 2006; Rothschild, 2009).

ORGANIZATIONAL STRUCTURE

As can be seen from our discussion thus far, organizational power, specifically authority, is closely tied to organizational structure. An understanding of the internal organizational structure is critical to the change process and has particular implications for how the change agent would approach and strategize efforts. In addition to the attributes of organizations broadly discussed in chapter 1, three important aspects to the internal structure have been identified: complexity, formalization, and centralization (Gitterman & Germain, 2008).

Complexity

This term refers to the degree of task specialization, power centers, and number of disciplines involved in an organization. A hospital is an example of a highly complex organization in that there are many professions, many tasks, and many power centers (medicine, nursing, pharmacy, social work). A children's advocacy agency made up only of social workers would be a much less complex organization. Generally, complex organizations made up of staff from a variety of professional disciplines are more conducive to change than are less-complex settings. This is in part due to the tendency of professionals to be more identified with their professions than they are with their employing organizations, and therefore more open to innovation. Also, the more complex the organization, the greater the variety of perspectives influencing decision makers, which in turn can serve to increase staff openness to change (Hage & Aiken, 1970).

There is a caveat, however, to the positive influence of complexity on an organization's receptivity to change. Different disciplines wield different amounts of power in an organization. In most health-care settings, for example, physicians have considerable power and social workers have relatively little. In host agencies, where social work provides services that are ancillary or secondary to the organization's purposes, the influence of social workers over more-powerful disciplines is weak. Thus, complexity may not always be advantageous for organizational change.

Formalization

This term refers to the degree to which organizations have elaborate and enforced systems of rules and regulations. For example, public welfare agencies tend to be highly formalized whereas grassroots community agencies tend to be much less so. Formalization can be a barrier or an aid to organizational change. In a highly formalized organization, innovations can challenge the status quo, which is protected by rules. The more codified a rule, regulation, or policy, the more resistant to change it is likely to be. Also, in more-formalized organizations the change agent may be forced to use the formal decision-making structure, even when the informal structure provides greater leeway and ambiguity, both of which are associated with greater openness to change. Formalization is not without its benefits, however. Change aligned with organizational rules can take advantage of formalization. Also, it may be easier for the change agent to know where she or he stands in a more formalized setting. In addition, data collection necessary to advance the change proposal is often easier in an organization with high formality because more is written and recorded about organizational life.

Centralization

This term is used to describe how the authority structure works in an organization. In highly centralized organizations, power rests in the hands of a small number of people at the highest levels of the hierarchy. In contrast, decentralized organizations are characterized by multiple, dispersed power centers. For example, state social service agencies are often very centralized with a commissioner or director making most of the decisions. In contrast, hospitals are an example of decentralization since there are many departments and sources of authority (heads of various departments, hospital director, other administrators). It has been suggested that centralization can inhibit change (Gitterman & Germain, 2008), because the powerful decision makers in the organization are likely to seek to protect their privilege and maintain the status quo. Proposals for change may appear as criticism of the decision makers and hence be rejected. Also, there is a tendency for centralization to limit the free flow of communication (Brager & Holloway, 1978). Finally, in a centralized setting, the change agent may not have access to the center of power. Organizational distance refers to how many levels of authority (hierarchy) an individual (such as the change agent) is away from the decision makers. Usually, the shorter the organizational distance between the change agent and the decision maker(s), the easier it will be to bring about change.

Centralization can facilitate change in some instances. This is likely to occur when the proposed change increases the power of high-level decision makers. The authority structure in a centralized setting may also lend itself to ready analysis by the change agent who knows who she or he needs to persuade, and who controls the decisions.

Complexity, formalization, and centralization interact with each other in predictable ways. Centralization and formalization tend to be found together in rigid hierarchies with many formal rules. Complexity and decentralization also tend to co-occur. The complex nature of the organization often generates a need for trained staff to perform intricate tasks. This situation tends to create a need for some delegation of authority and autonomy to trained staff, creating a more decentralized decision-making structure. This scenario is in contrast to the organization whose tasks are predictable and repetitive and where a high degree of centralization and formalization is sufficient for task monitoring and completion (Brager & Holloway, 1978).

STRUCTURE AND DECISION MAKING

Neugeboren (1991) defines the purpose of organizational structure as minimizing the influence of individual variations on organizational activities. Thus, structure provides a degree of uniformity in the carrying out of various organizational tasks. By limiting individual discretion, structure promotes conformity to the organization's goal. Neugeboren states that organizational structure "is a mechanism for achieving organizational control, which is required in order to integrate the individual staff member with the organization's goals" (p. 61). This description speaks to the formal organizational structure. It is important to distinguish between formal and informal agency structure; all organizations have both and both are relevant to organizational decision making.

Formal Structure

Decision making in a bureaucratic system is controlled by top-down, formal mechanisms. Human service organizations require an authority structure to manage the flow of decisions in an orderly fashion. Hierarchically structured human service organizations are characterized by a chain of command with progressively higher levels of decision making having progressively greater authority and responsibility for decision making (Seabury, Seabury, & Garvin, 2011). This kind of authority structure has critical implications for efforts to create change from below. By definition, nonmanagerial staff are low-power actors with limited means to make decisions and bring about change. These workers need to influence higher-level managers with decision-making power as to the desirability of the change they seek. Because of the chain of command, workers often must rely on influencing the managers in the level above them, who then must influence those in the level above them, and so on.

Many settings include discrete departments, such as foster care, adoption, and group home services. But there is most often a hierarchical chain of command and decision-making structure in each department (Seabury et al., 2011). As mentioned above, agencies range in their degree of bureaucracy. Large organizations tend to be characterized by highly formal decision-making hierarchies, with many layers of decision makers and decision-making processes codified in written rules and regulations. Smaller settings may be less formal and allow for some leeway in who can make decisions.

As we will further examine in chapter 3, organizational structure is a critical factor in facilitating or constraining organizational practice. Organizational structures can be functional or dysfunctional. It is important for the social worker seeking to make change to assess the decision-making structure to determine its functionality and who needs to be influenced to bring about change. It is not enough to examine just the formal organizational structure, however: the change agent also needs to assess the informal structure.

Informal Structure

Decision making in a human service organization is also affected by the informal structure, which may be less apparent than the influence of the more formal structure discussed above. This aspect of organizational life includes unofficial roles and relationships that do not appear on organizational charts. It is not uncommon to find administrative assistants and secretaries who exert considerable influence and power in an organization, power that is not reflected in the formal agency structure. Another example of an informal organizational relationship is the line staff person who has a personal relationship (friend, relative, neighbor) with a high-level decision maker. This person may have unofficial access and even influence with management. The line staff member seeking to influence management might be able to make use of these informal decision-making relationships. This is why examining organizational structure needs to go beyond an assessment of the formal structure.

Table 2.1 presents a summary of how these various facets of structure combine to produce different types of organizations.

ORGANIZATIONAL LEADERSHIP

Types of power, authority, decision-making processes, and structures serve as the parameters for the kind of leadership that is found in a given agency.

TABLE 2.1. Organizational Types by Division of Labor, Formalized Rules, and Centralization

Organizational Type	Division of Labor	Degree of Formalized Rules	Centralized Decision Making
Classic bureaucracy	High	High	High
Horizontal bureaucracy	Moderate	High	Moderate
Participatory democracy	Moderate	Moderate	Moderate
Modified collective	Moderate	Low	Low
Collective	Low	Low	Low

Being an organizational leader can be a challenging and rewarding responsibility. Effective leaders typically exhibit the following traits:

- Self-awareness: an understanding of one's strengths, limitations, values and aspirations
- Self-regulation: the ability to gather information and assess a given situation in nonjudgmental ways, and make purposeful, rather than reactive, decisions
- Motivation: the capacity to challenge and inspire others and oneself
- Empathy: an awareness of the feelings of other organizational members, specifically in situations that result in anxiety or stress, and an ability to understand different viewpoints
- Social skills: an ability to foster positive, supportive relationships with and between organizational members (Brody, 2005, pp. 15–16)

Leaders need to be adept at communicating, analyzing, working across multiple systems (known as boundary spanning), fostering creativity, implementing the mission and goals, and delegating tasks appropriately (Austin, Brody, & Packard, 2009). Unfortunately, we also are probably familiar with flawed leadership styles such as the micromanager, the arrogant individual, or the person who constantly puts others down. These types of leaders, who usually are leaders because of their positions or roles, generate considerable stress and mistrust, and damage the overall morale of the organization (Brody, 2005).

In human service agencies, the executive director (or the CEO) holds authority within the organization by virtue of the position and usually is seen as the organization's leader. Typically, these individuals have the following primary responsibilities:

- Plan and coordinate with governing body policies for program of services
- Guide staff in achieving organization's objectives
- Manage personnel

If the agency is a nonprofit, then a board of directors holds authority over the organization (Gibelman & Furman, 2008). A board of directors is responsible for the overall fiscal, legal, and programmatic health of the organization; the board as a whole, as well as individual board members, also serve as organizational leaders. Board members serve on a voluntary basis and are supposed to represent the interests of the community, client populations, or constituent groups. The functions of this governing body include the following:

- Appointing, monitoring, and evaluating the director or CEO
- Setting organizational policy

- Delegating responsibility for agency management and policy implementation to the director or CEO
- Facilitating strategic planning
- Fundraising and developing other resources

Board members do not get involved in the day-to-day tasks or activities of the agency. In nonprofit agencies, the CEO has the additional responsibilities of implementing board policy, attending board meetings, and informing the board about day-to-day finances, operations, and programs.

Leadership does not come, however, solely from those that hold positions of organizational authority. Depending on the circumstances, external actors such as funders or clients can serve as leaders of specific initiatives. Staff at all levels of an organization can also serve as leaders, particularly in organizational change efforts.

THE LOW-POWER ACTOR

Low-power actors are organizational members who, "for whatever reason, are currently in relatively weak or low-status positions vis-à-vis other actors" (Bouquet & Birkenshaw, 2008, p. 478). Brager and Holloway (1978) speak to the limited influence of practitioners, stating, "Although low and middle-level staff at times contribute to agency decision making . . . they are relatively powerless" (p. 1). Low-power actors typically lack decision-making power and resources, and may also lack the structural opportunities for interacting with key participants and obtaining necessary information. This is in contrast to high-power actors, who often act in ways to preserve their dominant status within groups and organizations (Lovaglia, Mannix, Samuelson, Sell, & Wilson, 2005; Seabury et al., 2011). Within human service agencies, low-power actors may include those personnel such as line staff at or near the bottom of the organizational chart, clients, constituents, or community members. It should be noted, however, that staff who are low-power actors may nonetheless exercise decision making and resource allocation control over clients, even when they have relatively little influence on their own jobs or work settings.

Being a low-power actor does not mean that change is unattainable. Some studies on power and exchange relationships in organizations suggest that low-power actors may have more accurate perceptions of organizational functioning (Simpson, Markovsky, & Steketee, 2011) because they need to negotiate the various protocols and procedures put forth by organizational elites. That is, low-power actors are more active in understanding the structures and processes of their organizations. Such insights can be the basis for change rationales. It is possible for low-power actors to join with other marginalized or low-status persons to collectively engage in change (Simpson &

Macy, 2004). Often, however, a low-power actor must rely on other higher status staff with whom he or she has relationships, to obtain information and influence key decision makers. Indeed, research underscores the importance of networking for low-power actors as a strategy for building power and influence (Scully & Segal, 2002). This use of facilitating actors, who have greater organizational status and can gain access to decision makers, will be discussed further in chapter 3.

In addition to facilitating change, networks can serve as protective factors for a low-power actor engaged in organizational change. O'Day (1974) identified a series of intimidation rituals that management engages in when threatened by change (see also Roscigno, Lopez, & Hodson, 2009). A key aspect of these rituals is isolation of the change agent. A primary strategy for countering this isolation is to maintain support networks rather than engaging in change by oneself and to document the change process.

When low-power actors become agents for organizational change, they become leaders within their agencies. This is perhaps not true in the traditional or formal sense, but an effective change agent knows how to encourage and how to inform others who wish to be involved in the effort. Often, while pursuing their change initiative, they help facilitate the empowerment of others, which is what we consider next.

EMPOWERMENT IN ORGANIZATIONS

Empowerment is a central value in social work and any organizational change should have empowerment as a guiding principle. As defined in *The Social Work Dictionary*, empowerment is "the process of helping individuals, families, groups, and communities increase their personal, interpersonal, socioeconomic and political strength and develop influence toward improving their circumstances" (Barker, 2003, p. 101). Empowerment often is thought of in terms of both process and outcome, and is associated with self-efficacy, awareness, control, participation, advocacy, and change. An empowerment orientation to practice includes addressing stigmatization, marginalization, and disenfranchisement of client or constituent populations (Gutiérrez & Lewis, 1999; Lauffer, 2011).

In a synthesis of the empowerment literature for agency management, Hardina (2005) identifies ten characteristics of empowerment-oriented organizations:

1. Includes clients/consumers in organization decision-making
2. Creates partnerships to design and evaluate programs
3. Delivers culturally appropriate services
4. Minimize [*sic*] power differentials between clients and staff
5. Promotes team-building and collaboration among staff members

6. Promotes psychological empowerment of workers by giving them more autonomy to make decisions that affect their work

7. Creates an administrative leadership structure that is ideologically committed to empowering clients and staff members

8. Increases employee job satisfaction through the provision of fringe benefits and other incentives

9. Encourages staff to advocate for improvements in service delivery and client resources

10. Increases the political power of organization constituents (p. 28)

Hardina further notes that organizational policies, structures, and processes need to support an environment in which members are empowered to participate in decisions. Similarly, Gutiérrez and Lewis (1999) state that an "empowering organization maximizes the power of its workers and constituents to participate fully in the governance of the organization" (p. 82). The following case example illustrates many of these points.

EXAMPLE: COMMUNITY HOUSING CORPORATION

The Community Housing Corporation (CHC) is a comprehensive organization that provides low-income housing in the northeastern part of the United States. In addition to operating twenty-five housing sites (typically apartment buildings), the CHC provides financial counseling and education to qualified individuals. When it became time for the development of a comprehensive strategic plan, the administrators at CHC decided that it was essential that staff from all parts of the agency participate in and benefit from the work. Working with a consultant, the CHC put together a strategic planning committee that had representatives from management, administrative support, service and outreach, housekeeping, and maintenance departments.

The initial task of the consultant was to assist the committee members in developing processes in which all could engage. This took a fair amount of work, because managers and program staff often dominated committee meetings (or at least tried). The consultant created work groups, with various staffing combinations, that were charged with gathering and analyzing information that would frame the strategic plan. Work group members were trained in basic research skills so that everyone could participate in this part of the process.

Once the work groups had completed their assessments, a few patterns became clear. First, people of color were hired into the organization, but did not rise through the organization in ways that were comparable to white staff. To address this issue, the committee recommended that an internal mentoring and career ladder program be created. Second, service and outreach staff needed assistance in meeting the needs of an ever-diversifying client population. In response, the committee designed a series of workshops that would be co-facilitated by key leaders of the various client groups and suggested that a peer-education program be instituted so that program staff could check in with each other around diversity issues in a purposeful way. Third, the committee learned that the maintenance and custodial staff at the various housing sites often became aware of problems that residents were experiencing (e.g., food shortages, children skipping school, domestic violence) well before program staff did. The committee undertook a series of focus groups with these staff to obtain a more accurate understanding of what they were witnessing. Based on this information, CHC administrators offered a series of workshops that focused on responsive steps to take regarding resident concerns to these staff members. Workshop attendees indicated that this was the first time an employer had thought to listen to their perspectives and offer assistance through training and resources.

Eighteen months into the planning and subsequent programming, the consultant did a comprehensive evaluation of the processes and outcomes. While some staff members (primarily managerial staff) complained that the overall initiative took too long and was too involved, most organizational members indicated that they appreciated how participation and inclusion were the guiding principles. Many mentioned that they felt empowered because they felt more involved, had received useful training or skill development, or saw real change in the agency in terms of more-diverse staffing, greater input into decisions, or better relations with client communities. Overall, there was a level of collective ownership and engagement in the agency that had not existed prior to the start of the strategic plan.

Empowerment needs to be central to any organizational change that is undertaken. It serves as an underlying theme in many of the chapters of this book. A change agent needs to consider how to maximize skill building, competence, self-efficacy, and participation for those involved in and benefitting from the effort. One goal for organizational change should be greater cohesion and collaboration within the agency, and this will necessitate addressing power differentials among staff and between staff and the client and consumer.

CONCLUSION

In this chapter, we discussed the characteristics of organizational structure, including the realities of organizational power and power discrepancies, particularly within the context of bureaucracies. We identified the aspects of organizational structure with great relevance for organizational change as complexity, formalization, and centralization. We explored the process of decision making within both the formal and informal realms of agency structure. We identified organizational leadership and the characteristics and authority of organizational leaders. We highlighted the status of low-power actors with regard to their role in initiating organizational change from below. Finally, we discussed the centrality of empowerment in organizational change practice. In the following chapter, we will discuss the process of organizational change from below and the assessment of specific forces that can be harnessed for change.

DISCUSSION QUESTIONS

1. Who has, and what is the basis for, power and authority in your agency setting?
2. How would you describe the organizational structure of your agency setting?
3. What elements of this structure promote organizational change? In what ways?
4. Who do you consider to be leaders in your agency and why? Are they the same individuals as those you identified in your answer to question 1?
5. What elements can serve to inhibit agency change? In what ways?
6. How can you best address power differentials between staff and clients or consumers in your organization? What do you need to keep in mind as you do this?
7. How can the empowerment of clients and workers be maximized in your agency setting? What would this look like?

REFERENCES

Austin, M., Brody, R., & Packard, T. (2009). *Managing the challenges in human service organizations.* Thousand Oaks, CA: Sage Publications.

Barker, R. (2003). *The social work dictionary* (5th ed.). Washington, DC: National Association of Social Workers.

Bouquet, C., & Birkenshaw, J. (2008). Managing power in the multinational corporation. *Journal of Management, 34*(3), 477–508.

Brager, G., & Holloway, S. (1978). *Changing human service organizations: Politics and practice.* New York: Free Press.

Brody, R. (2005). *Effectively managing human service organizations* (3rd ed.). Thousand Oaks, CA: Sage Publications.

French, J., & Raven, B. (1960). The bases of social power. In D. Cartwright & A. Zander (Eds.), *Group dynamics* (pp. 607–623). New York: Harper & Row.

Gibelman, M., & Furman, R. (2008). *Navigating human service organizations* (2nd ed.). Chicago: Lyceum Books.

Gitterman, A., & Germain, C. (2008). *The life model of social work practice* (3rd ed.). New York: Columbia University Press.

Gutiérrez, L., & Lewis, E. (1999). *Empowering women of color*. New York: Columbia University Press.

Hage, J., & Aiken, M. (1970). *Social change in complex organizations*. New York: Random House.

Hardina, D. (2005). Ten characteristics of empowerment-oriented social service organizations. *Administration in Social Work, 29*(3), 23–42.

Hyde, C. (2006). The women's co-op: The clash of two cultures. In D. Fauri, E. Netting, & S. Wernet (Eds.), *Case studies in macro social work* (2nd ed., pp. 29–44). Boston: Addison-Wesley-Longman.

Lauffer, A. (2011). *Understanding your social agency* (3rd ed.). Thousand Oaks, CA: Sage Publications.

Lovaglia, M., Mannix, E., Samuelson, C., Sell, J., & Wilson, R. (2005). Conflict, power and status in groups. In M. Poole & A. Hollingshead (Eds.), *Theories of small groups: Interdisciplinary perspectives* (pp. 139–184). Thousand Oaks, CA: Sage Publications.

Lunenburg, F. (2012). Power and leadership: An influence process. *International Journal of Management, Business, and Administration, 15*(1), 1–9.

Neugeboren, B. (1991). *Organization, policy and practice in the human services*. Binghamton, NY: Haworth Press.

O'Day, R. (1974). Intimidation rituals: Reactions to reform. *Journal of Applied Behavioral Science, 10*(3), 373–386.

Roscigno, V., Lopez, S., & Hodson, R. (2009). Supervisory bullying, status inequalities and organizational context. *Social Forces, 87*(3), 1561–1589.

Roth, G., & Wittich, C. (Eds.). (1978). *Max Weber: Economy and society* (Vol. 2). Berkeley: University of California Press.

Rothschild, J. (2009). Workers' cooperatives and social enterprise: A forgotten route to social equity and democracy. *American Behavioral Scientist, 52*(7), 1023–1041.

Scully M., & Segal A. (2002). Passion with an umbrella: Grassroots activists in the workplace. *Social Structure and Organizations Revisited, 19*, 125–168.

Seabury, B., Seabury, B., & Garvin, C. (2011). *Foundations of interpersonal practice in social work: Promoting competence in generalist practice* (3rd ed.). Thousand Oaks, CA: Sage Publications.

Simpson, B., & Macy, M. (2004). Power, identity, and collective action in social exchange. *Social Forces, 82*, 1375–1411.

Simpson, B., Markovsky, B., & Steketee, M. (2011). Power and the perception of social networks. *Social Networks, 33*, 166–171.

3

Organizational Assessment for Change

Marcia B. Cohen and Cheryl A. Hyde

Key topics of this chapter:

- Nature of planned organizational change
- Force field analysis
- Choosing change tactics
- Evaluating outcomes

INTRODUCTION

We have now examined basic characteristics and culture; and structure, policies, programs, and processes of human service organizations agencies, and have discussed some of the dynamics of organizational power and empowerment. In this chapter, we turn to the practice of planned organizational change and the assessment of specific forces that can be harnessed for change by low-power actors. This discussion will include identifying the nature of planned change, delineating the steps necessary in identifying an organizational problem for change, framing a change goal, determining participating actors in the change process, analyzing the forces promoting and inhibiting the accomplishment of the change goal, and determining appropriate change tactics. We will examine at length the methodology of the force field analysis, which is at the heart of organizational change practice. The chapter will conclude with a discussion of how to evaluate the outcomes of organizational change efforts.

THE NATURE OF PLANNED ORGANIZATIONAL CHANGE

Before discussing the steps necessary for identifying an organizational problem that necessitates change, we first need to explore what we mean by change. As Meenaghan and Gibbons (2000) point out, the process of effecting social change within organizations and communities is a highly complex process. As suggested by Mayer (1972), social change is inherently socially structured. Mayer describes organization structures as including status, role, and social relationships; these elements are integral to the concept of organizational functioning and change. *Status* is related to positional power within an organization, which influences organization participants' ability to bring about change. *Role* encompasses participants' activities within the social system of the organization, including the role of the social worker as a change agent. The behavior of organizational participants takes place within the context of *social relationships* and is influenced by participant self-interest (Meenaghan & Gibbons, 2000). The social worker seeking change needs to weigh these socially structured aspects of organizational life and be a deliberate participant in the change process.

It is also important to note that all social change is inherently political. Thus, organizational change takes place within a political context. Efforts by the social worker to bring about change are generally motivated by client interests that are not being met. The worker must consider the political dynamics and participant self-interest at play in the organizational decision-making process. These considerations are important to the process of planned organizational change, which we will now turn to.

GETTING STARTED ON PLANNED ORGANIZATIONAL CHANGE: SELECTING A CHANGE GOAL

As will be discussed in more detail below, the individual seeking organizational change (the change agent) begins by identifying a problem or concern in the organization that is having a negative impact on clients, constituents, and/or staff. The problem may be unmet or inadequately met client needs. Often the change agent learns of this problem directly from clients. The change agent then identifies a change goal that addresses this problem. This goal should be realistic in terms of agency values and available resources. The more specific the goal and the more it can be framed in operational terms, the more readily the change agent can determine its feasibility.

Organizational Participants and Self-Interest

The change agent next must identify organizational participants who would effect, and be affected by, the desired change. The change agent should evaluate the likely responses of these participants, including their self-interest in regards to their prestige, autonomy, influence, or authority. A change that will enhance participants' self-interest is likely to engender support whereas one that is perceived as threatening self-interest is likely to result in resistance. The worker seeking change should pay attention to participant behavior during formal and informal contacts, as these can reveal their self-interests (Gitterman & Germain, 2008).

Change agents also should evaluate their own organizational position and resources, formal and informal. Low-power actors may lack the structural opportunities for interacting with key participants and obtaining necessary information. However, an alliance with a key player, an administrative assistant for example, may improve the position of change agents and enhance access to essential data. For example, although a student intern is likely to have a relatively limited structural position in the organization, student status may generate access to key decision makers and other influential participants and possibly result in opportunities for experimentation. Finally, the change agent needs to develop organizational self-awareness, which is the ability to evaluate how others in the organization view him or her.

Such attributes as perceived competence, knowledge, and skill are valuable resources. A realistic appraisal of the change agent's availability of time and energy to work toward the desired change are also important components of organizational self-awareness. Thus, the change agent must assess not only the self-interest of decision makers and other actors of influence, but also her or his own resources.

Brager and Holloway (1978) suggest the following resources as being available to staff seeking change: knowledge and expertise, social appeal, social rewards, shared norms, collegial relationships, energy, tenure, and solidarity with other staff groups. Perceived knowledge and expertise enhances a change agent's prestige in the organization. Social appeal refers to the social attraction of the change agent: the greater the appeal, the more likely the change agent is to be able to influence others in the organization. Social rewards are those resources that the worker can bestow on other organizational staff, including gratitude, deference, recognition, and approval. Collegial relationships include shared norms, values, and social relationships. Tenure or longevity (the length of time the change agent has been with the organization) can be a potent source of influence. The social worker who has been in the organization for many years is more likely to have developed relationships with other staff, have familiarity with the organization's history with regard to the proposed change, be cognizant of agency rules and formal and informal decision-making structures, and be perceived as a stable and loyal staff member. Another powerful resource available to low-power change agents is their potential solidarity with other staff. This can be crucial for the building of alliances. We would also add solidarity with clients, rarely discussed by other theorists, who can be effective partners in the change effort.

THE FORCE FIELD ANALYSIS

Assessment is of critical importance in social work practice with all system sizes. Organizational assessment can be particularly complex because it involves the consideration of a large number of forces and actors. As our earlier discussion has demonstrated, in organizational practice there is a wide range of variables, within and without the organization, that change agents must carefully consider. Force field analysis, the tool to be discussed in this section, is particularly appropriate for organizational change assessment. Force field analysis is derived from Kurt Lewin's field theory (1951). Brager and Holloway (1978), among others, further developed this framework for purposes of assessing organizational readiness for change. Field theory conceptualizes stability within social systems as being in a constant state of dynamic equilibrium, rather than being static. Seeming organizational stability results from the presence of opposing and countervailing forces that operate to produce and maintain systemic equilibrium. Change occurs when the forces shift, creating disequilibrium in the system. Force field analysis enables the change agent to identify the forces that support or oppose the proposed change, particularly those that will influence key decision makers and other influential participants. This information is critical in guiding the change agent as to which forces can be shifted in the direction of the change.

This analysis begins with data collection and framing the goal for change, continues with identifying key organizational actors and decision makers, and proceeds to a careful categorization of forces for and against the proposed change. This assessment methodology is time tested and widely recognized as a tool for organizational change practice (Meenaghan & Gibbons, 2000; Netting, Kettner, & McMurtry, 2008).

Data Collection and Framing the Goal for Change

Once the change agent has determined the problem, he or she needs to collect the relevant data to determine the forces for and against the success of the change effort. The change agent needs to carefully assess external and internal forces (see chapters 1 and 2) to determine their likely influence on efforts to promote the desired change. Since the change agent needs to be concerned about how organizational actors will behave with reference to the change goal, the focus of data collection is on the meaning a potential change has for the relevant participants. Data gathering can include discussions with staff at other agencies, library research, and internet research. However, most of the data collection will come from within the change agent's organization. This information can be formal, and includes surveys, focus group interviews, content analysis of agency publications, mission statements, and other internal documents. Typically, much of the change agent's data gathering will be informal: observing, talking informally to staff and clients about how they experience the problem, discovering what its history in the agency has been, determining the outcomes of any earlier change efforts, and learning the prior behavior of organizational actors in response to change in general as well as change regarding the specific identified problem. A change agent may send up a trial balloon, asking a seemingly innocuous question related to the problem for change for the purpose of surfacing the responses of key participants. Much of the data gathering may initially need to be unobtrusive. If agency decision makers become aware of the proposed change prematurely, they may reject it out of hand, potentially ending the change effort before it has begun.

Information gleaned from organizational and environmental assessment can be used to determine how the change agent can best frame the change goal to increase its likelihood of acceptance. As stated earlier, it is important that the goal be specific and stated in operational terms that can serve to focus the change effort and facilitate the evaluation of its success. Often there are multiple goals that can address the problem. A preliminary assessment of available data can be extremely helpful in determining which goal will be pursued and how it will be framed. An example will illustrate this point.

EXAMPLE: INITIAL ASSESSMENT FOR CHANGE

A social work student placed in an elementary school observed that a large number of the teaching staff appeared to be experiencing considerable stress, which was impairing their work with students. She began her data collection by interviewing the teachers. They confirmed her perception that they were under a great deal of stress, which was having a negative effect on their work with students. For some, this stress was a function of overwork and poor working conditions. For others, it was the intrusion of personal and familial difficulties into their work life. The student continued her data collection through discussions with the school social worker (her field instructor), who concurred with her assessment of the problem.

The student considered a range of possible change goals to ameliorate the severe staff distress she was observing. Some, such as helping the staff form a union, did not seem feasible, based on prior unsuccessful efforts to unionize at the school. Decreasing workloads and improving working conditions, while highly desirable, seemed unlikely in a time of school budget cuts and retrenchment. Also, such remedies would not address the personal problems staff was contending with. After talking with staff and researching how other school systems in the state were managing similar situations, the student framed her change goal as having the school implement an employee assistance program (EAP).

Assessing the wider environment, the student determined that there were two schools in the school district that already provided EAP services. Discussions with the social workers at those schools suggested that the provision of EAP services, while not addressing the systemic organizational dysfunction, had been successful in improving teacher morale and effectiveness. Inter-

nally, the student learned from the social worker that the principal had proposed an EAP the previous year, but that the plan appeared to have stalled at the level of the school superintendent. This suggested openness to the change goal on the part of the principal, but potential organizational resistance from the superintendent, a higher-level administrator.

It was clear to the student that if she framed her change goal ambitiously as implementing an EAP in the elementary school she would need to collect data that would persuade the superintendent. She also framed an alternative change goal, which could be implemented without the need for approval at the level of the superintendent. This goal was to have the school hold a series of brown bag seminars with outside experts on a variety of topics that would address many of the areas of stress that staff was experiencing. The student saw this considerably more incremental change goal as a backup plan in the event that the EAP effort proved unfeasible.

Once having made a preliminary determination of possible goals, the student was ready to take the next steps: identifying key organizational actors and decision makers, and assessing the array of forces, those that appear likely to promote the desired change and those that seem likely to inhibit it.

Identifying Key Organizational Actors and Decision Makers

Earlier, we discussed the importance of identifying key participants in the change process. Once the change agent has gathered the relevant data and framed a potentially feasible goal for change, she or he can refine this identification. The relevant actors need to be identified in order to determine their potential support of the change goal and the extent to which they can be influenced. These actors are critical actors, facilitating actors, and allies. *Critical actors* are organizational participant(s) who have formal or informal power to implement the change goal. These are the individuals whose support is essential for the goal to be accomplished. They are frequently, but not always, administrators and other high-level decision makers. *Facilitating actors* are organizational participants with the formal or informal power to help or hinder the change agent's efforts to get to the critical actor(s). Facilitating actors can serve as gatekeepers to access higher-power actors or can influence them for or against the change effort. *Allies* are participants who support the change goal and can be called on to help in the change efforts.[1]

---

[1]The earlier literature does not include the category of allies. We include it here because allies can enhance change efforts through their support and potentially be mobilized as part of a change strategy.

Allies often are low-power actors who can bring strength in numbers or provide support, and frequently are coworkers and agency clients.

Constructing a Force Field Analysis

Once external and internal forces have been identified, data have been gathered, a change goal framed, and the relevant actors identified, the force field analysis can be constructed. A force field analysis is a listing of the key actors and the array of forces, those that appear likely to promote the change (driving forces) and those that seem likely to inhibit the change (restraining forces), particularly in relation to their influence on key actors. If the driving forces are increased or the restraining forces decreased, organizational participants will be more likely to support the proposed change. A force field analysis template (as used by the authors of the case studies in chapters 5–14) is presented in figure 3.1.

FIGURE 3.1. Template for a Force Field Analysis

Change Goal:

Critical Actors:
1.
2.
3.

Facilitating Actors:
1.
2.
3.

Potential Allies:
1.
2.
3.

Driving Forces for Change:	*Restraining Forces for Change:*
1.	1.
2.	2.
3.	3.
4.	4.

The change agent constructs a balance sheet, with driving forces listed on one side and restraining forces on the other. He or she should list these forces with as much specificity and precision as possible. For example, listing "the agency's mission" as a driving force for change is too general to be useful in determining strategy. It is more helpful to specify the particular aspect of the mission; an example would be "client empowerment" as the relevant force (Brager & Holloway, 1993). The purpose of creating this balance sheet is to identify all of the relevant forces and determine which of the driving forces can be increased and which of the restraining forces can be decreased. This determination can be used as a predictor of the likelihood of success in achieving the change goal.

Once the change agent has developed the balance sheet, he or she can evaluate each force to determine its potential for modification and impact with regard to the change goal. The change agent assesses the forces with regard to three characteristics: amenability to change, potency, and consistency. *Amenability to change* refers to the likelihood of modifying a force, particularly the potential to increase it if it is a driving force or decrease it if it is a restraining force. The worker may modify the forces directly or through the efforts of others. *Potency* refers to the impact of the force on achieving the goal—in other words, how much impact will an increase or decrease in the force have on the desired change? As with the assessment of amenability, evaluating the potency of a force provides important information about the feasibility of the change goal and may also suggest the next steps the worker needs to take in advancing the goal. *Consistency* refers to the presumed stability or predictability of the force. Can the worker anticipate that the force will remain stable, or that if increased or decreased in the desired direction the force will remain in its new state?

Once the worker has assessed the forces as to their amenability, potency, and consistency, he or she is in a position to estimate the likelihood of achieving the change goal through a further examination of the driving and restraining forces. Forces are categorized as working, framing, or unpredictable. *Working forces* are those that can be used to advance the change goal. These forces are those that are judged to be amenable to influence, potent, and consistent. The likelihood of success is directly related to the number and strength of the working forces. The greater the percentage of working forces, the more likely the change effort will succeed. *Framing forces* are low in amenability and high in consistency. They make up the predictable organizational and environmental context within which the change effort will take place. Although not subject to the worker's modifications, it is important to evaluate these attributes. Driving forces that are framing can have a positive impact on the worker's change efforts, whereas framing forces that are restraining can have a negative impact and impede success. An example of the former are accreditation standards that must be met and that support the desired change. An example of the latter would be statewide funding cuts. A force is judged to be framing if it is low in amenability and high in consistency. Framing forces can vary in potency. *Unpredictable forces* are those that lack consistency or are uncertain with regard to amenability or potency. If the force field analysis includes unpredictable forces, then this may be an indication that the worker needs to obtain more data or proceed with caution. When the stakes are high and there is considerable unpredictability in the forces, it is generally too risky to proceed. Under these circumstances, the worker may need to consider other change goals related to the problem or wait until the situation becomes more predictable.

EXAMPLE: CONTINUING THE ASSESSMENT

The student in the EAP example above conducted a force field analysis, including the relevant attributes in the field of forces. She began by identifying the driving and restraining forces relevant to her change goal. Her driving forces included

1. support for the change goal from the principal who has proposed developing an EAP in the past;
2. support from the school social worker who has high credibility within the school;
3. communication with the teachers who have said that they need help with the stress they are experiencing;
4. documented research showing that EAP services can improve teacher morale, effectiveness, and productivity, resulting in a better learning environment for students; and
5. increased teacher productivity can enhance the school's compliance with the federal No Child Left Behind Act (2001).

Her restraining forces included

1. the high cost of providing EAP services;
2. the fact that the economy has been weak and there has been some talk of cutbacks in funding for schools in the state;
3. the school superintendent's recent position of not being receptive to this idea; and
4. the fact that an EAP will not directly address the problems of overwork and poor working conditions.

The student's force field analysis (see figure 3.2) included her analysis of forces and culminated in a categorization assessment of the forces as working, framing, and unpredictable. When she looked over her force field analysis with her field instructor, several things were quickly apparent. Three of her five driving forces

FIGURE 3.2. Force Field Analysis for Student School-based Change Plan

---

Change Goal:

To implement a support structure such as an employee assistance program (EAP) based in the school with the goal of improving interactions between staff and students.

Critical Actors:

1. Superintendent of schools

Facilitating Actors:

1. Principal

2. School social worker

3. Lead teacher

Potential Allies:

1. Teachers

2. Parents

Driving Forces for Change:	*Restraining Forces for Change:*
1. Principal supports EAP services in the school (Amenable, Potent, Consistent; A Working Force)	1. Providing an EAP would be costly. (Potent and Consistent; A Framing Force)
2. School social worker supports EAP services and has credibility within the school (Amenable, Potent, Consistent; A Working Force)	2. The weak economy has threatened funding for the school system. (Potent and Consistent; A Framing Force)
3. Teachers have indicated that they would like some help with the stress they are experiencing. (Amenable, Potent, Consistent; A Working Force)	3. The superintendent did not act on the previous proposal for an EAP. (Potent and Consistent; A Framing Force)
4. EAP services can improve teacher morale, effectiveness, and productivity, resulting in a better learning environment for students. (Potent and Consistent; A Framing Force)	
5. Increased teacher productivity may enhance the school's compliance with the federal No Child Left Behind Act. (Potentially Potent but low in Amenability and Consistency; Unpredictable)	

were working forces and one was a driving, framing force. These forces were considered working because they suggested support that might be mobilized to influence the superintendent in the direction of the change goal, in addition to possibly mobilizing parents as allies. Furthermore, the data (from the two schools that had EAP services and the literature) that pointed to the benefits of an EAP could be persuasive. However, on the restraining side the three framing forces (high cost of EAP services, possible budget cuts, and the superintendent's historical lack of support for the plan) seemed insurmountable, all of them being potent and consistent and none being amenable to influence. The student and school social worker consulted with the principal, who agreed with this assessment and indicated that, for financial reasons, she believed it was just not the right time to renew her EAP proposal to the superintendent. She indicated that the data supporting an EAP would be useful when funding was more stable and promised to reintroduce the plan then. The student then returned to her force field analysis to assess her back-up goal of providing a series of seminars to teachers to address some of their concerns. While this was a far more modest and incremental goal, it proved successful and ultimately beneficial. The original change goal was not abandoned but rather put on hold temporarily until the circumstances became more favorable.

CHOOSING CHANGE TACTICS

Once the force field analysis is complete, the change agent should have a good idea of the change goal's feasibility and which driving forces need to be brought to bear on the key actors and which restraining forces need to be reduced. The next step is to determine which tactics to employ in order to modify the forces in the direction of the change goal. Tactics are the specific short-range behaviors that are linked together to form strategies. Tactics have been conceptualized as being either collaborative, campaign, or contest in nature (Brager & Holloway, 1978; Netting et al., 2008). These form a continuum of tactics that range from least conflictual to most conflictual (see table 3.1). It is important to remember that when choosing change tactics the change agent should involve clients in the process as much as possible while ensuring that their interests are protected (Netting et al., 2008).

Collaborative tactics include open communication, provision of information, recommendations, problem solving, education, and mild persuasion. These tactics imply a degree of teamwork and reciprocity. Collaboration is most effective in situations where there is a general agreement (goal consensus) that the problem for change exists, and where all parties are operating in good faith (Resnick & Patti, 1980). The change agent may begin by simply making the decision maker (target actor) aware that the problem exists and sharing the data that he or she has collected. If the target actor shares the change agent's perception and concern about the problem,

TABLE 3.1. Range of Change Tactics

Tactic	Level of Conflict	Action Repertoires
Collaborative		
Agreement, or high potential for agreement, between constituent and target systems that change is needed and resources are available.	• Least conflictual • Overt methods • Beginning point in keeping with the principle of least contest	• Open communication • Education • Mild persuasion • Presenting recommendations, alternatives, demonstration projects • Cooperative planning
Campaign		
Target system willing to communicate with constituent system, but • Presenting little consensus that change is needed; and • Unwilling to allocate resources.	• More conflictual • More covert methods • Principle of least contest dictates starting with campaign strategies before moving to contest	• Negotiation and bargaining • Hard persuasion/ education • Hidden agendas • Social marketing via media use • Threats (of using conflict tactics) • Lobbying and testifying • Informational picketing
Contest		
Target system opposes change or allocation of resources and is not open to further communication.	• Most conflictual • Covert and overt methods	• Demands, call for sanctions • Public criticism • Demonstrations, protests, rallies (legal or illegal) • Boycotts (acts of non-compliance) • Strikes and picket lines • Class action lawsuits

mutual problem solving can take place and the change goal discussed. Sometimes the worker will need to try to convince the target actor, using mild persuasion (i.e., expressing ideas and arguments regarding the problem and the merits of the change goal).

Campaign tactics fall in the middle range of the hierarchy of tactics. They are best used in situations where the decision maker(s) does not agree that the problem exists, is indifferent to the problem, or gives lip service to looking into the problem but takes no action and is unwilling to explore the issue further. This would be characterized as issue difference. Campaign tactics can include bargaining, negotiation, hard persuasion, political maneuvering, and mild coercion. Bargaining and negotiation generally take the form of the change agent making requests or demands, arguing them, and arriving at a point of compromise. The term "hard persuasion" refers to a mode of advocacy for the change agent's point of view that is aimed at the specific interests of the target actor. The change agent carefully selects which facts to present and which to omit in order to increase the strength of his or her argument. Mild coercion refers to the mobilization of pressure directed at the target actor aimed at increasing the likelihood of his or her acceptance of the goal (Brager & Holloway, 1978). An example of mild coercion would be a petition signed by staff or clients, or both, advocating for the change. Organizing a petition campaign is also an example of political maneuvering. Campaign tactics can be covert. For example, while the worker may organize the petition drive, his or her role in this activity may not necessarily be revealed. It is important, however, that this activity not jeopardize clients in any way. Similarly, the deliberate selection of which facts to include and which to omit has a covert quality. The potentially controversial issue of using covert tactics will be discussed at greater length below.

Contest tactics are the most conflictual and are used in situations where there is total goal dissensus (complete divergence in perspective) between the change agent and the target actor concerning the problem for change. They are most often used when there is a sharp difference in power between the change agent and the target actor, and when there is considerable organizational distance between them. Contest tactics are characterized by the mobilization of public pressure or sanctions directed at the target actor in order to bring about acceptance of the change goal. These tactics include demands, calls for sanctions (e.g., by funding or accrediting bodies), public criticism, protest demonstrations, use of the media, whistle-blowing, acts of noncompliance including boycotts, and acts of interference such as strikes and picket lines. These actions can bring swift results with regard to the change goal but they can also have negative consequences for the change agent and his or her allies, including clients. Hence, they must be entered into cautiously. The change agent needs to ensure that clients and allies will not be jeopardized by their actions, and that they understand and are fully prepared to risk potential consequences. The worker also needs to ensure his or her safety from reprisals or make a deliberate decision to take serious risks. These risks can range from the target actor assailing the worker's credibility, to demotion, or even firing. Contest tactics are not to be used lightly. They are generally not invoked unless less-adversarial tactics have proven unsuccessful and the stakes are high. The change agent must make certain that she or he has sufficient resources in the form of strong support from internal and external allies before initiating adversarial tactics. In the case of whistle-blowing, there are legal protections available to the change agent. However, even when support and protections exist, it is generally unwise to begin change efforts at the level of contest.

The Principle of Least Contest

The principle of least contest dictates that change agents begin at the least conflictual tactical level that is appropriate to the change goal and the organization. Beginning with campaign or contest tactics before attempting more collaborative approaches can easily backfire, leaving the change agent open to the charge of irresponsibility for not first discussing the plan with the key participants. "It is important not to escalate the change effort unnecessarily. If the change agent begins with campaign or contest tactics, it may then be impossible to deescalate to more collaborative methods" (Netting et al., 2008, p. 355). In contrast, the worker who begins with a series of collaborative tactics that prove unsuccessful, and who then gradually escalates to campaign tactics, will have greater credibility because of the initial, more-collaborative approach.

EXAMPLE: CHOOSING TACTICS

Many of the issues involved in choosing change tactics are illustrated in the following example of organizational change in a hospital-based drug rehab center. The change agents in this example were two social work interns, one of whom was also employed by the facility. These workers became aware from their many immigrant clients that the agency provided little more in the way of culturally sensitive services for immigrant clients than the provision of interpreters for non-English speakers. They framed a broad change goal of increasing cultural sensitivity in the delivery of the facility's services through the provision of staff training and collaboration with outside agencies providing multicultural services. They gathered data through discussion with staff and analyzed staff handbooks and agency policy manuals. They also compiled a list of multicultural resources in the community that might provide support and assistance to the rehab facility through trainings, referrals, and collaboration.

The students conducted a force field analysis that identified the presence of four working driving forces:

1. The Joint Commission on Accreditation of Healthcare Organizations (JCAHO), the facility's accrediting body, mandates the provision of culturally sensitive services.

2. The facility's Process Improvement Team (PIT), a standing committee in the facility with responsibility for making policy recommendations and improving services, supports the change goal.

3. There was an increased need for culturally sensitive services as the community had become more diverse.

4. Several multicultural community agencies had agreed to provide support and resources.

The change agents also identified three restraining forces: (1) cost; (2) insufficient staff time; and (3) the staff's potential fear of increased workload demands. The first two restraining forces were assessed as framing forces, while staff concerns about the impact on their workload were assessed as unpredictable.

Once securing external support from multicultural agencies and developing internal support from staff, the students began with collaborative tactics directed at the program director, a critical actor. Their tactics included open discussion, education of the program director as to the increase in number of non-English speaking patients served by the facility, and problem solving as to what services were most needed. They recommended that the facility begin with intensive staff training, utilizing the resources of outside agencies. When the program director appeared to be unconvinced, stating limitations in time and funds, the students moved into more of a campaign mode by mentioning the JCAHO requirement and implying that JCAHO might become aware of the facility's noncompliance in this area.

This veiled threat got the director's attention. They were able to move back into a collaborative problem-solving mode, with the students offering to organize the first training session and involve multicultural experts from the community who would not charge for their services. The program director agreed, and subsequently mandated all staff of the rehab facility receive the training. The training itself was videotaped for future use and a collaborative relationship between the facility and multicultural community agencies was forged. The threat of JCAHO noncompliance proved sufficiently potent to overcome the restraining forces. While the overall strategy used by the students was collaborative in nature, this one campaign tactic, a threat, proved sufficient to overcome resistance. These students followed the principle of least contest. Had they begun with the threat, it might have created a hostile environment and the subsequent, problem-solving discussion and successful outcome might not have been achieved.

Covert Behavior

While the students in the above example used the campaign tactic of a threat, they did not need to resort to covert behavior. That is not always the case. Covert behavior includes all efforts to influence the target actor(s) that are unobtrusive or disguised in some manner. In extreme situations, it can involve deception. Sometimes the change agent needs to be unobtrusive during the data-gathering process so as not to reveal her or his plan prematurely, resulting in a negative response from the key actors early in the process, which prevents the change effort from going forward before it has begun. Covert behavior is distinguished from overt behavior in which the change agent's activities are fully transparent.

As Netting and colleagues (2008) point out, change often involves the shifting of power from those who have it to those who do not. Under these circumstances, there can be a risk that open actions will fail. This circumstance can create a need for secrecy on the part of the change agent. They also point out that actions begun in secret often do not remain secret. Hence, the change agent needs to be prepared for the consequences of covert actions becoming known, and needs to ensure that the tactics used will hold up to ethical standards.

Brager and Holloway (1978) offer clear guidelines regarding the ethical use of covert tactics. They note that the norms and ethics of the social work profession assume a commitment to serving clients to the best of that profession's ability. When this concern for the interests of clients is ignored or replaced by personal or organizational interests and more open methods to promote change have failed, it is ethical to use covert methods. They suggest that covert tactics are appropriate when the following conditions are present: (1) Agency officials are ignoring the needs of clients in service of personal interests. (2) The worker is unable to access legitimate sources of influence without jeopardizing clients, colleagues, or himself or herself. (3) Overt tactics have been tried and failed or are not feasible (see also Morrill, Zald, & Rao, 2003). The complex issue of ethics in organizational practice is discussed at length in Seabury, Seabury, and Garvin (2011), who point out differences in both the client–worker and the agency–worker relationships. This discussion is elaborated in chapter 4.

EVALUATING OUTCOMES

It is important that the change agent evaluate the outcome of the change efforts. Often, the success or failure of these efforts is self-evident. In the prior example of students seeking an increased focus on the needs of patients from diverse cultures, the mandated provision of multicultural training for staff constituted success. Had the students set a further goal of increased multicultural knowledge and expanding services and referrals resulting from the training, measuring outcomes might include several types of evaluation. Such measurement might take the form of participant evaluations of the training, evaluation of staff knowledge through testing before and after the training, and interviews with staff and clients. If the provision of multicultural services is documented by the facility, an assessment of this documentation would also be useful in evaluating outcomes. If the outcome of the training remained unclear, an alternative measure might take the form of a measurement scale (Seabury et al., 2011). In this example, a scale measuring staff sensitivity to and knowledge about multicultural issues would be appropriate.

Evaluations of outcomes can be made at more than one point in time. The training may appear to have been successful shortly after it took place, but it is important to determine whether multicultural services are still being used six months later, and whether there appears to be a need for additional training. The more specific and operational the framing of the change goal, the more readily it can be measured.

CONCLUSION

The primary focus of this chapter was how to facilitate planned organizational change. We have discussed the importance of collecting information and teasing out forces that are relevant to the change goal. The change agent gathers data regarding these forces and any other information that is relevant to the problem for change. Once data have been gathered and considered, the change agent selects a change goal that is specific and operationalizable. Once the change goal has been framed, the key actors in the organization are identified.

Next, we reviewed the process of constructing a force field analysis that will serve to determine the change agent's next steps. With the change goal specified and the key players in the organization identified, the change agent should have sufficient information to begin developing a force field analysis. Forces are assessed as being driving or restraining in relation to the change goal and their potential to influence key actors. They are further categorized as to their amenability (openness to influence), potency (impact), and consistency (stability). This information is then used to determine which forces are working forces (usable in influencing key actors), which are framing (fixed aspects of the organizational environment that cannot be modified), and which are unpredictable forces (lacking in consistency or certainty). An examination of the completed force field analysis, particularly the number and strengths of the working forces, should provide the change agent with enough information to determine the feasibility of the change goal and to begin developing tactics.

We discussed three types of tactics: collaborative, campaign, and contest. These tactics move from the least to the most conflictual. We described the basis for choosing among tactics and presented examples. We introduced the principle of least contest, emphasizing the importance of beginning at the lowest level of conflict appropriate to the change goal and organization and escalating to more-conflictual tactics only when less-conflictual tactics prove unsuccessful. We explored the use of covert tactics, and discussed the circumstances in which they constitute ethical, professional behavior.

We concluded the chapter with a discussion of the evaluation of outcomes. This evaluation is an important step in organizational change practice and is consistent with the current emphasis on evidence-based practice. We introduced a number of methods for measuring success, along with the caveat that these may need to be repeated over time to determine whether the change goal is still in force.

DISCUSSION QUESTIONS

1. Identify a problem or gap in your agency's provision of services to clients or constituent groups. How would you go about gaining information regarding this organizational problem?
2. Who would you want to talk to? What are some other sources of information that might be helpful to you in obtaining data?
3. How would you frame your change goal(s) based on your organizational assessment? What are some alternative frames?
4. What would you do if your force field analysis suggests a great deal of unpredictability in the external or internal agency environment?
5. Under what circumstances, if any, would you feel comfortable about engaging in covert tactics? Why or why not?

REFERENCES

Brager, G., & Holloway, S. (1978). *Changing human service organizations: Politics and practice.* New York: Free Press.

Brager, G., & Holloway, S. (1993). Assessing the prospects for organizational change: The uses of force field analysis. *Administration in Social Work, 16*(3/4), 15–28.

Gitterman, A., & Germain, C. (2008). *The life model of social work practice* (3rd ed.). New York: Columbia University Press.

Lewin, K. (1951). *Field theory in social science.* New York: Harper & Row.

Mayer, R. (1972). *Social planning and social change.* Englewood Cliffs, NJ: Prentice Hall.

Meenaghan, T., & Gibbons, W. (2000). *Generalist practice in larger settings: Knowledge and skills concepts.* Chicago: Lyceum Books.

Morrill, C., Zald, M., & Rao, H. (2003). Covert political conflict in organizations: Challenges from below. *Annual Review of Sociology, 29*, 391–415.

Netting, F., Kettner, P., & McMurtry, S. (2008), *Social work macro practice* (4th ed.). Boston: Pearson Education.

No Child Left Behind Act (2001). P.L. 107-110. 107th Congress, Sess. 1. http://www.govtrack.us/congress/bills/107/hr1

Resnick, H., & Patti, R. (1980). *Change from within: Humanizing social welfare organizations.* Philadelphia: Temple University Press.

Seabury, B., Seabury, B., & Garvin, C. (2011) *Foundations of interpersonal practice in social work: Promoting competence in generalist practice* (3rd ed.). Thousand Oaks, CA: Sage Publications.

4

Social Justice and the Ethics of Organizational Change from Below

Brett A. Seabury, Marcia B. Cohen, and Cheryl A. Hyde

Key topics of this chapter:

- Economic context of and for organizational change
- Ethics of a profession committed to social justice
- Ethical organizational change
- Revisiting change tactics

INTRODUCTION

In this chapter, we address some of the ethical issues that inform the practice of change agents, social workers in particular, who are in low-power agency positions. We do so from a social justice perspective, which is a core value in social work. The ethics of working to change "target systems" (i.e., communities and organizations) has not been elaborated with the same depth as are the ethics involved in helping "client systems" to change (but see Bloom & Farragher, 2010; Hyde, 2012; Minkler, Pies, & Hyde, 2012). When clients and social workers come together to change aspects of the client's environment, their work usually places them in low-power positions compared to the organizations or community structures targeted for change (Patti, 1974). This chapter presents some of the major economic issues that confront social workers and their clients, provides a summary of how ethical practice is linked to broader social justice values, discusses how to engage in ethical organizational change, and describes some of the basic tactics and countertactics of organizational change. We conclude the chapter with a case example that illustrates these points.

THE ECONOMIC CONTEXT OF AND FOR ORGANIZATIONAL CHANGE

In order to put this discussion of ethics in context, we begin with a brief overview of the economic issues faced by poor and working families who find themselves receiving social work services (Bloom & Farragher, 2010). There is an unprecedented income gap between the very rich and everyone else, with wealth and attendant power concentrated among a small percentage of Americans (Edelman, 2012). Recent years have seen increasingly severe cuts in funding available to human service organizations, a growing scarcity of services, elimination of worker rights programs, welfare reform, and the deregulation of banking and housing sectors.

This is the context for work in human service organizations (see chapter 1 for a more general discussion) that can result in regressive actions against workers when agencies run into financial difficulties. Line workers are converted into contract workers so the agency no longer pays for health or retirement benefits and in some cases no longer has to comply with a union contract that previously protected workers' rights. Contract workers are paid on the basis of client contacts and the client's ability to pay, so that agencies screen and take only those clients with good insurance or the economic resources to pay the full fee. Poor clients without insurance are pushed to the end of the waiting list (Collins & Mayer, 2010; Figueira-Mcdonough, 2007; also authors' information from local agencies).

It should be the responsibility of persons in powerful positions to address and find remedies for their misguided decisions that harm others. This notion of redistributive justice does not exist today in powerful organizations and institutions that are more likely to cover up, minimize, or blame others for the chaos that they have created. Challenging these systemic problems, therefore, becomes the ethical imperative of social workers.

When a social worker is involved in organizational change, he or she negotiates three primary arenas: the client system, the worker system, and the target system. All three systems are affected by the aforementioned economic trends, albeit differentially. The client system includes various individual, family, and group networks and resources. The worker system comprises agency- and profession-based networks, policies, and procedures. The client usually is part of one (and probably more) communities, and has affiliations with a number of organizations; these communities and organizations constitute the target system. The target system manifests the problem or issue of concern and also hopefully holds the key to rectifying the situation. When change occurs, the social worker needs to interact with the client and target systems, though this can get complicated if, for example, the practitioner's place of employment also is the target system, or if the client is a nonvoluntary "member" of the target system. Figure 4.1 presents the basic relationships among these three systems.

The relationship that a social worker has with the client system is based on a contract, which signifies an agreement to work together to solve some problem in the client's life and to achieve some goal that both parties agree to pursue. The target system represents those aspects of the client's life that must be changed in order to realize the goals in the contract. The relation-

FIGURE 4.1. Worker's Relationship to Client and Target Systems

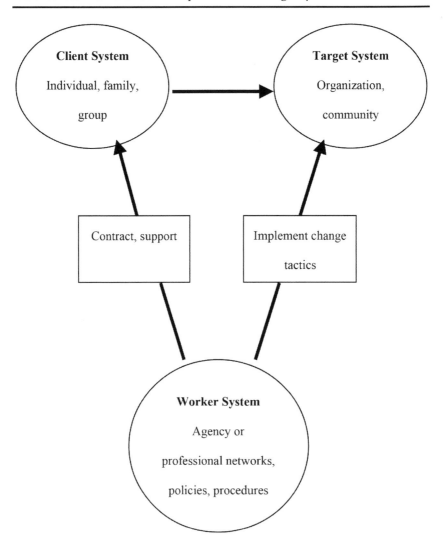

ship that the social worker has with the client system differs from the relationship that the social worker develops with the organization or community in the target system. Moreover, a challenge for the practitioner is to engage in change while maintaining one's professional ethics and commitment to social justice.

THE ETHICS OF A PROFESSION COMMITTED TO SOCIAL JUSTICE

When entering social work, students learn about the context and systems described above and can feel overwhelmed by the progressive ideology of social work. Some may wonder why they have to deal with the errors of the political economy or how they can be expected in such a "lowly" profession to make changes in such vast social problems. Many arrive in social work hoping to work with children and families or to create nonprofit agencies focused on some special client group, but are uncomfortable looking at the implications and consequences of the larger sociopolitical environment. Most students are the products of privilege (i.e., race, gender, or class), and may resist examining the implications of their cultural identities.

Addressing these struggles, for students as well as practitioners, is part of embracing the profession's tradition of engaging in progressive actions to alter the societal arrangements that negatively affect individuals and communities in vulnerable or low-power positions. At the end of the nineteenth century and beginning of the twentieth century, the settlement house movement addressed the oppressive living conditions of immigrants and their exploitation in sweatshops. Social work pioneers promoted laws to eliminate child labor and support women's suffrage (Addams, 1935), and supported the peace movement that advocated for the United States to stay out of World War I. In the 1940s, social workers mobilized to stop the internment of Japanese Americans in camps in the wake of Pearl Harbor and rallied against fellow social workers who staffed the Relocation Administration (Nickel, 1942a, 1942b). In the aftermath of World War II, Bertha Capen Reynolds, the premiere social work educator of her time, worked endlessly to promote a progressive agenda for the profession by looking at the political and economic issues that were negatively impacting poor and working class families (Reynolds, 1964). She was a staunch supporter of workers' rights, a position that brought down the wrath of the House Un-American Activities Committee.

During the Vietnam War, the National Association of Social Workers (NASW) went on record opposing that war, and later opposed the Iraq War. More recently, NASW promoted policy positions including support for affirmative action in hiring and education; the rights of lesbian, gay, bisexual, and transgender (LGBT) populations and undocumented immigrants; and women's reproductive choice, including abortion. Many of these progressive policy positions by NASW may not be popular with the rest of society, but they are consistent with the views of the majority of social workers; while social workers are not monolithic in their political ideologies, studies repeatedly indicate that most of them hold liberal to progressive views on health and welfare issues (Rosenwald & Hyde, 2006).

These examples suggest some of the ethical principles that guide social workers in social justice work. But what are current ethical guidelines for their actions to change the institutions in society, their communities, and the organizations that hire them when change is indicated? The NASW *Code of Ethics* outlines a number of ethical principles that pertain to the actions of its members and delineates responsibilities to clients, colleagues, practice settings, the social work profession, and the larger society (National Association of Social Workers Delegate Assembly, 2008). Specifically, "Unlike the expectations in the codes of conduct of many other professions, such as psychology, medicine, law, business, etc., social workers are expected to engage in social and political action that will improve the lives of clients. Social workers should act so that all people have equal access to the resources, employment, services, and opportunities to meet their basic human needs. Social workers should act to expand choice and opportunity for vulnerable, disadvantaged, oppressed, and exploited people and to promote conditions that encourage respect for cultural and social diversity" (Seabury, Seabury, & Garvin, 2011, p. 45).

The NASW *Code of Ethics* is clear that social and political action is a responsibility of professional social workers. The *Code* also states that social workers have a responsibility to improve their employing agencies' policies and procedures, to prevent and eliminate discrimination in the employing agencies' work assignments, and to improve the efficiency and effectiveness of agency services. These prescriptions to engage in social and political actions and to change the policies and practices of employing agencies clearly identify environmental institutions and agencies as potential target systems of social work practice. Yet what is missing in the *Code* are details about what kinds of actions are permitted when engaging in target system change.

What is clear, however, is that social workers cannot engage in actions that involve violence or that will potentially lead to harm of clients, colleagues, and others in the client's environment. For example, the International Federation of Social Workers (IFSW) states that "social workers should not allow their skills to be used for inhumane purposes, such as torture and terrorism" (International Federation of Social Workers and International Association of Schools of Social Work, 2004). Social workers oppose corporal punishment of children and capital punishment for convicted inmates, even those who may have committed heinous crimes. Social workers cannot threaten or use deadly force to influence clients, nor can they use such tactics to influence decision makers in agencies or communities. Social workers have an ethical responsibility to prevent clients from engaging in harmful acts toward others (i.e., the duty to warn and the duty to inform) and themselves. Group workers make it clear in ground rules that the Association for the Advancement of Social Work with Groups (2006, p. 18) will not tolerate violence in groups; family practitioners will not allow violence in family sessions and must take care that issues raised in sessions do not result in violent consequences for any family members when the family returns home. The bottom line: in the practice of social work, any form of violence is proscribed and cannot be employed as a change strategy.

ETHICAL ORGANIZATIONAL CHANGE

The economic and political context (described above), as well as the commitment to social justice of the profession, shape the ethics of organizational change in two ways. First, in the broadest sense, for social workers to act ethically means they must practice in ways that enact social justice. That is, practitioners need to continuously ask these questions: Are my actions and interventions promoting social justice and social change? If so, for whom? Second, ethical practice means understanding the difficult choices that challenge us, choices that are circumscribed by the realities of our clients and constituencies, as well as by our own realities. Ethical practice often is defined as making the best choice when none of the options is good (Harrington & Dolgoff, 2008; Hyde, 2012). Selecting the lesser of two (or more) evils typically is dictated by economic, political, and cultural forces beyond our control.

It is essential that the practitioner be clear as to what constitutes the client and target systems, and as to whether there is any overlap, because social workers do not necessarily have the same ethical responsibilities to each of these systems. There are some instances when the same values apply to both. For example, social workers are prohibited from engaging in activities that endanger the client's life; likewise, they are prohibited from engaging in any activity that will endanger lives in the target system, such as members of the organization or community. As noted above, violence is anathema in social work practice.

Other ethical principles manifest differently depending on the system with which one is working. For example, the *Code of Ethics* clearly states that social workers must protect the information they have about clients and this information can only be disclosed under strict situations. This kind of privileged communication is protected by law in many states as part of licensure. Confidentiality, however, does not operate in work with changing organizations and communities. In fact, the threat and even disclosure of information about a target system is a common tactic in organizational change and may even be protected by law. Many states, and the federal government, have whistle-blower laws that protect workers who disclose compromising information to outsiders, including the press and funding sources. These laws are designed to protect the whistle-blower from organizational retaliation. The very act of disclosure and deliberately violating confidence is a tactic that is used in organizational or community change, but it would never be sanctioned as a tactic in client change.

When social workers engage in organizational change, competing interests or conflicting priorities may emerge as the process unfolds. These create dilemmas for the social worker when the interests of the client system have negative impacts on other groups within the organization or community. By way of illustration, consider the expansion of Wal-Mart into low-income communities:

EXAMPLE: WAL-MART EXPANSION INTO LOW-INCOME COMMUNITIES

Wal-Mart has begun to expand and build large stores in poor inner-city communities. In some communities, there have been protest movements and political action to keep the company out. The opening of a Wal-Mart store in a poor, inner-city community will bring the opportunity for many new, low-skilled jobs and lower prices for the many consumers in the community. This store may also increase local taxes for the community and may act as a magnet for other stores to move into the shopping area around the Wal-Mart store. But Wal-Mart's model is viewed by some as predatory and likely to drive the small ma-and-pa grocery stores, shoe stores, hardware stores, and clothing stores out of business. In that case, the poor community will gain jobs and inexpensive goods, and the working-class members of the community will lose their jobs and family businesses. How does a social worker respond? Do we help to mobilize poor clients to promote Wal-Mart's request to build the store before the community planning board, or do we join the advocacy groups that are fighting to keep Wal-Mart out of the community?

Another major difference in the relationships between the social worker and client system in contrast to the relationship between the worker and target system concerns empowerment. Social workers seek to empower client systems, yet the opposite is often going on in their work with target systems. Because the client and worker are in the lower power position in relationship to the target system, the social worker's tactics often are to attempt to disempower or diffuse or shift power from the target system to the client system. Workers rarely attempt to empower the organizations they are trying to change on behalf of clients. Most of a worker's efforts in trying to change organizations or communities involve mobilizing support for the client's position and simultaneously attempting to reduce the power inherent in the target organization.

Because of the power differentials between clients and organizations, there are tactics that the social worker might use with organizations, yet they would not use these same techniques with clients. For example, such tactics as manipulation and surprise are not considered desirable tactics in the relationship between client and worker because these tactics do not build trust. With organizations, however, trust may not be as essential to the relationship as power dynamics. In fact, in some organizations there may be little trust between the management of the organization and the social worker who is trying to influence the organization to make a decision on behalf of the client.

A social worker may help clients connect with advocacy groups or consumer groups in the community, but he or she would not help the organization in the target system connect with other organizations to prepare and protect it from the actions of client or consumer groups. Social workers may plan with clients to prepare a public demonstration in front of the target organization and notify the press at the last minute, but the social worker would not warn the organization that the demonstration was being planned. Surprise and disclosure of injustice are tactics that are used by clients and social workers to pressure organizations to change harmful policies and procedures.

Another ethical difference concerns the primacy of client interests (Reamer, 2006). In the NASW *Code of Ethics*, it is clear that the needs of the client are the primary concern of professional practice. Even when one section of the *Code* conflicts with another, resolution should favor the client's interests (Harrington & Dolgoff, 2008). For example, social workers are expected to comply with their employing agencies' policies, practices, and procedures. In situations in which such practices may not be helpful to clients, social workers may bend the rules and not follow explicitly stated agency procedures, placing the client's needs ahead of the agency's procedures. Nowhere in the *Code* are the needs and interests of a target system, which usually is made up of organizations and community structures, placed over the needs of the client and worker.

Other unique ethical dilemmas for practitioners who are engaged in change efforts within, or against, a target system include

1. the eliciting of real, rather than symbolic participation;
2. the challenges of conflicting priorities;
3. the dilemmas posed by funding sources and regulatory organizations;
4. the perils of cultural conflict, including challenging the –isms (racism, sexism, etc.);
5. the unanticipated consequences of organizing; and
6. the matter of whose "common good" is being addressed through the organizing effort. (Minkler et al., 2012, pp. 111–112)

Taken together, these particular dilemmas touch on issues of account-ability, self-determination and participation, commitment to one's mission or goals, and cultural conflict. The practitioner needs to become adept at nego-tiating this ethical terrain in order to support the client system while simul-taneously challenging the problems present in the target system.

REVISITING CHANGE TACTICS

As was discussed in chapter 3, conceptualizing the change effort can be understood by applying force field analysis to the identified situation. From a systems perspective, any effort to change the organization will be met by resistance due to the homeostatic nature of all organisms to resist change. The driving forces of change on a given issue will stir up restraining forces in the target system.

There is an extensive advocacy literature in social work about the kinds of tactics and techniques that social workers employ when working to change larger systems that have a negative impact on clients' lives (Buchanan & Badham, 2008; Lens, 2004, 2005; Patti, 1974; Schneider & Lester, 2001). These various tactics span a range from collaborative to cam-paign to conflict tactics; social workers are encouraged to follow the princi-ple of least contest when engaging in social change tactics (see chapter 3). This principle frames ethical choices that are made during the change process. We revisit the information presented in chapter 3 on tactics and add to that the consideration of countertactics employed by members of the tar-get system in their efforts to sabotage change. Figure 4.2 summarizes this information.

Collaborative tactics are employed when the social worker believes that the target system can be approached openly. In order for collaborative tac-tics to have an impact on the decision maker, the social worker and client should carefully document the issue or problem before presenting it to the decision maker in the target system ("We thought you would want to know that Ms. Smith has not received all of the hot meals that were originally planned, and that the driver has skipped delivery of meals on Tuesdays and Thursdays"). The social worker and client may also point out the negative consequences for the client ("Losing two meals a week is significant for Ms. Smith who is a homebound elder who cannot get out of her apartment to replace the missing food"). In some situations, the decision maker may not be aware of the problem and will take the documented issue seriously and investigate. The social worker may offer to help the decision maker in the investigation of the issue.

Documentation eliminates a common countertactic that may appear at this point in the process. The decision maker may deny that the problem exists or minimize the issue ("It seems unlikely that missing delivery days would happen in our agency, and if this did happen once, I am sure that it

FIGURE 4.2. Force Field Analysis of Tactics and Countertactics

Driving Forces Change Tactics	Restraining Forces Countertactics
Collaborative:	Deny Problem Exists:
Provide information about the issue.	Minimize the problem.
Document the issue.	Distract, refocus, reframe the issue.
Suggest changes or alternatives.	Cover up or destroy evidence of issue.
Encourage experimentation.	Avoid experimentation.
Campaign:	Delay, Stall, Drag Out:
Is persistent.	Say "non mea culpa" (it is not our fault).
Appeals to emotion or conscience.	Blame the victim.
Points out negative consequences.	Blame the change agent.
Creates worst case scenarios.	Side-track change into an ad hoc committee.
Presents petition of supporters.	Send intermediaries to "cool out the mark."
Contest:	Coopt, Blame, Attack:
Go over decision maker's head.	Delegitimize the change agent.
Confront in public meetings.	Suggest change agent is mentally ill.
Testify in public forums.	Rumor, slander, or frame-up.
Blow the whistle.	Choose a scapegoat to blame within agency.
Boycotts or strikes.	Direct threats to harm client and change agent.
Pursue litigation and lawsuits.	Concede the case to avoid the class issue.

rarely occurs. We do not want homebound elders to miss meals and will check into what happened with Ms. Smith"). Now the decision maker may follow through and discover that the meals are not being delivered to a number of families on Tuesdays and Thursdays. She or he may also find out that the particular driver who delivers meals on those days seems to be at fault. When the decision maker discovers this driver is selling meals on the side to a local soup kitchen, and subsequently fires the driver, the issue will have been resolved without having to escalate to more contentious tactics. It is better if the issue can be resolved with these gentler tactics because in this way the relationship between the social worker and the decision maker will not be put in jeopardy (Mailich & Ashley, 1981; Richan, 1973; Simmons, 1972).

Now suppose the decision maker in the target system does not accept the information provided and does not follow through in investigating the issue. Ms. Smith continues to lack meal delivery on Tuesdays and Thursdays. The social worker and client will have to put more pressure on the decision maker. Common campaign tactics involve being persistent, petitioning, appealing to emotion or conscience, pointing out negative consequences of the issue if nothing is done or positive consequences if the issue is resolved, developing a worst-case scenario and presenting it to the decision maker, and so on.

The social worker may *persist* by recontacting the decision maker to learn what the investigation has uncovered and by providing a negative consequence about doing nothing: "The meals still did not appear last week. Ms. Smith has been eating cat food on the days the meals do not appear. Ms. Smith and I were wondering what your investigation has revealed. I'm sure you would agree that cat food is not a nutritious substitute for a hot meal." The decision maker in the target system may stall and explain that the investigation is ongoing and offer excuses that many other important issues have occupied the agency: "Our agency is in a major expansion of our services to a number of communities with elders who need hot meals, and we have not been able find a solution to the issue you have raised." In response, the social worker may apply a little more pressure by suggesting a way that she can help: "Would it be helpful if I explored whether other residents in the community are also missing meals and who is responsible for delivering those meals on Tuesday and Thursday?" This simple tactic is an example of moving a private trouble into a public issue, making it much harder to ignore and minimize (Mills, 1959; Riley, 1971; Sunley, 1970).

Now if this pressure still does not result in any change, then the social worker may have to consider more-contentious actions in the form of contest tactics. In some situations, the decision maker may be apathetic about the issue and feel there are many more-important tasks that need to be addressed. Examples of contest tactics include going over the decision maker's head, being confrontational in meetings, testifying in public meetings, whistle-blowing, organizing boycotts and strikes, and pursuing litigation and lawsuits. For example, the social worker may locate other elders who are not getting their meals and ask them to sign a petition stating that lost meals are a hardship for them: "I'm calling in to follow up to Ms. Smith's situation. I have located eight other elders in Ms. Smith's neighborhood who are not getting their meals on Tuesdays and Thursdays. They have all agreed to sign a petition testifying to this problem. I'm concerned that there may be many other elders in other neighborhoods who are not getting all of their meals." If such a petition seems to have no effect, then the social worker may decide to go over the head of the decision maker to a higher power person in the agency. Going over the decision maker's head is an adversarial tactic that works with administrators who are climbers. A climber has aspirations to move up the organizational hierarchy and is always looking for a way to take credit for positive things in the organization but also is easily threatened when negative things happen on his or her watch (Patti & Resnick, 1972).

Common countertactics to contest techniques are to shift the blame to someone else, or "non mea culpa": "It's not my fault that the food was not delivered" or "Why are you making such a big issue of this problem? Do you have some kind of hidden agenda?" In some situations, the social worker will have to threaten and be ready to do a version of whistle-blowing and take the issue outside the agency to funding sources or the news media: "Well, it doesn't look like you are taking this issue seriously so I am prepared to take this issue and your inaction to the director of United Way, a major funding source for your agency. I am also willing to talk with the consumer advocate at the local TV channel, and get them to take up this issue." A common countertactic to this contest tactic is to suggest that the social worker's action may do much more harm than good: "Do you realize that we are a small, underfunded agency and we are the only agency that provides meals to these homebound elders? Your behavior may jeopardize all of the elders in the community if we are closed down."

There are many other tactics that have been discussed in the literature on organizational change, including: organizing others who will support the change and attend public meetings to present their complaints, taking out advertisements in local media, writing Op-Ed pieces in a local paper, organizing boycotts, and initiating lawsuits. The point of this discussion is that contest tactics involve power dynamics in order to move the target system to change behavior. Social workers often are not comfortable with deliberately initiating adversarial tactics because they want to avoid conflict in practice, yet it is through conflict that these higher-power people in organizations are likely to take notice and do something about the issue.

A CASE EXAMPLE

Even though organizations have more power and resources to resist the efforts of clients and social workers to make changes, it is possible to bring about change in organizations. This chapter concludes with a real case example of the first author in working to change a community resource, a resource that had a long record of not meeting the needs of its clients. The target system in the case was a large halfway house with more than two hundred deinstitutionalized patients as residents. The institution had been a motel that a group of physicians had purchased; they were running it as a private nursing facility. The first floor areas of the old motel had been converted into a large day room in which most of the residents congregated, and the basement area was converted into a large dining area and kitchen facility that could feed the two hundred plus residents. Even though the purpose of the halfway house was to reintroduce patients to the community, most were disoriented and disabled, and the electronic lock on the front door did not allow them to leave the building. Only a few patients had the privilege to go in and out of the building. Psychiatric aides who once worked in the state hospitals and still wore white uniforms that designated them as attendants staffed this institution.

The department of welfare and a local school of social work gave me (the first author) permission to participate in a first-year graduate student field placement designed to teach graduate social work students about the welfare system and how to work with poor, urban, welfare clients. The focus of this unit was supportive counseling, brokerage, resource development, and advocacy. I was assigned a man in his late sixties, Mr. Z, who was elderly, white, and Polish American. Mr. Z had been a resident in this halfway house for about a year. He was not placed in this institution because of a prior psychiatric history; rather, he had no family, had been homeless and living on the streets, and voluntarily took up residence in this facility. The costs of residing in this facility were covered by his small social security pension and SSI (Supplemental Security Income). Because of his voluntary status, he was allowed to come and go as he pleased.

I entered Mr. Z's life by sending him a letter explaining who I was, and saying that I wanted to meet and talk with him about any problems he might be having and how I might help. When I arrived at the facility and was buzzed in through the locked front door, the receptionist explained that I would probably find Mr. Z in the day room. The day room was filled with cigarette smoke; people milled around, lay on the floor, or sat in old furniture scattered around the room. Someone pointed out Mr. Z to me. He shook my hand and suggested that we go outside and sit on a stoop on a nearby abandoned building in order to talk privately. For the three months that I worked with Mr. Z, we met on this stoop.

The first point that Mr. Z shared with me was that he was not "crazy" like most of the other residents, and had never been in a mental hospital. The second point that he shared was that he was appalled at the way the staff treated the patients. He recounted many injustices that he had seen over the past nine months in the residence. He recounted how fearful patients were of staff and how quickly everyone learned not to complain about conditions in the residence.

Much of my work with Mr. Z involved supportive counseling and exploring options to his living situation. At that time, large state-run facilities were being closed down and patients were being outsourced into the community, such that readmission was impossible. Nursing care facilities were in very short supply. Even when relatives could be located, they were unwilling to consider letting these patients come and live in their homes. Homelessness was on the rise, there were very few shelters or other resources for the homeless population, and there was a severe shortage of affordable housing. The movement to deinstitutionalize the mentally ill had promised that community-based resources would abound because the costs of caring would be much lower than the cost of caring in large state institutions—but this promise was a sham.

Mr. Z and I agreed that the likelihood of him finding an alternative living arrangement other than the street was slim, so we agreed to think of ways that we could improve the living conditions in the halfway house. Though this decision was somewhat of a forced choice for Mr. Z, he was adamant that it was wrong for people who were mentally ill to be treated the way they were in his residence. The first change we decided to pursue involved the discretionary funds that were supposed to be given to residents each month so they could buy personal items such as cigarettes, candy, snacks, personal hygiene products, and so on. This was a small amount of cash (around $20) that residents were supposed to receive from their SSI grants that paid for their room and board in the residence. Very few residents understood that they had this personal resource and how much it entailed. Mr. Z had only been sporadically successful in getting this money during the nine months of his stay.

Mr. Z and I decided that we would go to the business manager of the residence and talk about these funds and the difficulty Mr. Z had in obtaining them. We would begin with the "private trouble" that Mr. Z experienced before presenting the "public issue" that many other residents were not getting these funds, either. (This is "case advocacy" because it involved the private trouble of an identified client; in "class advocacy," the public issue would be experienced by many clients who for the most part would not be identifiable.) The business manager agreed that Mr. Z was eligible for these funds and also agreed to a procedure so that Mr. Z would get these funds each month. If this procedure did not produce results for Mr. Z, then the business manager suggested that Mr. Z should contact him and he would remedy the situation. Up until this point in the interview, except for the introductions Mr. Z had done all of the talking and had successfully self-advocated for his interests. From an empowerment perspective, this had been a successful tactic.

When I raised the broader issue that many other residents were also eligible for this payment and did not seem to know about it, the business manager became much less congenial. He stated that these funds were a private matter between the residents and the halfway house and therefore was basically none of my *business. He then announced that the interview was over and he had to "get back to work." At this point in the interview Mr. Z got up from his chair, and we both left the business manager's office.*

When we talked later about this encounter, Mr. Z was clear that he did not want to pursue the broader issue. He said he agreed with the business manager that this money issue was an issue between each resident and the halfway house. He also pointed out that he did not want the business manager to change his mind and renege on the deal to guarantee his money. Mr. Z gently refused to go back and advocate for the other residents.

The next issue we decided to pursue involved strange behavior that residents performed at mealtimes. The first time Mr. Z witnessed this behavior he asked staff about it; they told him that this behavior demonstrated how mentally ill many of the residents were. When the door to the dining area was opened at mealtime, residents would not rush to get a tray and start a line at the cafeteria area, but instead would rush to the condiments area and start grabbing napkins until they were all gone. This behavior had nothing to do with cleanliness during mealtime, but did have to do with cleanliness from the consequences of mealtime. The facility did not provide rolls of toilet paper to the bathrooms in the rooms. The custodial staff was not allowed to put toilet paper in the rooms because on many occasions residents had flushed these rolls down the toilets, which clogged the plumbing system.

Mr. Z, who was able to leave the residence and purchase toilet paper with his discretionary funds, was not interested in pursuing this issue. He stated that he would allow his roommate, a very quiet, withdrawn, and reclusive chap, to have some of his toilet paper so that it did not smell bad in the room. Mr. Z agreed that this was an example of the kind of neglect that went on in the institution, but he agreed with the staff that the hoarding behavior before meals was better than clogging the plumbing system that would have ramifications for all of the residents.

The final issue in this case example involves a change to this institution that addressed a class issue that impacted all of the residents. During the time I spent working with Mr. Z, he often complained about the food; he had lost a lot of weight since coming to this halfway house. For over a month I ignored these complaints because I had heard them many times before from institutionalized mental patients and even from college students who did not like their food service. When I arrived to see him one day, he had a sling and bandage on his left hand, and the left side of his face was swollen and the skin covered with scabs.

He told me that several days earlier he had been walking on the sidewalk with his buddies when suddenly he collapsed on the sidewalk and lay there unconscious while his friends went for help. He was taken by ambulance to a nearby emergency room (ER) and revived. The ER doctor told him that he wanted to run some routine tests and x-rays to check for any broken bones. When the tests were complete, the doctor informed him that he was lucky and had not broken any bones. The tests, however, revealed that he suffered from malnutrition and probably fainted as a result. The ER doctor provided a note to take back to the halfway house that stated that Mr. Z needed to eat more food and be monitored to make sure he ate sufficiently.

The response of the halfway house to this note was to inform the kitchen staff that Mr. Z would receive double portions of all food at meals for one week. This countertactic was a minimal response to Mr. Z while covering up the larger issue of malnutrition in this facility. This was a wake-up call for me that Mr. Z's complaints were valid, and I began to focus on this issue. I learned that several residents had been taken to the ER with heart problems and many of them had complained about the food. Others had also complained about weight loss. I asked Mr. Z and his two buddies about what actually was served at meals and they had trouble remembering specifics. I asked them if they would be willing to carefully keep track of what was served at each meal, as to both quantity and quality, and they agreed.

Mr. Z and his two buddies carefully recorded and compared notes about what was served for one week in the dining room. Because of the age of the population in the residence and the fact that many were missing teeth and had received inadequate dental care in the state hospital, almost all of the food was ground up and served with a scoop on the partitioned trays. At some meals, they could not identify what kind of meat they were being served. When I saw them the following week, I could see how proud they were of their daily meal log and how carefully they had completed this task. I congratulated them on the detail in their food log and explained that it would be easy for the nutritionist at University Hospital to judge the adequacy of the diet.

I took the handwritten food log to the nutritionist at University Hospital and explained who I was. I asked whether she could help me understand the adequacy of these meals for a population of middle-aged and elderly residents in a nursing care facility. She explained that all nursing care facilities are required by law to have a licensed nutritionist make up weekly meal plans. The nutritionist was usually a consultant who submitted plans to management with the expectation that these plans would guide the food preparation staff as to what to purchase and cook.

She looked over the log and exclaimed that this log could never have been planned by a nutritionist because it was totally inadequate—both in balance and quantity. She wanted to know where this log came from and told me she wanted to do something about this "right away!" I thanked her for her help and explained that I still needed to talk with a physician in the ER before taking any action in the residence. I asked her for a ballpark figure as to how much an institution must budget for food for a week for an adult in order to provide an adequate diet. She looked at some tables for the University Hospital and gave me a general figure for a month. I asked her, if it came to a legal proceeding against the nursing home, would she be willing to testify to the inadequacy of the meals? She readily agreed, and I thanked her for being so helpful to me and to the residents of this facility. I told her I would get back to her and let her know about the next steps I would be taking.

I then went to the ER and was able to locate the physician that had treated Mr. Z. Luckily, he was a resident who was eager to help answer my questions and who gave up about fifteen minutes of his break (this event was pre-HIPAA [Health Insurance Portability and Accountability Act of 1996] so the confidentiality policies were not as stringent as they are today). I learned that a number of patients from the halfway house had come into the ER with a heart condition associated with malnutrition. The resident stated that he was glad to see someone trying to improve this large facility and wished me luck. I ended the contact by asking him if he would be willing to testify in a legal proceeding about the information about malnutrition in these patients. His eagerness rapidly disappeared, and he said it would not be possible for him to testify but he would help behind the scenes in order to prepare a case against the facility. I thanked him for his cooperation and the information he had shared about malnutrition.

In my next interview with Mr. Z and his buddies, I shared the responses of the nutritionist to their food log, and they were pleased with the result. In the discussion that followed, we discussed what we would do with this information and who in the organization we should approach. The decision came down to who in the institution would have the power to remedy the inadequacy of the meals. Mr. Z shared the information that he had only been at the facility for about a year, yet the facility had recently hired a third director who had been on the job for only about one month. She had introduced herself to the staff and patients in a morning meeting and seemed to be friendly and concerned about patient care. We agreed that she seemed like the person to approach because she was in an executive position with the power to investigate and make changes. Mr. Z and his two buddies, however, made it clear to me that they would not go with me to a meeting to present the information they had collected. They worried about retaliation and being thrown out of the facility onto the street. This was a risk I did not have to bear, so I agreed to meet with the director alone and to share the results of the food log and what the ER physician had stated, but not to disclose who collected the information for the food log.

I made an appointment with the director, explained who I was, and said that I was planning to share some information that I hoped she would be concerned about in her new position. We began the interview by sharing some small talk about our respective careers. She had no education in mental health but had a background in management, which was why she had been hired to run the facility.

I shared the food log with her and asked if she would be willing to compare the log with the weekly plan that had been submitted by the nutritionist. She located the plan and discovered that there were a number of differences between the plan and the food log created by my clients. She seemed genuinely concerned about the discrepancies so I shared my concern about the adequacy of the diet for residents. I explained that because I was not a nutritionist, I had shared the food log with a registered nutritionist. She was uncomfortable with this act of sharing so I explained that the nutritionist did not know the source of the food log. I then explained that the nutritionist found the diet inadequate and told me that it was unlikely that a nutritionist would have planned it. She agreed that because of the discrepancies between the food log and the facilities food plan there must have been some kind of breakdown in the food service.

I stated that I did not know where the discrepancy arose and assured her that I was confident that she would be able to explore the reasons for the discrepancy. I also stated that I was concerned that the discrepancy might emerge in the facility's budget process. I explained that the nutritionist was the director of nutrition at University Hospital, and that she had given me a ballpark figure about how much money should be budgeted to feed a resident for a month. I stated what this figure was, and she reassured me that the budget process allowed more money per resident than that number.

I thanked her for taking time to listen to my concern and asked if I might see her again in two weeks to find out what she had discovered about the discrepancy. She thanked me for bringing the information to her, and (serendipitously for the residents) exclaimed, "I am a Jewish mother and no one in my house shall go hungry!" She then shared that she planned to check out the accuracy of the food log by arriving at work early and going to breakfast, as well as randomly attending the noon meal, which is the largest meal of the day. I expressed my delight in how she planned to follow up and to take my concerns seriously.

In the next two meetings with Mr. Z and his buddies, I asked them if they had noticed any changes in the food service. They explained that they were surprised to see the director at several meals during the week in which she ate the same food that the residents were eating. They felt this must have been unpleasant for her because of the "lousy" food and the pestering of many of the residents while she tried to eat. I explained that it had been her idea to check up on the food that was being served. I also explained that there were large discrepancies in the facility's food plan with the food log that they had carefully recorded. In my second week after my meeting with the director, I asked Mr. Z and his buddies if the director was still coming to meals. They reported that they had only seen her once, but they felt there was more food offered to residents, which was a change in the right direction.

Coda: The director discovered that the problem with the food served in her facility was a function of the cook and several food personnel in the kitchen. The cook had a small restaurant across town and had been siphoning off some of the food as it was delivered to the facility and taking it over to his restaurant. In effect, the facility was helping to subsidize the cook's restaurant. The cook and several of the food service personnel were fired and a new food service was contracted to provide food in the facility.

The case example demonstrates that empowered clients and their social worker can make changes in an institution without having to resort to highly contentious, adversarial strategies. In some cases those strategies may be necessary, but not in this case. By no means was this facility perfect; there were many other issues that could be addressed, but the changes in the food service had the result of improving the health and well-being of residents.

CONCLUSION

This chapter has focused on ethical issues inherent in organizational change from below. We distinguished between the relationship that exists between social workers and client systems and that between social workers and target systems (e.g., organizations and community institutions). This difference is embodied in the NASW *Code of Ethics*, which reflects our primary commitment to the well-being of clients while our responsibilities to our employing organizations include improving policies, procedures, and effectiveness of services on behalf of clients. Thus, clients are the primary beneficiaries of our practice while community institutions and agencies are potential targets of our efforts. Moreover, the social justice values of social work have implications for our involvement in organizational change efforts that promote equal access to resources and opportunities, particularly for vulnerable and oppressed populations.

We discussed organizational change tactics (collaborative, campaign, and contest) within a context that takes into consideration the power differentials that exist between client, social workers, and organizations. We explored potential countertactics that may be employed by target systems in order to resist change efforts. The chapter concluded with a case example that highlighted several organizational change efforts, illustrating the possibilities of significant change that can be brought about by workers in collaboration with clients.

DISCUSSION QUESTIONS

1. What tactics did the worker in the case example use? Why do you think he chose those?
2. The chapter refers several times to turning "private troubles" into "public issues." What is meant by this? What would be an example?
3. In what ways do social workers' relationships with client systems differ from their relationships with target systems, and why?
4. How does ethical practice in organizational change work reflect a social justice perspective?

REFERENCES

Addams, J. (1935). *Forty years at Hull House*. New York: Macmillan.

Association for the Advancement of Social Work with Groups. (2006). Standards for Practice with Groups. Retrieved from http://iaswg.org/docs/AASWG_Standards_for_Social_Work_Practice_with_Groups2010.pdf

Bloom, S., & Farragher, B. (2010). *Destroying sanctuary: The crisis in human service delivery systems*. New York: Oxford University Press.

Buchanan, D., & Badham, R. (2008). *Power, politics, and organizational change: Winning the turf game* (2nd ed.). Thousand Oaks, CA: Sage.

Collins, J., & Mayer, V. (2010). *Both hands tied: Welfare reform and the race to the bottom in the low-wage labor market*. Chicago: University of Chicago Press.

Edelman, P. (2012). *So rich, so poor: Why it's so hard to end poverty in America*. New York: New Press.

Figueira-Mcdonough, J. (2007). *The welfare state and social work: Pursuing social justice*. Thousand Oaks, CA: Sage Publications.

Harrington, D., & Dolgoff, R. (2008). Hierarchies of ethical principles for ethical decision making in social work. *Ethics & Social Welfare, 2*(2), 183–196.

Health Insurance Portability and Accountability Act. P. L. 104–191, 110 Stat. 1936. (1996). http://library.clerk.house.gov/reference-files/PPL_HIPAA_HealthInsurance PortabilityAccountabilityAct_1996.pdf

Hyde, C. (2012). Ethical dilemmas in human service management: Identifying and resolving the challenges. *Ethics & Social Welfare, 6*(4), 351–367.

International Federation of Social Workers (IFSW) and International Association of Schools of Social Work. (2004). *Ethics in social work, statement of principles.* Retrieved from http://www.ifsw.org/p38000324.html

Lens, V. (2004). Principled negotiation: A new tool for case advocacy. *Social Work, 49,* 503–513.

Lens, V. (2005). Advocacy and argumentation in the public arena: A guide for social workers. *Social Work, 50*(3), 231–238.

Mailich, M., & Ashley, A. (1981). Politics of inter-professional collaboration: Challenge to advocacy. *Social Casework, 62*(3), 131–137.

Mills, C. (1959). *The sociological imagination.* New York: Grove Press.

Minkler, M., Pies, C., & Hyde, C. (2012). Ethical issues and practical dilemmas in community organizing and community capacity building. In M. Minkler (Ed.), *Community organizing and community building for health* (3rd ed., pp. 110–129). New Brunswick, NJ: Rutgers University Press.

National Association of Social Workers Delegate Assembly. (2008). *Code of ethics.* Retrieved from http://www.socialworkers.org/pubs/code/code.asp

Nickel, G. (1942a). Evacuation, American style: Part one. *The Survey, 78,* 99–103.

Nickel, G. (1942b). Evacuation, American style: Part two. *The Survey, 78,* 262–265.

Patti, R. (1974). Organizational resistance and change: The view from below. *Social Service Review, 48,* 367–383.

Patti, R., & Resnick, H. (1972). Changing the organization from within. *Social Work, 17*(3), 48–57.

Reamer, F. (2006). *Social work values and ethics* (3rd ed.). New York: Columbia University Press.

Reynolds, B. (1964). The social casework of an unchartered journey. *Social Work, 9*(4), 13–17.

Richan, W. (1973). Dilemmas of social work advocates. *Child Welfare, 52,* 220–226.

Riley, P. (1971). Family advocacy: From case to cause and back to case. *Child Welfare, 50,* 374–383.

Rosenwald, M., & Hyde, C. (2006). Political ideologies of social workers: An under explored dimension of practice. *Advances in Social Work, 7*(2), 14–26.

Schneider, R. L., & Lester, L. (2001). *Social work advocacy: A new framework for action.* Belmont, CA: Wadsworth.

Seabury, B., Seabury, B., & Garvin, C. (2011). *Foundations of interpersonal practice: Promoting competence in generalist practice* (3rd ed). Thousand Oaks, CA: Sage Publications.

Simmons, L. (1972). Agency financing and social change. *Social Work, 17*(1), 62–67.

Sunley, R. (1970). Family advocacy: From case to cause. *Social Casework, 51,* 347–357.

Part II

Case Studies

Part II consists of seven chapters written by social work academics and practitioners, each of which reflects and expands on the material in part I and provides a detailed case illustration of organizational change from below. As a whole, these case studies provide the reader with a range of issues, strategies, settings, outcomes, and practitioner roles. These differences aside, the cases all demonstrate effective use of the force field analysis, sometimes as the sole means of strategic assessment and sometimes in combination with other change paradigms. The array of concepts from part I of this text and the case study chapters that highlight them are summarized in table II.1.

TABLE II.1. Concepts from Part I

Theme	Chapter						
	5	6	7	8	9	10	11
Advocacy		x		x		x	
Assessment	x						x
Board of directors			x				
Coalitions/Collaborations						x	
Community	x		x	x	x	x	x
Diversity/Differences		x		x	x	x	
Empowerment/Efficacy	x			x			x
Leadership development				x			
Media						x	
Networks	x		x				
Organizational culture	x		x	x			
Organizational mission, goals, values			x	x	x	x	
Organizational power/Authority			x	x			
Organizational structure	x		x	x	x		
Social protest						x	
Staffing	x				x		
Vulnerable populations		x		x		x	x

Understanding and managing relationships is often at the heart of a change effort. The significance of relationships is demonstrated in chapter 5 through a detailed discussion of social capital in a settlement house setting.

Social capital is defined as the value generated by the social networks or connections among individuals. According to social network theory, an efficient and effective strategy is one of engaging and strengthening existing social networks in order to provide assistance. In this chapter, an assessment of the change agent's use of social networks, and the social capital within them, is joined with a force field analysis to provide the strategic framework for successful change from below. In documenting these networks, the case weaves together the importance of understanding the external environment with internal organizational properties of structure and culture.

A common impetus for organizational change is a lack of access to essential programs and services. Chapter 6 provides a case example of a class action suit and the resulting Burgos Consent Decree to illustrate how direct service staff was able to influence social and organizational change from below in order to secure the right to translation for Latino families. The case began with social workers recognizing a pattern of discrimination that led them to pursue various forms of advocacy for clients. Initially, practitioners engaged in microlevel client advocacy. Eventually, they moved toward macrolevel strategies including cause, legal, and administrative advocacy as well as organizational change. This case demonstrates that line social service practitioners can play a critical and vital role in advocacy. In particular, the decision of two settlement house caseworkers to access the court system and file a class action on behalf of their clients helped convey an important message to the Illinois child welfare system—that the availability of language-appropriate services was a matter of civil rights.

Chapter 7 presents another paradigm for understanding change from below: a social movement within an organization. This change effort takes the form of an internal insurgency in which a few organizational members join with sympathetic outsiders to pursue their goal. Set in a domestic violence shelter that has drifted from its more political roots, the change focuses on altering the composition of the board of directors so that more profeminist and activist-oriented individuals become board members. Spearheaded by a newly minted social worker, this internal social movement succeeded in its initial goal of getting profeminist change supporters and allies elected to board positions, and in recruiting a number of new, sympathetic members as well as reengaging some of the existing membership.

Chapter 8 also addresses a shift in organizational orientation with its focus on the efforts of women in a homeless shelter who, with the assistance of a social work student, created a new, empowerment-oriented, client-centered shelter environment. Specifically, empowerment, discussed at some length in part I, is a key theme in this case. The process and outcome emphasized the structural causes of homelessness in its service provision rather than the more individual and victim-blaming approaches that characterized the original shelter setting. The initial goal of this change effort was to remove the women from the shelter that also housed men. The focus then was to change the location of shelter for single women. Hence, the shelter became the target of change. An initial secondary goal was to help the women gain a sense of power and control over their lives. This secondary goal became primary as the change process proceeded. The chapter illustrates the importance of force field analysis as a means of determining change strategy and also as a model for program maintenance.

The topic of diversity, discussed in several chapters, is the specific focus of chapter 9. This chapter explores some of the organizational challenges in meeting the needs of diverse external customer groups. The chapter presents an inclusion framework that helps identify alternative strategies designed to respond more effectively to customer needs. It demonstrates the application of this framework through the case example of a change initiative undertaken by the Special Projects Team of the Social and Community Service Department in the regional municipality of Halton, Canada. This organizational change process emphasized the inclusion of members of groups other than those of the dominant culture, particularly groups marginalized due to their social position and lack of power. The chapter illustrates how an organizational change process can address inclusion and diversity as core organizational values in the delivery of client-centered services in ways that are measurable and accountable to those working in the organization and those affected by its decision. The experience of the Special Projects Team demonstrates the effectiveness of force field analysis in combination with a logic modeling, set within an overarching framework that guided a sequential, reflective assessment of processes and actions to meet a change goal.

Chapter 10 also addresses matters of inclusion from more of a community perspective. The case presented here describes a five-year grassroots organizing campaign that changed the perception of people with disabilities within a community. The efforts of a statewide advocacy organization in promoting equal rights for people with disabilities are chronicled, with particular emphasis on their campaign to make public transportation accessible to people with mobility impairments. A thorough force field analysis; the strategic use of collaborative, campaign, and contest tactics; and organizing across disabilities expanded the base of the organization and resulted in a highly successful effort. The experiences of the members of this organization demonstrate the importance of building community, using the media, educating the public, and identifying disability rights as a civil rights issue.

Part II concludes by looking at a failed change effort, thus illustrating the adage that multiple attempts, informed by analysis of prior actions, often are needed before real transformation occurs. Chapter 11 underscores the importance of organizational assessment in successful organizational change practice, and describes an unsuccessful attempt to bring about organizational change in a program serving homeless people. Organizational analysis was employed as a means of examining what went wrong in the organizational change effort. It shed light on the sources of the strong organizational resistance encountered by change agents who sought to increase consumer voice in the organization through the establishment of a consumer advisory board. Conducting an "in hindsight" force field analysis proved useful in analyzing the errors made and suggested a more informed approach to this goal. Issues such as timing and the need to bring staff on board with the change goal before moving ahead proved to be particularly salient to this change effort. One year after the initial organizational change effort failed, a consumer-directed action group was successfully organized at the agency, with goals very similar to those originally envisioned. The pitfalls encountered in the original organizing effort were avoided through the use of a well-thought-out force field analysis and change strategy.

5

Social Capital and Social Networks

A Strategy for Organizational Change from Below

Jacqueline B. Mondros

INTRODUCTION

Youth Paradisio House was a mid-size settlement house agency serving a multicultural population in an inner-city neighborhood of a large city. A staff of fifty, not all of whom were social workers, offered a variety of services including programs for youth, in-home case management for seniors, classes in English as a second language (ESL) and in preparing for the general educational development (GED) tests, mental health, and family counseling. The agency also housed a credit union, a food cooperative and green market, a community organization, and a financial counseling program.

The agency had a long-time, charismatic director, much beloved by the staff and neighborhood residents. Youth Paradisio House had developed a fine reputation for service, despite its unstable financial situation and meager infrastructure; it was known for doing things the old-fashioned way, but doing them very well. The organizational culture was always described as informal and close, and there had been little staff turnover for many years. The one problem was an ongoing conflict between the mental health staff (all clinicians with master of social work [MSW] degrees) and the program staff, many of whom had no social work training. The director of mental health services, Rachael Ortiz, was a psychotherapist, and was committed to excellent therapeutic service. The director of programs was Tony Smith, a brilliant but erratic administrator who disdained therapy in favor of program development and community organizing. Both Rachael and Tony held strong, though polar, views about the best way to help community residents.

When the longtime director retired, the agency's board chose not to promote from within, hiring instead Jim Cavanaugh, a social worker from outside the organization. That decision increased the tension between the clinical and program staff, with Tony and Rachael jockeying for the new director's attention and support. Jim was introducing change slowly. He remained somewhat distant from both Rachael and Tony, avoiding direct confrontation with them. He had hired some new program staff members and that action did not sit well with the clinicians who were hoping to improve their status and numbers in the agency.

The program staff had recently received a new grant from the city that would establish several supportive housing units for persons with mental illness. They were planning the service component for the housing without involvement from the clinical staff. The clinical staff resented being left out of the planning process. Despite their request to intervene, Jim had stayed out of the discussions, which had also increased tension in the organization.

Julie Chen was a recently hired social worker on the clinical staff who arrived just before Jim became director. A well-respected and experienced clinician, her initial energy and enthusiasm for her job was waning because of all the conflict and resistance to change in the clinical department. Her experience and knowledge had convinced her that clinical work should be asset based and focused on resilience and recovery. She had come to Youth Paradisio expecting to do such work. Her former agency had not made a sharp division between program and clinical services. She had been trained that rather than using long-term and deficit-focused interventions, program and clinical services could and should be easily combined, using approaches of self-help, peer support and mutual aid, and community-based support services that strengthened existing client assets. The new housing units, she felt, were an opportunity to develop a broad community-based resiliency service model that would feature self-help; programs of all sorts; employment, education, and mentoring opportunities; as well as supportive counseling. But her position in Rachael's clinical services department allowed her no access to the housing.

To assess her chances for influence, Julie completed a force field analysis (shown in figure 5.1). Julie's force field analysis showed little hope for change. There were strong forces opposing innovation, an organizational culture that was committed to individual psychiatric services, an organizational structure that impeded the introduction of a new clinical service, conflicts among staff, and a critical actor unwilling to take a position. Those forces were much stronger than the driving forces. While the new housing offered opportunity for change, there was little impetus for the organization to capitalize on it. The most hopeful sign was that new staff had been hired with new ideas and energy. That one driving force got Julie thinking about the use of social capital and social networks in the agency to achieve her change goal. She vowed to learn more to further assess her capacity to influence organizational change.

FIGURE 5.1. Force Field Analysis for Youth Paradisio House Change Effort

| *Change Goal:* |
| To introduce into the agency clinical services based on self-help, peer support, and mutual aid in the new supportive housing program |

| *Critical Actors:* |
| 1. Jim Cavanaugh |

| *Facilitating Actors:* |
| 1. Rachael Ortiz |
| 2. Tony Smith |

Driving Forces for Change:	*Restraining Forces for Change:*
1. New housing that offers an opportunity for new services	1. Organizational culture and history emphasize individual psychothera-
2. Broad acceptance of newer practice models outside the agency	peutic services
3. The presence of new staff who were not part of the organization's conflicts or service traditions	2. Conflict between Rachael and Tony, preventing open discussion of service issues
	3. Structural division of agency between programs and clinical services
	4. Newly hired director unwilling to take a stand
	5. Julie, who was new to the agency

SOCIAL CAPITAL AND SOCIAL NETWORKS

In the past three decades, scholarship on the relevance of social capital as an explanation for a range of social problems and conditions has grown substantially. Social capital may be defined as "connections among individuals—social networks and the norms or reciprocity and trustworthiness that arise from them" (Putnam, 2000, p. 19). Measured by participation and trust, Putnam contrasts social capital with human capital (i.e., individual skills, talents, and knowledge that results in individual productivity) and with financial capital (land, labor, and investment). Healy and Hampshire (2002) also contrast social capital with physical capital (housing, roads, and transportation systems) and cultural capital (access to characteristics, knowledge, skills, and forms of expression that are valued in the culture). Briggs (1997) notes that social capital is not a substitute for other forms of capital: "Rather, social capital makes the other kinds work well. It greases the gears of commerce, along with other areas of life" (p. 111).

The concept of social capital has moved well beyond Putnam's initial interest in civic engagement, and is now broadly applied by social scientists from a wide range of disciplines to describe and study a variety of social conditions. In this broader view, social capital refers to the resources stored in human relationships that are either casual or close. Over time, value or capital builds up through repeated exchanges among people or organizations, particularly in local contexts (Healy & Hampshire, 2002). Individuals then draw on the stored capital to solve human problems and receive support and assistance.

Social capital is stored in people's social networks. Social science researchers study these social networks to understand how people use them, what and how much is exchanged in them, under what conditions, and the impact of these exchanges on health and wellness, crime, enhanced government services, and education.

Social networks can be described in terms of strong, weak, and bridging ties (Briggs, 1998). *Strong* ties are relationships that are built on similarities, trust, and intimacy. Strong ties, particularly in closed local systems (known as dense networks), provide instrumental and emotional support, such as assistance with babysitting, lending money, and caretaking. The more personal the need, the more likely one is to look toward the most intimate ties to meet it. Because of the inherent support, dense networks may positively impact individual outcomes (Cattell, 2001) such as weight loss and smoking cessation (Christakis & Fowler, 2009).

Though supportive and intimate, there can be negative outcomes when people communicate solely among their close network ties. Closed networks can encourage shared dysfunctional behavior and confine an individual's opportunities, a phenomenon Sabar (2002) calls a *paradoxical social network*. For example, dense local ties foster the growth and strength of gang networks (Pattillo-McCoy, 1999) and increased drug and alcohol abuse, particularly in rural areas (Draus & Carlson, 2009). Networks may be overextended or inappropriately invasive, discouraging individual personal growth (Dominguez & Watkins, 2003). Rawsthorne (2000) found that strong ties among professionals and community residents sometimes prevented youth from reporting violence and compromised support and service delivery. Strong ties may also restrict information, innovation, and social opportunity. For example, if no one in the network has a job, then the network is unlikely to be able to help an individual locate employment (Livermore & Neustrom, 2003).

Once information gains currency in a dense network, however, it is likely to spread quickly and gain broad acceptance. Think, for example, about how quickly a new game or fashion becomes popular among teenagers. New ideas gain legitimacy through what Brenner (2002, p. 364) refers to as "social marketing."

Weak ties are relationships among people with greater heterogeneity, fewer commonalities, and less intimacy (Cattell, 2001). People are less likely to use weak ties for social support or assistance, but they often use these ties to seek information and advice that they cannot access from their closest friends and family members. For example, teachers frequently connect low-income youth with opportunities that are unknown to them or their circle of family and friends. They serve as references for their students, give them information about opportunities beyond their immediate social network, and recommend them for jobs, scholarships, and awards. Chaskin (2005) finds that professionals who are residents of the low-income neighborhoods in which they work frequently serve as bridging ties for others. They combine expertise and legitimacy, translating between neighborhood people and bureaucratic systems. Dominguez and Watkins (2003) note the importance of social workers as bridging ties, assisting low-income women when family or friendship networks are ineffective or unavailable. This is the role that settlement house workers traditionally play for newly arriving immigrant groups.

Finally, there are linking ties that connect people beyond those they know in their own networks. *Bridging* ties connect people to other networks, crossing social divides or cleavages to an external system (Healy & Hampshire, 2002). Professionals such as health-care providers, educators, librarians, social workers, politicians, bankers, and local business owners serve as linking ties because they have connections external to the local neighborhood. For example, if a resident needs housing, social workers may refer him or her to organizations that provide financial counseling or affordable housing. Bankers may identify available loan programs and grants. Together, banks, human service agencies, and local community organizations may establish community credit unions. By tapping into links, a resident can access resources far beyond his or her personal network.

Perhaps most important, when multiple linking ties are activated, they are particularly effective in bringing people together to create neighborhood change. This is a network attribute that Sampson, Morenoff, and Gannon-Rowley (2002, p. 457) call "collective efficacy."

Obviously, the most effective networks will have strong ties that offer social support, weak ties that promote new information and opportunities, and bridging ties that can be activated for collective action. There is clear evidence that people with small or no networks are vulnerable to a range of social problems. The absence of a social network or the presence of a paradoxical social network, for examples, are associated with homelessness (Shinn, Knickman, & Weitzman, 1991), drug use (Draus & Carlson, 2009), declining health status (Subramanian, Kim, & Kawachi, 2002), mental illness (Mitchell & LaGory, 2002), and poverty (Draus & Carlson, 2009). As Hawkins and Maurer (2009) note, "Combining bridging and linking with bonding social capital offers the best economic chances" (p. 13).

THE RELEVANCE OF SOCIAL CAPITAL FOR SOCIAL WORK

Social work has a rich tradition of working with natural helpers, natural groups, and community residents. Just as often, however, social workers see themselves as the primary instruments (drivers) of assistance, service provision, and change. Social network theory suggests that a parsimonious, cost-efficient, and effective service strategy may be to engage and strengthen the network as the means to providing assistance. Of particular interest to social workers is a significant body of social science research that explains how the poor use their social networks and the social capital stored within them (Cattell, 2001). This research is widely acknowledged in the social work literature in Sweden, the United Kingdom, and Australia, where it has been incorporated into government policy (Healy & Hampshire, 2002); it is increasingly finding its way into our work in the United States (Ersing & Loeffler, 2008; Loeffler et al., 2004).

Research suggests that social networks can be powerful allies for clinicians working with a range of populations. Assistance and support received through dense social networks have demonstrated impact on the racial and ethnic identities of young people and their families (Weller, 2010), on mental health (Pescosolido & Levy, 2002), on health outcomes (Cattell, 2001), on assisting youth to make the transition from foster care to independent living (Collins, Spencer, & Ward, 2010), and on reducing depression and psychological distress in youth transitioning from foster care (Perry, 2006). Victims of Hurricane Katrina benefited from their strong and linking ties (Hawkins & Maurer, 2009). Weak ties are shown to play a role in youth transitioning from foster care (Perry, 2006), and in helping low-income individuals access employment opportunities (Briggs, 1998; Livermore & Neustrom, 2003). Networks that include strong and weak ties provide both social support and social leverage, and may determine whether low-income mothers of color escape poverty (Dominguez & Watkins, 2003).

This research suggests that an important strategy for clinical social workers may be to focus on engaging, helping to strengthen, and assisting clients to access or establish a social network, and for the social worker to serve as a weak link to external systems to which the client networks have no access. For example, rather than working with low-income teenage mothers individually in a clinic, the social worker may want to position herself within public housing, and then link the mothers to citywide health clinics and job centers. In this model, the practitioner works with the existing social network, and serves as a weak link to an outside resource (Chaskin, 2005; Dominguez & Watkins, 2003).

Social capital and social network theory also is applicable to the area of prevention, specifically explaining how information, innovative ideas, and change in behavior can best occur. Dense local networks are likely to restrict innovation, either because the messages do not reach the networks or because the strong bonds encourage individuals to resist the innovation (Sabar, 2002). For example, mothers, aunts, sisters, and girlfriends may discourage young girls from pursuing educational or career opportunities. On the other hand, weak ties, like teachers, are effective communicators of new information and innovation (Chaskin, 2005; Dominguez & Watkins, 2003). However, if an innovative idea enters a dense network, the innovation is likely to be supported and sustained.

Consequently, the understanding of social networks can be utilized to develop programs for health prevention and promotion. Brenner defines social marketing as "the marketing of relevant programs, ideas, and behavior aimed at motivating all segments of the community to make changes" (2002, pp. 365–366) and notes that social marketing has been widely used in public health promotion. Messages about health risks are purposefully framed for and disseminated through social networks. The marketing saturates a network by (1) using a network of institutions, (2) targeting multiple audiences with multiple messages designed to influence each audience, and (3) offering many desirable outcomes (called products) with the goal of changing health behaviors (Altschuler, Somkin, & Adler, 2004). These ideas can be employed by social workers to use a combination of weak ties to introduce new ideas, and to use strong ties to reinforce and sustain changes in behaviors.

The relevance of social capital theory and research for community organization practice is obvious. Loeffler and colleagues (2004) argue that social capital is at the core of community organizing because of its ability to generate collective action. They write about social capital as "the process of building trusting relationships, mutual understanding, and shared actions that bring together individuals, communities, and institutions. This process enables cooperative action that generates opportunity and/or resources realized through networks, shared norms, and social agency" (p. 24).

Sampson and colleagues (2002) write that it is not the mere existence of ties but the activation of social ties that promotes shared expectations for action. Warren, Thompson, and Saegert (2001) describe how social capital creates bonds among people within communities, bridges people across communities, and links communities to financial and public institutions. They argue that an analysis of the bonds, bridges, and links emerging from the social capital of organizational participants could be studied for its influence on the organizations' capacity to solve problems. It may well be that knowledge about social networks and social capital is essential for community organizers to identify existing networks. Organizers serve as weak ties to link people internally, and as bridging ties to help local organizations make connections to external resources. Of particular importance to organizers will be the organization's ties to financial and public institutions achieved by their organizations, and how those linkages lead to problem solving (Mondros, 2008).

Consequently, as Schuller, Baron, and Field (2000) argue, social capital bridges the theoretical gap between individuals and their communities, and consequently is well suited to the person and environment perspective and the micro to macro continuum that characterizes the social work profession. Social workers can employ this construct to design and test interventions, making use of the assets of social networks suggested by this research (Castillo, 2010). As part of the effort to utilize this knowledge, I next suggest an application to the practice of organizational change.

SOCIAL NETWORKS AND CHANGE FROM BELOW

In their discussion of organizational critical and facilitating actors, Brager and Holloway (1978) anticipated the literature on social capital and social networks. Typically, critical actors have administrative responsibility for the area of the organization affected by the proposed change. Facilitating actors are of two types: those in the hierarchy who must approve plans before the change reaches the attention of the critical actor, and those whose views are valued by the critical actor (Brager & Holloway, 1978). A critical part of the change process is for the change agent to influence these actors to accept the proposed change goal. Brager and Holloway propose that workers try such tactics as developing relationships, building heterogeneous coalitions of actors, and framing distinctive arguments. These strategies assume that people have relationships, networks, bonds, and linkages, and that a change agent's job is to both join and work that network on behalf of the desired change.

Knowledge about social capital and social networks deepens and expands strategic options for influence. It suggests that change agents can analyze the organizational social networks so as to better assess their efficacy for the change goal. Based on that assessment, workers can then choose to strengthen the appropriate network or tie that is most likely to pursue the desired change. An analysis of social networks allows the practitioner to plan more carefully the connections that she or he might engage in to introduce, achieve, implement, and sustain the change goal.

We offer some principles of social capital and social networks that may contribute new insight to the social worker who is proposing an organizational change:

1. Brager and Holloway's original work (1978) placed importance on how the interests, personalities, and relationships of individuals influence change goals. If we assume that social networks exist within human service organizations just as they do in other social enterprises, potentially many more influential actors exist than Brager and Holloway assumed. Workers attempting to influence host organizations will want to assess the social connections among myriad actors, beyond those connections considered critical or facilitating. Since the networks may be extensive, with both internal and external links, knowing where everyone is connected (and conversely, who is isolated) may be critical information in pursuit of the change.

2. Social networks are more than just a sum of individual actors and their characteristics. The networks themselves have attributes that make them more useful with some functions and less useful with others. Dense networks with strong ties are good for social support and assistance, but not for innovation. Extended networks with weak

ties are effective at introducing new information and innovation, and at offering opportunity. Heterogeneous networks that cross divisions and reach beyond the local network are most likely to be activated for effective organizing. Information about the networks' character is also important, suggesting that different networks should be engaged throughout the influencing process. A weak link may most effectively introduce an innovation, particularly someone who is seen as both legitimate and an expert, though not well connected to others in the network. In social service agencies, the weak tie may be a consultant, an individual from another discipline, someone from another institution or agency, or an academic. Networks with strong connections that provide support, assistance, and encouragement are more likely to be needed if the change requires pressure rather than influence at the point of implementation and certainly to ensure that the change is institutionalized.

3. Facilitating and critical actors will have social networks (though socially isolated actors are not unknown in human services, and that, too, is important information). While Brager and Holloway (1978) assume that the close relationships of key actors must be assessed and engaged, social network theory suggests that the search for influence must be much broader, including both strong and weak ties, as well as possible external connections that can be engaged. If the organization's structure has a dense network, it will be difficult to induce change from within. That may mean engaging a more distant relationship, perhaps with someone the critical actor knows and respects but with whom he or she is not particularly close, to bring about change.

4. Though they mention contest tactics in their chapter on persuasion, Brager and Holloway (1978, p. 137) do not address the possibility of engaging external networks to influence organizational change goals. Social network theory's understanding of links that connect beyond the relationships extant inside the organization open up a range of new possibilities to the astute social worker. He or she can engage linking ties that cross social divides and can engage cleavages to create interest and pressure on the views of critical actors. Importantly, he or she can engage a linked social network to support an organization and its mission, and not only as part of a conflict strategy. Just the impression of a groundswell of sentiment and support for an idea, especially one that is emerging from a large and diverse external constituency, can be a very important factor in convincing a decision maker to approve a change.

5. Often social workers who propose organizational changes must sell an idea, a strategy that Brager and Holloway described as persuasion (1978, p. 132). Social network theory offers a new and

broader persuasion strategy, in which one saturates existing networks with messages supporting the change in multiple ways. The network bonds between people then reinforce the change message. For example, information about help for family violence is taught in schools, shared by the principal at parent meetings and by nurses at women's health clinics, and by hairdressers, who are trained to talk to clients about it in their salons. In this way, the preferred behavior is reinforced throughout the network. When used in an organization, such saturation makes the change attractive before a decision is made. Thus, critical actors may be influenced by popular opinion without much direct work from the social worker proposing the change. Also, a social marketing strategy may dispose many organizational actors toward the change once it is introduced, and promote its implementation and sustainability.

Finally, Brager and Holloway urged social workers attempting change to build and maintain a network of relationships, and to do favors in exchange for later assistance. Social capital theory and research gives new urgency to that advice. Ersing and Loeffler (2008) argue that social work students need to develop a "personal cache of social capital" (p. 234). Growing evidence about the utility of strong ties for support, weak ties for innovation and information, and links for collective efficacy that cross systems and divides suggests that the wise social worker will carefully build and manage her own network. Well in advance of attempting change, the astute social worker will begin by identifying her network, and by making a conscious effort to extend and build it to use for support, information, opportunity, and collective strength. Since social networks hold such great potential for influencing one's colleagues (and, conversely, such great possibility of alienating one's adversaries), the practitioner will want to examine the networks of her friends and opponents in order to counter obstacles wherever possible. It is not necessary for the social worker proposing the change to be connected to everyone in the organization, but it is highly desirable for everyone in the organization to be connected to someone in his or her network of supporters. In this way, everyone in the network can be lobbied and hopefully influenced by someone with whom they have a positive bond.

USING SOCIAL CAPITAL AND SOCIAL NETWORKS IN A CASE EXAMPLE

As we described earlier, Julie wanted to find a way to influence the development of clinical services in the new housing. She began to examine the existing social networks. When she assessed her clout in the agency, she reluctantly realized that her opinions at staff meetings were often overlooked—not so much by the executive director as by Rachael and Tony. Her two closest friends were Sam Wade, a somewhat burnt-out mental health worker, and Sonya Abety, also a new clinician, who had gained respect among some of the program staff for her expertise in culturally competent practice. She hoped that Lucy, a long-time clinician, friend of Sam, and ally of Rachael, who had opened many of the programs and services at the agency, would take the lead, but Lucy had so far remained out of the conflict between Tony and Rachael, and had not taken a leadership role in this area.

Julie then began to analyze the broader social networks in the organization in order to assess the likelihood of success (see figure 5.2). She noticed that, contrary to popular belief, there were not many close relationships

FIGURE 5.2. Social Networks at Youth Paradisio

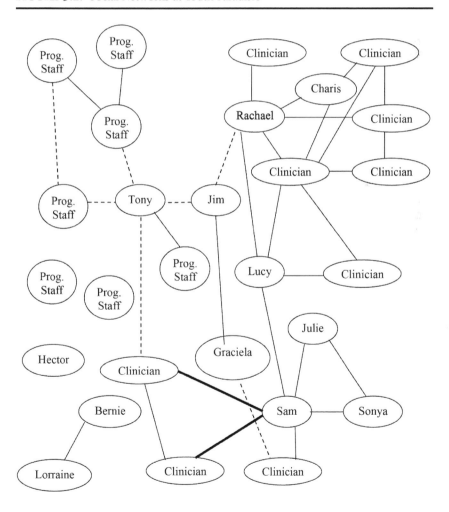

among staff members. The weak links in the organization suggested that change was more possible than she had originally thought. Rachael was the only person with a dense network of strong overlapping bonds among clinicians of long standing. Julie might have tried to introduce her change in a clinical staff meeting, but the nature of Rachael's relationships suggested that this network would probably oppose innovation. On the other hand, Tony's program staff network had few strong links and several weak links, suggesting that it might be easier for her to introduce ideas in the program staff discussions.

Julie then assessed her own social network. While she had only two close relationships, her analysis showed that Sam had several strong ties to clinical staff members who were not strongly bonded to Rachael. Also, Julie had a relationship with a newly hired clinician, Graciela, whom Jim had brought to the agency from his former organization. Graciela had ties to another small clinical network, and, importantly, she had a connection with Jim. Julie reasoned that Sam and Graciela's network of clinicians might serve as a countervailing force to Rachael's network if she needed clinical staff support for her ideas.

Finally, Julie set about the task of analyzing Jim's relationship network. As a new executive director, Jim did not have long-standing ties with existing staff, including Tony and Rachael. Julie's observation was that Jim had not committed himself to either Tony or Rachael, but had concentrated instead on hiring new staff. Jim, however, had brought two of his former employees, including Graciela, on to the staff at Youth Paradisio House. Additionally, he had hired three new program staff members (Bernie, Hector, and Lorraine), as well as the new clinician (Sonya). This information told Julie that Jim intended to build his own network within the agency. While most of the new employees were program staff, Graciela was linked to both Julie and Jim.

Julie used this information to develop her strategy. Julie asked Graciela to reach out to Jim informally to see what he was planning for the new supportive housing. She posited that, based on their prior relationship, Jim would be more open with Graciela than with anyone else. She asked Sam to talk with his network of clinicians to see whether they were open to other ideas about services in the new program. She knew that Sam's network would need to be strong in order to counter Rachael's network's resistance to change. Julie would plan next steps once she had received initial feedback from these networking efforts.

Graciela reported a very positive lunch with Jim. Jim told Graciela that he hoped more resiliency and recovery approaches could be introduced into the agency. He knew of interesting asset-based models using peer support, employment, and coaching that he thought could easily be implemented in the new supportive housing. Graciela reminded Jim of someone who had developed a similar program in another city, and suggested he talk to this person about what he had learned since instituting this model. She told him she would explore available funding for this model of service. Although Jim was attentive and open, he made clear that he was not ready to insist that either Rachael or Tony accept change. He signaled, however, that he would be responsive to change that bubbled up from others in the organization. Jim believed that Tony would have to be convinced of the value of resiliency approaches, and might be open to these ideas, but would resist any inclusion of clinical staff members on his planning committee.

Sam reported that his friends, with the exception of Lucy, were very interested in including more intervention approaches in their work. He said that his network members were chafing at the restrictive views of clinical practice held by Rachael and members of her network. They all were intimidated by Rachael and no one would challenge her. Most important, he reported that Lucy would not lead or support the change because of her long-standing relationship with Rachael, but he believed she would not vocally challenge it if others agreed.

Armed with this information, Julie convinced Sam and Sonya to ask for a meeting with Tony to explore his plans for services in the new housing. She asked Sonya to set up the meeting since she could be viewed as a neutral newcomer. Julie helped Sam and Sonya plan how to describe a resiliency model of service to Tony. They planned to focus on how this model would be different from the agency's current approach to clinical service, especially emphasizing that it employed program activities as therapeutic intervention. She also helped Graciela search for possible funding sources that could be used to sell the idea to Tony and Jim.

During the meeting with Sam and Sonya, Tony said he had few preconceived notions about the appropriate service model for the housing, but was clear that a resident council should be established. That is what he cared about. Sonya asked if Tony would consider including some clinicians in planning the services for the new housing, saying how interested they were in new ways of working with consumers of service and how much they could learn from the program staff. She stressed that she thought a resident council was an important component of models based on resiliency, offered several examples of programs that had such councils, and offered her knowledge about funding for this.

Although Tony was open to all their ideas about service, he wanted to ensure that any clinical services offered in the new housing be accountable to him rather than to Rachael. Sam and Sonya supported this position, arguing that the services had to be consistent with the housing. Seeking to maintain his control, Tony agreed to add one clinician to the planning committee for the housing, but did not want to make that decision without talking with Jim. Jim almost certainly would want to assign the staff person to work on the service delivery plans.

Graciela informally stopped by Jim's office. She quickly updated him on the meeting between Sam, Sonya, and Tony. Jim asked her advice on who should serve, and she suggested that it would be important to have more than one clinician there so they could fully develop the services, and perhaps extend the resiliency model beyond the new housing. Jim was reluctant for staff to spend time with responsibilities for the planning committee, but said he would consider it. Graciela left a folder with Jim that included many articles on use of the model in community programs, and also all of the information about funders who were interested in these resiliency approaches. Julie's hope was that Jim would see that resiliency approaches were gaining traction in the city and with funders.

In his regular supervision with Jim, Tony asked whether Jim wanted to assign a clinician to help design the services for the new housing. Tony's idea was to have one clinician join the current planning staff team. Jim was immediately supportive of this idea, and, surprisingly, asked Tony who he would like to see involved. When Tony suggested Sonya be assigned, Jim suggested that a separate services committee be formed. Sonya could be asked to include two other colleagues, and Rachael could also choose one staff member to participate. Jim also said that he would want Tony to chair the committee since the housing fell under his auspice. He gave Tony the funding information, telling him he thought it looked like there might be many options for resources to support the services.

Jim announced at the next staff meeting that a service planning committee would be established for the new housing. The planning committee included Sonya, Sam, and Julie. Rachael appointed Charise, one of her closely linked allies. Graciela asked that she be excused from serving on the committee. She felt she was too new to be a legitimate member, but promised Julie that she would continue to serve as a link to Jim. Tony chaired the committee, but relied heavily on Sonya's advice about how to proceed. She suggested that they study similar programs and conduct a literature review on best practices. Graciela continued to update Jim on the progress of the planning committee, making certain to credit Tony's openness and work. Julie went to work on grant proposals to fund the service component. Sam made sure that his network of clinicians supported the plans for clinical services in the new housing, and reported on the progress at clinical staff meetings. The development of the services was protected within the organization's culture and structure, and Rachael and Charise could do little to challenge the committee's work.

The service planning committee met for six months; at the end of that time, the committee had written and adopted a concept paper, "Residents' Resilience Program." Tony took the draft to Jim who took it to a staff meeting with his full endorsement. Julie was able to obtain seed funding from a small local foundation to support the development of the services. As the housing moved toward completion, the agency advertised for a director of resident life to oversee the facility and program, and a director of resident services to oversee the support services. Tony asked Sonya to interview candidates for these positions. Julie applied for the position and Tony hired her as the director of resident life. Tony hired a new staff member, a clinician with experience in resilience models, to fill the services job. Julie's appointment was the first time a clinician had held a program job, opening the opportunity for more integration among the staff. The new clinician was quickly added to the Sonya/Julie/Sam/Graciela network. Julie also worked to build strong ties with Bernie, Hector, and Lorraine, the newly hired program staff. A new network of program and clinical staff was beginning to form.

Jim asked Rachael to see if there were ways she might introduce resiliency models to the existing work of the clinical staff. He gave Rachael responsibility for choosing and arranging site visits to other programs, and he paid for her and two of her staff to attend a two-day training in another state. At staff meetings, Jim praised Rachael's efforts to innovate clinical services and gave her great credit for instituting clinical services in the new housing. Julie was careful to thank Rachael publicly for her support and expertise.

CASE ANALYSIS

The case study of Youth Paradisio House includes much of what Brager and Holloway (1978) describe as a change process. Julie was the initiator of the change. She had an ambitious change goal: to introduce asset-based clinical services to a traditional agency.

While it was possible to develop a force field analysis of this change effort, Julie's analysis of the organization's existing social networks added much needed insight to the strategy for change. She found that despite the agency's reputation for close and informal relationships, there were not many strong ties, and almost no ties between individuals in different departments. Instead, the critical factors that influenced Julie's change work were the conflict between the program and clinical staff and Jim's reluctance to get involved in the conflict. Jim, the person who would ordinarily be assumed to be the critical actor, would only respond to pressure from below. Graciela could be considered a facilitating actor, but she alone could not have convinced Jim to make the change. Julie used a social network strategy.

Julie realized that Rachael's network, with its strong bonds and resistance to innovation, would have to be avoided if change were to occur. Even Lucy would not challenge Rachael. Tony had a very weak network, suggesting that perhaps there might be an opening for change there, but his staff was too weak to carry out and implement a change. No one in his network, not even Tony himself, cared very much about the services in the new housing. Julie's only hope was to create a new network that would introduce, cheer on, implement, and sustain the change.

The existing relationship between Graciela and Jim was quite fortunate. Graciela's assistance allowed her to judge Jim's interest and encourage his indirect support. That support was implicit and would not have emerged without a groundswell from below. Julie was helped a great deal by Sonya and Sam. Their network allowed the group who supported the change to appear larger and more powerful than it was. As long as Tony thought he was in control of the group, he was willing to allow the change to occur.

Furthermore, Julie used a social marketing approach that convinced Jim and Tony that resiliency models had currency in the city and among the funding sources. This external information reinforced Jim's interest in the change. As a new director, he would want to appear to be informed and forward thinking. The information probably convinced Tony that he could further strengthen his program department with more funding.

Importantly, the network of change agents was diverse (what Brager and Holloway called a heterogeneous coalition) and so it could not be attacked as homogeneous. Sonya and Graciela were Latina, Julie was Chinese, and Sam was African American. They were all experienced clinicians. This made it difficult for the clinical staff to challenge them. Because they were clinicians who were not part of Rachael's network, Tony was open to their inclusion. When he wanted to include only Sonya, they found a way to involve Sam and Julie as well so that the change goal could be protected and championed by several people. Importantly, Julie accepted a program job, rather than the clinical position. With Julie in the program job and new connections between the clinicians and Hector, Bernie, and Lorraine, a linking network that crossed the divide between clinical and program staff was formed. Linking networks are more successful at collective efficacy, and therefore Julie's network will presumably have an easier time making changes in the future.

CONCLUSION

In sum, using theories of social capital and social networks strengthens our ability to assess the likelihood of change. It also helps practitioners plan and execute strategy that moves change forward. This knowledge builds upon and enriches Brager and Holloway's original work (1978).

DISCUSSION QUESTIONS

1. Assess the social networks in your organization. What do the relationships among people tell you about the best way to influence the system?
2. What relationships in your organization will be likely to resist the change goal you have proposed? What are the relationships that are most likely to carry the change forward?
3. Would a different part of your organization's social network be best for implementation and institutionalization of the change than its introduction? Why?

REFERENCES

Altschuler, A., Somkin, C. P., & Adler, N. E. (2004). Local services and amenities, neighborhood social capital, and health. *Social Science & Medicine* (59), 1219–1229.

Brager, G., & Holloway, S. (1978). *Changing human service organizations: Politics and practice.* New York: Free Press.

Brenner, B. (2002). Implementing a community intervention program for health promotion. *Social Work in Health Care, 35*(1/2), 359–375.

Briggs, X. (1997). Social capital and the cities: Advice to change agents. *National Civic Review, 86,* 111–118.

Briggs, X. (1998). Brown kids in white suburbs: Housing mobility and the many faces of social capital. *Housing Policy Debate, 9*(1), 177–221.

Castillo, J. T. (2010). The relationship between non-resident fathers' social networks and social capital and the establishment of paternity. *Child and Adolescent Social Work Journal, 27*(3), 193–211.

Cattell, V. (2001). Poor people, poor places, and poor health: The mediating role of social networks and social capital. *Social Science and Medicine, 52*(10), 1501–1516.

Chaskin, R. (2005). Democracy and bureaucracy in a community planning process. *Journal of Planning Education and Research, 24*(4), 408–419.

Christakis, N., & Fowler, J. (2009). *Connected: The surprising power of our social networks and how they shape our lives.* New York: Little, Brown and Company.

Collins, M., Spencer, R., & Ward, R. (2010). Supporting youth in the transition from foster care: Formal and informal connections. *Child Welfare, 89*(1), 125–143.

Dominguez, S., & Watkins, C. (2003). Creating networks for survival and mobility: Social capital among African-American and Latin-American low-income mothers. *Social Problems, 50*(1), 111–135.

Draus, P., & Carlson, R. (2009). Down on Main Street: Drugs and the small-town vortex. *Health Place, 15*(1), 247–254.

Ersing, R., & Loeffler, D. (2008). Teaching students to become effective in policy practice: Integrating social capital into social work education and practice. *Journal of Policy Practice, 7*(2–3), 226–238.

Hawkins, R., & Maurer, K. (2009). Bonding, bridging and linking: How social capital operated in New Orleans following Hurricane Katrina. *British Journal of Social Work, 39*(2), 1–17.

Healy, K., & Hampshire, A. (2002). Social capital: A useful concept for social work? *Journal of Australian Social Work, 55* (3), 227–238.

Livermore, M., & Neustrom, A. (2003). Linking welfare clients to jobs: Discretionary use of worker social capital. *Journal of Sociology and Social Welfare, 30*(2), 87–103.

Loeffler, D., Christiansen, D., Tracy, M., Secret, M., Ersing, R., & Fairchild, S. (2004). Social capital for social work: Towards a definition and conceptual framework. *Social Development Issues*, 26(2/3): 22–38.

Mitchell, C., & LaGory, M. (2002). Social capital and mental distress in an impoverished community. *City and Community, 1*(2), 199–222.

Mondros, J. (2008). Introduction to a dissertation: Posing questions on perceived empowerment and community problem solving. In R. Cnaan, M. Dichter, & J. Draine (Eds.), *A century of social work and social welfare at Penn* (pp. 288–301). Philadelphia: Penn Press.

Pattillo-McCoy, M. (1999). *Black picket fences: Privilege and peril among the Black middle class.* Chicago: University of Chicago Press.

Perry, B. (2006). Understanding social network disruption: The case of youth in foster care. *Social Problems, 82*(6), 727–746.

Pescosolido, B., & Levy, J. (2002). The role of social networks in health, illness, disease and healing: The accepting present, the forgotten past, and the dangerous potential for a complacent future. In J. Levy & B. Pescosolido (Eds.), *Social networks and health* (pp. 3–28). Oxford: Elsevier Science Ltd.

Putnam, R. (2000). *Bowling alone.* New York: Simon and Schuster.

Rawsthorne, M. (2000). Complex negotiations: Discourses that shape rural young people's understanding of sexuality and sexual violence (Doctoral dissertation). University of Sydney, Australia.

Sabar, N. (2002). Kibbutz L.A.: A paradoxical social network. *Journal of Contemporary Ethnography, 31*(1), 68–94.

Sampson, R. J., Morenoff, J., & Gannon-Rowley, T. (2002). Assessing "neighborhood effects": Social processes and new directions in research. *Annual Review of Sociology, 28*, 443–478.

Schuller, T., Baron, S., & Field, J. (2000). Social capital: A review and critique. In S. Baron, J. Field, & T. Schuller (Eds.), *Social capital: Critical perspectives* (pp. 1–38). Oxford: Oxford University Press.

Shinn, M., Knickman, J., & Weitzman, B. (1991). Social relationships and vulnerability to becoming homeless among poor families. *American Psychologist, 46*(11), 1180–1187.

Subramanian, S., Kim, D., & Kawachi, I. (2002). Social trust and self-rated health in U.S. communities: A multilevel analysis. *Journal of Urban Health, 79*(4), Suppl. S21–S34.

Warren, M., Thompson, J., & Saegert, S. (2001). The role of social capital in combating poverty. In S. Saegert, J. Thompson, & M. Warren (Eds.), *Social capital and poor communities* (pp. 1–30). New York: Russell Sage Foundation.

Weller, S. (2010). Young people's social capital: Complex identities, dynamic networks. *Ethnic and Racial Studies, 33*(5), 872–888.

6

Combating Discriminatory Practices in Child Welfare Services

The Burgos Consent Decree

**Edward Gumz, Maria Vidal de Haymes, Luis Barrios,
Vicky Ha, and Nicole Howver**

INTRODUCTION

Advocacy is a well-established method of intervention in the social work profession; indeed, it is "one of the activities that may distinguish social work from other helping professions" (Kaminski & Walmsley, 1995, p. 53). Social workers use various strategies of advocacy to assist their clients at different system levels. The dimensions of advocacy can include speaking on someone's behalf, representing another, taking action, accessing rights and benefits for someone, serving as a partisan, demonstrating influence and political skills, securing social justice, empowering clients, identifying with the client, and using legal maneuvers (Schneider & Lester, 2001).

This chapter presents the Burgos Consent Decree as a case example of how direct service staff can influence social and organizational change through a number of advocacy strategies. This case began with social workers recognizing a pattern of discrimination that led them to work on behalf of their clients. Initially, the strategies were on the micro level of individual client advocacy and they eventually moved toward more macro levels to include

The research for this chapter was supported by the Provost Fellowship Program, Loyola Undergraduate Research Opportunities Program (LUROP), Loyola University Chicago.

95

cause, legal and administrative advocacy, and implementation. Throughout the advocacy process, numerous barriers presented themselves that eventually led to different actions, interventions, and strategies to create change.

THE CASE

The Burgos and Mendez Families

In 1970, Leopoldo and Iris Burgos migrated from Puerto Rico to the United States with their nine children. They lived in a small apartment in the West Town neighborhood of Chicago. Upon their arrival, the family had a difficult time adjusting to an urban setting. The family longed for their homeland and incorporated traditions and practices from their rural Puerto Rican lives into their new home. For example, absent a yard, they kept native plants in their apartment windows and live chickens roamed the apartment. Members of the Burgos family were monolingual (Spanish). Neither parent was formally educated and both were unemployed, Mr. Burgos due to the loss of four fingers on his right hand in a factory incident. The couple received $700 in public aid and $560 in food stamps each month, and paid a monthly rent of $300 (Davidson, 1987, para. 23).

The Burgos family came into contact with the Illinois Department of Children and Family Services (IDCFS) in 1972, when an English-speaking social worker visited the family at their home. Two children—Henry, age six, and Olga, age three, were removed from their family home at this time. The parents understood from the IDCFS worker that the children were being taken to have their blood tested for lead. Instead, the children were taken into custody by IDCFS, which reported that the children were unclean and that they were being pecked by the chickens. Both children spoke Spanish exclusively and were unable to understand English.

IDCFS placed Olga and Henry in long-term foster families. The families that cared for the Burgos children did not speak Spanish. In addition to language barriers, these foster families were also unfamiliar with the Latino culture and the religious customs of the children. When interviewed decades later, Sheila Wymore, Olga's foster mother, recalls that Olga had scars that could have been from leather belts or human hands. Other marks were round like cigarette burns. She also had lead poisoning. "'She was not speaking any language, not even Spanish,' Wymore said. 'She wouldn't say anything'" (Casillas, 2007, para 9).

While in foster care, the children began speaking English and lost their ability to communicate with their Spanish-speaking parents. During this time, the Burgos parents were never assigned a Spanish-speaking caseworker and failed to receive written notices or information in Spanish from IDCFS (Winter, 2008).

The children remained in foster care for four years before being reunited with their family of origin. Henry and Olga spoke only English at reunification, and were unable to communicate with their birth family. This made the process of reintegration into the family system nearly impossible. As Wallace Winter, the Legal Assistance Foundation (LAF) attorney that represented the Burgos family said, "The crime is that IDCFS did not act quickly to bring this family back together. As a result, they were totally estranged. The children lost their language and their cultural identity. . . . It was beyond hope" (Winter, 2008).

The Burgos parents found it difficult to communicate with Olga, who had remained in foster care from three to seven years of age. This experience created a great linguistic and cultural divide, making readjustment into her natural family difficult, due to the newly formed cultural differences. In order to aid in her reassimilation, Olga, then seven, was sent to Puerto Rico to live with her grandmother and learn Spanish. Years later, at the age of eighteen, she returned to Chicago.

In 1973, five of Miguel and Idaina Mendez's children were taken into guardianship or custody by the IDCFS. Their case was very similar to the Burgos family. The Mendez children were placed in non-Spanish-speaking long-term foster homes that were neither Catholic nor familiar with Latino culture. Both Mr. and Mrs. Mendez were of Puerto Rican ancestry and birth. They spoke Spanish exclusively and had recently relocated to Chicago's West Town community from rural Puerto Rico. Similar to the Burgos case, the Mendez family were not assigned a Spanish-speaking social worker, nor did they receive any notices in Spanish regarding their children. They were not offered any counseling or other supportive services that would facilitate the return of their children.

As with the Burgos parents, the attending worker required Mr. and Mrs. Mendez to speak solely in English during supervised visits. In both cases, the parents were unable to communicate with their children in foster care without the assistance of an interpreter. The children had lost their ability to speak Spanish while interacting in an English-speaking environment. Furthermore, the foster parents changed the names of two of the Mendez children from Bienvenido and Idiana to the more Anglicized names of Dean and Christie, without the knowledge of their parents but with the consent of IDCFS (Winter, 2008).

From Client to Cause:
Recognizing a Pattern of Discrimination

Both the Burgos and Mendez families came in contact with Association House of Chicago, a settlement house established in the Chicago West Town community in 1897. Association House has been recognized for providing bilingual and bicultural social services to the ethnically diverse community. Knowing this, both the Burgos and Mendez families sought their assistance.

Leopoldo and Iris Burgos went to Association House's West Town Youth Services Program independently seeking counseling and assistance in regaining custody of their children. Mrs. Mendez, on the other hand, was already working as a volunteer in the West Town Youth Services Program when she sought assistance regarding her children from one of the program social workers. Both social workers attempted to work directly with the assigned foster care workers for each case to resolve the issue, but encountered numerous barriers, and their efforts were futile. Working individually on a client advocacy level, the Association House social workers came to realize the injustice that the Burgos and Mendez families were subjected to by the IDCFS. Together they noticed a pattern of discrimination regarding the placement of Latino children in foster care based on their work with the Burgos and Mendez families. After numerous unsuccessful attempts at resolution, the cases of the two families were referred to the West Town LAF of Chicago.

Both families sought legal counsel and aid from the LAF regarding their children. Attorney Wallace Winter, then the director of Latin American Special Projects for the LAF, took an interest in the Burgos and Mendez cases due to a language discrimination case he was working on at the time of referral. That case focused on challenging state agencies such as the Department of Public Aid and the Department of Labor for failing to develop Spanish language materials. Given the LAF's public interest legal work on language discrimination issues, Mr. Winter agreed to represent the families, beginning a new direction in advocacy for the Burgos and Mendez families.

The Role of Advocacy in Change

Client Advocacy. Most advocacy efforts begin with the individual (Hunter, 1979). While individual advocacy is the most commonly used form of advocacy, client advocacy is much more expansive and can include working with an individual, a family unit, a group, or an entity such as an organization or a community as a whole.

The mission of a client advocate is to ensure that a client receives the proper services, rights, benefits, and resources to which they are entitled (Herbert & Mould, 1992; Sheafor, Horejsi, & Horejsi, 1994). As the Burgos family sought help from Association House regarding their children in the state child welfare system, this agency advocated for the parents on a client level to help them regain custody of their children. Their efforts at client advocacy were ineffective, however, and they confronted one barrier after another.

Cause Advocacy. When Association House social workers recognized that their individual cases reflected a pattern of language discrimination and learned that there were more cases like those of the Burgos and Mendez families, they understood that another form of advocacy would be needed to address the systemic problems this population faced. The confluence of the failed attempts at client advocacy and the recognition of a broader systemic discrimination led them to move from case microlevel to cause macrolevel advocacy.

Legal Advocacy. With the transition to a cause focus, agency social workers employed new forms of advocacy, both legal and administrative. The strategy of legal advocacy utilizes legal assistance as a form of intervention. The form of legal advocacy advanced in the Burgos case was that of a class action suit, which is a legal suit filed by a party as a complaint on behalf of themselves and others, typically a larger group that is affected by the same claims. Class actions can offer several advantages by aggregating a number of individual claims into one representational lawsuit. They can increase efficiency and lower costs of litigation and may be brought to purposely change behavior of a class or the procedures and policies of an institution of which the defendant is a member. Class action suits have led to significant reforms when brought against federal, state, and local officials and offices. Such cases are typically presented in federal courts and have led to actions to end discriminatory practices, enforce civil rights laws, or ensure due process. Two exemplary cases are *Goldberg v. Kelly* and *Brown v. Wade*. In *Goldberg v. Kelly*, the U.S. Supreme Court ruled that recipients of public assistance must be given notice and the opportunity for a hearing prior to termination of benefits. The *Brown v. Wade* class action lawsuit yielded a Supreme Court decision striking down segregated schools (Lehman & Phelps, 2005a).

A consent decree eventually became the resolution for the class action lawsuit in the Burgos case. This decree, entered into January 1977, is known as the Burgos Consent Decree (hereafter the Decree). A consent decree is a binding order that memorializes a voluntary agreement between parties to a lawsuit and brings a close to civil litigation. Once entered, a consent decree is binding. If the party against whom the judgment is rendered violates the terms of the consent decree, the nonbreaching party can undertake enforcement through a contempt action (Lehman & Phelps, 2005b). The Decree called for system reforms that addressed the language, translation, and communication needs of Hispanic families and required that children with Spanish-speaking parents be placed in Spanish-speaking foster care. The specific provisions of the Decree will be discussed later in the chapter.

By 1979, it was clear that IDCFS was unable to satisfactorily implement the Decree and was thus out of compliance with it. In response, that year the LAF filed a motion of contempt against IDCFS (Suleiman, 1998). This was the first of numerous contempt motions filed by LAF against IDCFS for its failure to fully comply with the provisions of the Decree. A contempt action can be taken when there is deliberate disobedience or disregard for an order, a failure to comply with a request, or a defiance of a public authority, such as a court or legislative body (Lehman & Phelps, 2005c).

Through the 1980s and 1990s, advocates continued to turn to the courts for remedy. LAF filed several contempt of court motions. A motion is an application for an order. In the Burgos case, these motions led to several court orders. An order is a decision of a court or judge regarding a motion that is entered in writing, determines some point, and directs some step in the proceedings, which can include a timetable and procedure for managing a civil lawsuit (Lehman & Phelps, 2005d).

Administrative Advocacy. The court orders directed IDCFS to take administrative measures to fully address Burgos requirements that led to additional reforms, creating internal and external monitoring positions and provisions and changes in administrative procedures and practices. Implementation of these additional reforms called for administrative advocacy to create organizational change needed for IDCFS to come into compliance with the Decree. This form of advocacy focuses on promoting change internally from within an agency (Schneider & Lester, 2001). In the Burgos case, the administrative advocacy primarily occurred through the internal and external organizational procedural and practice changes promoted by newly created administrative and monitoring positions. Internally, the new positions of Burgos coordinator and the coordinator of Hispanic services were charged with coordinating enhanced efforts to fully implement the decree orders. In addition, the external positions of special master and later court monitor were charged with monitoring and reporting implementation and compliance (see appendix 6.1).

Progression of Advocacy Efforts

The advocacy efforts in this case, initiated by the two Association House social workers, progressed through several stages and produced various results. Commenting on the significance of their efforts, Mr. Winter stated, "It's a good example of proactive, alert, advocacy oriented social work. If it had not been for these two workers a motion may never have been filed on behalf of the non-English speaking family members and there would not have been a Burgos Decree" (Winter, 2008). Figure 6.1 presents the progression of advocacy on the Burgos and Mendez case that the two Association House direct practice social workers set in motion. A force field analysis summary (figure 6.2) and a case timeline (appendix 6.1) are tools that can assist the reader in following the progression of the Burgos case, as well as the many agents for and barriers to change that influenced this progression.

Advocacy and Legal Processes in the Burgos and Mendez Case. The social work profession becomes involved in the legal process when advocating for protection of the rights of clients (Raider, 1982). Social work advocacy "attempts to impact a specific decision, law, policy or practice on behalf of a client or group of clients" (Ezell, 1991, p. 5). In this case, the acknowledgment of a pattern of discrimination against a population of Latino families in

FIGURE 6.1. Progression of Advocacy in the Burgos and Mendez Cases

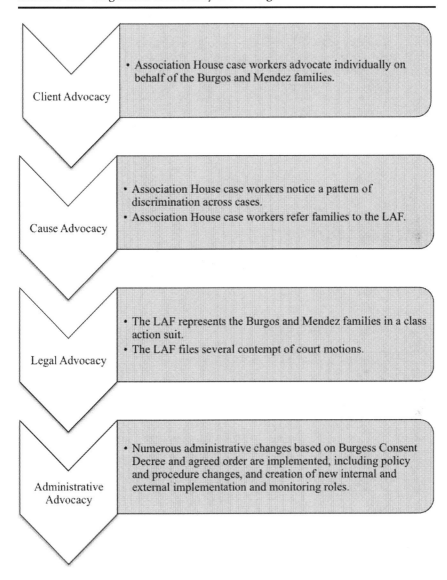

the child welfare system led to incorporation of legal advocacy as a form of intervention.

As the form of advocacy on the Burgos and Mendez cases took on a legal strategy, other direct service–level social workers became involved. One of the social workers from Association House put the LAF's attorneys in contact with six Latino IDCFS social workers. These IDCFS workers began to

FIGURE 6.2. Force Field Analysis for Access to Language Services

---

Problem:

Meaningful access to services for clients with limited English proficiency is guaranteed by Title VI of the Civil Rights Act of 1964, making language-appropriate services a matter of civil rights and cultural competency. The lack of bilingual capacity diminishes the ability of IDCFS to meet the child welfare service needs of these families.

Change Goal:

Ensure that all Spanish-speaking children and families receive services in the Spanish language and bring the agency in full compliance with the Consent Decree.

Critical Actors:

1. Director of IDCFS and his legal advisors

2. Federal court

3. Legal advocate representing the plaintiff

Facilitating Actors:

1. IDCFS senior managers from operations, clinical, purchase of services, and quality assurance divisions

2. IDCFS Burgos coordinator and Office of Latino Services (OLS)

3. IDCFS training office

4. Private sector representatives including Child Welfare Advisory Council, Child Care Association of Illinois, Latino Consortium

5. Juvenile court personnel

6. Community leaders

7. American Federation of State, County and Municipal Employees (AFSCME)

Driving Forces for Change:	*Restraining Forces for Change:*
1. Internal and external advocates	1. Resistance from the director's office
2. Training programs	2. Resistance from elected officials
3. Management and supervision	3. Plaintiff representatives and federal court
4. Quality assurance/Improvement programs	4. Child and Family Service review
5. Child and Family Service Review Program Improvement Plan (PIP)	5. Resistance from IDCFS inspector general
6. Council of accreditation	
7. Illinois Latino Family Commission	

provide LAF attorneys with information regarding similar cases that fit a pattern of language discrimination. This information provided from within IDCFS helped strengthen the case that the LAF was building against the state child welfare agency. The case proceeded as a class action lawsuit concerning the pattern apparent in the Burgos and Mendez families and other cases in IDCFS that were arguing similar claims. These claims all maintained that children of monolingual (Spanish) parents were being placed with monolingual (English) foster parents, and that the birth parents did not have access to services, notices, and other information in their primary language that would facilitate the return of the children to their biological families. The results of these actions created situations in which Latino parents could not effectively work toward reunification with their children. In addition, the children lost their ability to speak Spanish, which seriously compromised their ability to communicate with their birth parents. Common difficulties related to the intergenerational linguistic divide presented themselves upon reunification. The overriding tragedy was that the IDCFS failed to best serve the interests of the children and through its practices created significant barriers to family reunification.

While language was of paramount concern, culture was also a factor that merited serious attention. Latino children were often placed in non-Latino homes that could neither instill nor maintain their cultural identity, values, and practices. These placements heightened the anxiety, insecurity, and loss felt by the children upon removal and contributed to difficulties in their adjustment to their temporary foster homes. In cases where children remained in foster care for a long-term basis, the children often experienced a loss of their ethnic culture and confusion in regards to issues of identity. By distancing the children from their ethnic culture, language, religion, and values, the placement process subsequently weakened their family ties.

Cultural ignorance was not simply a problem associated with the foster homes. The IDCFS and the agencies contracted for the provision of services also lacked bilingual staff and lacked culturally responsive practice skills and familiarity with Latino cultures, as well as some of the factors associated with migration stress and accommodation. The following examples were shared by former IDCFS workers as illustrative of the types of cultural misunderstandings that were common, yet that carried heavy consequences for families. In one case, a child was not allowed to return home because the worker observed the father coaxing the child to drink a bottle of Malta India, a nonalcoholic malt beverage popular in Latin American countries that uses packaging similar to that used by the beer industry. Unable to read the content description of the package, the worker misunderstood the incident, and thought that the parent was forcing the child to drink beer.

Another worker expressed concern regarding a child's development because when asked the color of a banana during a cognitive assessment, the child responded that bananas come in many colors. Unfamiliar with the variety of bananas and plantains in many Latin American countries, the worker was concerned when the child did not respond with a simple answer of "yellow." The worker proceeded to make assumptions about the child's cognitive ability and the parents' neglect in supporting the child's learning.

As both issues of language and culture were intertwined, family reunification became difficult and in some cases impossible, yet the legal case proceeded solely on the basis of language, without addressing culture. Although best practices would consider the importance of culture, there was no legal basis to address this important factor, so the class action lawsuit was limited to language discrimination.

Both the Illinois Juvenile Court Act (1987) and Title VI of the Civil Rights Act of 1964 provided the legal basis of the complaint of discriminatory practices. Court documents presented the argument as follows:

> Pursuant to Illinois Revised Statute, Chapter 23, 5001, the Defendant IDCFS is obligated "to provide social services to children and their families . . . and such services must be delivered in accordance with the purposes of the relevant part: The purpose of the Act is to secure for each minor subject hereto such care and guidance preferably in his own home as will serve the moral, emotional, mental and physical welfare of the minor and the best interest of the community; *to preserve and strengthen the minor's family ties whenever possible . . . and when the minor is removed from his family, to secure for him custody, care and discipline as nearly as possible equivalent to that which should be given by his parents.*" (Illinois Juvenile Court Act of 1987, chap. 23, para. 5007, Sec. 7; emphasis added)

> Federal monies are allocated to the defendant IDCFS under various federal statutory programs and IDCFS is thereby obligated to comply with Title VI of the Civil Rights Act of 1964, 42 U.S.C. 2000d, which provides: No person in the United States shall on grounds of race, color, or national origin, be excluded from participation in, be denied the benefits of, or be subjected to discrimination under any program receiving federal financial assistance. (Title VI of the 1964 Civil Rights Act, Sec. 2000d, para. 1)

The discriminatory practices identified in the complaint included the failure of IDCFS to (1) employ a sufficient number of Spanish-speaking personnel, (2) license sufficient numbers of Spanish-speaking foster families, (3) provide counseling and other supportive services to the named plaintiffs and other Spanish-speaking individuals and families whose children have been placed under the guardianship and custody of IDCFS, and (4) print official notices and forms in the Spanish language.

The class action suit was filed on behalf of Spanish-speaking parents and children against the IDCFS under Title VI of the Civil Rights Act (1964). The lawsuit claimed that the Burgos and Mendez families, as well as other Spanish-speaking families, were subjected to discrimination on the basis of their national origin and race. The presence of language discrimination showed a violation of the Equal Protection clause of the Fourteenth Amendment to the U.S. Constitution and the Civil Rights Act (1964). Under the Civil Rights Act, a person shall not be discriminated against due to national origin or race, which includes language as a part of an individual's national origin. Rights are defined as protections and guarantees that are ensured by the Constitution to all citizens and cannot be denied without due process of law; substantive rights; and basic human rights (Hardcastle, Wenocur, & Powers, 1997; Kirst-Ashman & Hull, 2008). One of the most well-known and fought-for liberties in the United States is civil rights. The Thirteenth and Fourteenth Amendments to the U.S. Constitution and congressional acts guarantee these rights.

Schneider and Lester (2001) define legal rights as "rules or requirements that exist because of their mandate by the legal system, not based on concerns for outcomes or abilities to decide what could or should occur" (p. 153). The outcome of the class action lawsuit filed in 1975 for the Burgos and Mendez families against the IDCFS culminated in the Decree. Judge McMillen entered the Decree on January 14, 1977, creating an agreement between both parties to correct the injustice by ensuring that the IDCFS complied with language appropriate services to Spanish-speaking families. These services include language communication needs, placement and service monitoring, staff development, and the hiring of bilingual staff.

Initially, the Decree covered only the IDCFS regions of Cook and Kane Counties, but later was extended throughout the state. Building on the initial decree and subsequent court actions, the Decree became subject to judicial enforcement under the supervision of the U.S. District Court. Its purpose was to monitor and ensure the following (Suleiman, 1998):

- All Spanish-speaking children of Hispanic/Latino parents shall be placed only with Spanish-speaking foster parents.

- The IDCFS assigned social workers or its vendors providing child welfare and counseling services to Spanish-speaking Hispanic/Latino clients shall be bilingual employees. These social workers shall not have caseloads substantially higher than those corresponding persons in the same area office who work with English-speaking clients.

- All essential child welfare services provided by the Department or its vendors that involve direct contact and communication with Spanish-speaking Hispanic/Latino clients shall be provided by bilingual employees.

- The Department and its vendors shall make all reasonable efforts to provide adjunctive and supportive child welfare services for Spanish-speaking Hispanic/Latino consumers through bilingual employees. In no case shall the Hispanic/Latino consumer be denied such services by the Department or its representatives because the parent or child is unable to speak English.

- As of 1977, the number of bilingual staff shall be expanded by hiring additional workers in the Chicago and Northern regions.

- A Spanish language notice describing the above services shall be posted in a conspicuous location in the Chicago metropolitan area offices.

- The individualized written communication mailed to all Spanish-speaking plaintiffs and other Spanish-speaking Hispanic/Latino parents by IDCFS or its vendors shall be in the Spanish language. In addition, all informational books, pamphlets and posters listed in the decree are to be available and circulated in Spanish.

- Licensed Spanish-speaking foster parents within the Chicago metropolitan area are to be identified.

- The Department of Child and Family Services and its vendors must accurately identify the national origin of all Hispanic/Latino clients who are or should be receiving child welfare services in the language that the consumers primarily rely upon for oral and written communication. This will be documented by the use of language determination forms signed by the client.

Pairing Legal and Administrative Advocacy: The Challenge to Implement the Decree. Although a consent decree is a legal order and agreement between two parties, the Decree was not completely successful in resolving the presenting issues in 1977 when it was entered by Judge McMillen. In the early 1980s, the LAF returned to court, filing a contempt of court motion against the IDCFS. While the Decree granted many concessions and protections to Latino children and families, the IDCFS and its vendors were sufficiently out of compliance with the Decree in its entirety to warrant action. Although both parties agreed to the terms of the 1977 order, the problem was not solved, as IDCFS did not fully comply with the order, which resulted in further legal action. In April of 1979, a motion to show cause why IDCFS should not be held in contempt of the consent decree was filed. On March 3, 1982, a stipulation to withdraw the contempt motion was entered, wherein IDCFS agreed to take several measures to address requirements of the consent decree, including recruiting and obtaining additional Spanish-speaking foster parents, annual civil rights compliance, ensuring vendor compliance with the consent decree, and the filing of quarterly statistical information and semiannual reporting to verify compliance actions.

Yet the problems with compliance persisted, leading the plaintiffs to file several additional contempt of court motions between 1987 and 1989. To remedy this situation, the U.S. District Court Judge James B. Zagel entered an agreed order in 1990 to resolve the pending contempt motion. The agreed order between IDCFS and the LAF of Chicago established several measures to ensure compliance with the Decree. One such change was the requirement for the Burgos coordinator to report directly to the director on issues of compliance. Other measures included ensuring that a child will not be used as an interpreter, the removal of waivers to receive services in the Spanish language, training of direct client workers and supervisors regarding the Decree and its implementation, and the appointment of a special master to prepare a compliance report. The compliance report was issued the following year and included numerous recommendations, including the establishment of a permanent court monitor to scrutinize compliance. The first permanent court monitor was appointed in 1992.

Despite the agreed order, implementation remains problematic to this day. However, during the mid-1990s and early 2000s, IDCFS participated in the development of a new Latino services administrative initiative. This effort created a service provision network called the Latino Consortium (hereafter the Consortium), comprising eight private agency member organizations. This significant effort aimed to address the issue of inadequate service delivery by bringing together a number of agencies with noted leadership, capacity, organizational focus, and track records for providing culturally and linguistically appropriate quality services to Latino clients. The creation of the Consortium presents an ongoing vehicle for autonomous yet contractually connected administrative advocacy on behalf of the clients. The agencies that compose the Consortium are independently contracted by IDCFS to provide services. However, IDCFS provides a contract to the group as a whole through the Consortium fiscal agent, to support collective service planning, coordination, and training to develop workforce and agency capacities to provide culturally and linguistically responsive programs and services for the Latino population.

Currently, the IDCFS and many of its stakeholders, including the Consortium member agencies and advocates, are making a strong good faith effort to fully implement the Decree. Although much remains to be achieved to fully implement this consent decree, it is important to recognize the many agents of change that were involved in bringing forth the case that led to the consent decree, the subsequent efforts to push IDCFS into compliance, and the ongoing efforts to implement the various provisions of the Decree. Clearly, there has been an ongoing struggle since 1977 to fully implement the Decree to realize the reforms it promised and remedy the problem it targeted.

CONCLUSION

While the Burgos Consent Decree has led to many reforms in Illinois, it did not prevent the Burgos family from facing the devastating consequences of an inappropriate intervention. A newspaper interview conducted ten years after the Decree reveals the troubling fate of Henry, Olga, and the Burgos family. After returning home at age ten, Henry was unable to adjust: "He never relearned Spanish and began running away from home. At 15, he went to live with black friends, adopting their culture and assuming the last name 'DeBarge,' for the black music family. He has had no contact with his biological family in nearly a year, family members say" (Davidson, 1987, para. 17).

Upon her return home, Olga also experienced great difficulty in adjusting to her biological family. She was removed from her family's home at the age of three and returned at the age of seven. Her parents were concerned by her adjustment difficulties and rebellious behavior. Unsure of what to do, they sent her back to Puerto Rico to live with her grandmother; she later returned to her biological parents at the age of eighteen. In an interview at that time, she indicated, "I feel like I never lived here. My grandmother is going back to Puerto Rico in maybe a week, and I'm scared. I don't talk a lot. I don't know anybody. I don't know if I will stay" (Davidson, 1987, para. 19). Recalling the day her children were removed from their home, Iris Burgos commented through an interpreter, "They did not explain anything; they just gave me papers in English to sign. I felt like I lost my babies and I never got them back" (Davidson, 1987, para. 15).

There is general agreement today among researchers and practitioners that our large public child welfare agencies are in trouble. Faced with more severe cases, fewer resource, and conflicting mandates, they have come under attack from the media, from advocacy groups, and from the social work profession itself (Cohen & Austin, 1994). It is clear that there is a continued need for advocacy and reforms. While the Decree brought great reforms to the Illinois child welfare system, more than three decades later IDCFS continues to struggle with the implementation of the Decree due to a limited number of bilingual social workers and licensed Spanish-speaking foster homes, among other persistent systemic problems.

In analyzing the role of consent decrees such as the Burgos example, Buttrick (1995) discusses how these decrees bring about institutional reform. Increasingly, in the field of public child welfare these decrees have become comprehensive and sometimes intrusive from administrative and executive vantage points. The monitor of the consent decree is an arm of the court and has the authority to demand compliance. Buttrick (1995, p. 80) asks, When is the agency "perfect" enough to be free of such intensive control? Guidelines in this area are few. While consent decrees can bring about needed mandates for change in the social services, we are still left with the dilemma of implementation. That is an entitlement issue often with few resources, and is something for which continued advocacy is needed.

The Burgos and Mendez cases demonstrate on a client level, as well as on a systemwide level, the need for advocacy for institutional reform. As this case illustrates, consent decrees are an additional, albeit limited, tool available to advocates for change to improve and advance the various systems of care that society can offer to vulnerable populations. This case also demonstrates that social service practitioners can play a critical and vital role in advocacy. In this particular case, the decision of two settlement house case workers to advocate on behalf of their clients helped to convey an important message to the Illinois child welfare system: services for Spanish-speaking families are guaranteed by federal law, making language-appropriate services a matter of civil rights, not just cultural competency.

Discussion Questions

1. Identify and discuss the various forms of advocacy that were exercised in the Burgos case.
2. What factors and forces should a social worker consider when determining what form of advocacy they should take on behalf of their clients?
3. What factors and forces made it difficult to implement the Burgos Consent Decree at an administrative level?
4. What are the implications of viewing language-appropriate services as a matter of cultural competency? Of civil rights?

References

Buttrick, S. (1995). Remedy and remorse: Judicial control of social welfare. *Administration in Social Work, 3*, 75–82.

Casillas, O. (2007, May 13). Finding mom: Pulled apart by the state three decades ago, a woman and her foster mother reunite. *Chicago Tribune*. Retrieved from http://articles.chicagotribune.com/2007-05-13/news/0705130002_1_foster-parents-birth

Civil Rights Act. P. L. 88-352, 78 Stat. 241. (1964). Retrieved from Lexis/Nexis Academic database.

Cohen, B., & Austin, M. (1994). Organizational learning and change in a public child welfare agency. *Administration in Social Work, 18*(1), 1–19.

Davidson, J. (1987, June 14). Reunited family still torn apart. *Chicago Tribune*. Retrieved from http://articles.chicagotribune.com/1987-06-14/news/8702130638_1_hispanic-children-family-services-consent-decree

Ezell, M. (1991). Administrators as advocates. *Administration in Social Work, 15*, 1–18.

Hardcastle, D., Wenocur, S., & Powers, P. (1997). *Community practice: Theories and skills for social workers.* New York: Oxford University Press.

Herbert, M., & Mould, J. (1992). The advocacy role in public child welfare. *Child Welfare, 71*(2), 114–130.

Hunter, J. (1979). Advocacy in action for the elderly. *Practice Digest, 1*(4), 15–17.

Illinois Juvenile Court Act of 1987. Retrieved from http://codes.lp.findlaw.com/ilstatutes/705/405

Kaminski, L., & Walmsley. C. (1995). The advocacy brief: A guide for social workers. *The Social Worker, 63*, 53–58.

Kirst-Ashman, K., & Hull, G. (2008). *Understanding generalist practice.* Chicago: Nelson-Hall.

Lehman, J., & Phelps, S. (Eds.). (2005a). Class action. *West's encyclopedia of American law* (2nd ed., Vol. 2, p. 423). Farmington Hills, MI: Gale Cengage.

Lehman, J., & Phelps, S. (Eds.). (2005b). Consent decree. *West's encyclopedia of American law* (2nd ed., Vol. 3, pp. 103–104). Farmington Hills, MI: Gale Cengage.

Lehman, J., & Phelps, S. (Eds.). (2005c). Contempt. *West's encyclopedia of American law* (2nd ed., Vol. 3, p. 154). Farmington Hills, MI: Gale Cengage.

Lehman, J., & Phelps, S. (Eds.). (2005d). Order. *West's encyclopedia of American law* (2nd ed., Vol. 7, p. 322). Farmington Hills, MI: Gale Cengage.

Raider, M. (1982). Protecting the rights of clients: Michigan sets a model for other states. *Social Work, 27*(2), 160–163.

Schneider, R., & Lester, L. (2001). *Social work advocacy: A new framework for action*. Belmont, CA: Brooks/Cole.

Sheafor, B., Horejsi, C., & Horejsi, G. (1994). *Techniques and guidelines for social work practice* (3rd ed.). Boston: Allyn & Bacon.

Suleiman, L. (1998). Burgos Consent Decree summary. Retrieved from http://cssr .berkeley.edu/cwscmsreports/LatinoPracticeAdvisory/IL_Burgos%20Consent%20 Decree%20Summary.pdf

Title VI of the Civil Rights Act. (1964). 42 U.S.C. Sections 2000d–2000d-7, Title 42, The Public Health and Welfare, Subchapter V, Federal Assisted Programs. Retrieved from http://www.justice.gov/crt/about/cor/coord/titlevistat.php

Winter, W. (2008). Interview. In Orland, T. (Producer and Director), *Culturally responsive child welfare practice with Latino children & families: Child welfare staff training video*. Loyola University Chicago Latino Child Professional Training Project. Maria Vidal de Haymes, P.I., U.S. (DHHS CFDA: 93:648, Child Welfare Training Projects).

APPENDIX 6.1. BURGOS TIMELINE

Year	Landmark Events
1975	Burgos vs. IDCFS Class Action Suit is filed.
1977	Burgos Consent Decree is entered by Judge McMillen.
1979	April. Motion for a rule to show cause why state defendants should not be held in contempt of consent decree is filed.
1982	March 3. Stipulation to withdraw the contempt motion wherein IDCFS agrees to take several measures to address Burgos requirements. Includes the following: recruit and obtain additional Spanish-speaking foster parents, annual civil rights compliance, vendors' compliance with the Consent Decree, quarterly statistical information, and semiannual written report to verify compliance actions.
1987	Burgos coordinator position is relocated to the central office, within the office of the coordinator for Hispanic services.
1987–1989	Plaintiffs file several contempt of court motions.
1990	Plaintiffs and IDCFS have the court enter an agreed order appointing a special master to prepare a compliance report.
1991	July 17. Special master issues an extensive report making numerous recommendations, including a permanent court monitor.
1991	Office of Hispanic coordinator is split. Burgos coordinating function is moved to the Office of Litigation Management.
1992	March 16. The first permanent court monitor is appointed.
1994	The first court monitor resigns.
1995	A new court monitor is appointed.
1998	Court monitor prepares compliance report.
1999	Burgos compliance work plan is finalized and entered in the federal court.
2000	Burgos coordinator position is relocated to the clinical division.
2004	Burgos coordinator position is relocated to the Office of Latino Services

7

Social Movements within Organizations

Insurgency at the Shelter

Cheryl A. Hyde

INTRODUCTION

Typically, social movements are viewed as societal level transformations—significant and widespread actions through which collective grievances are recognized and addressed. Social movements such as those enacted by civil rights, feminist, environmental, and labor sympathizers and activists result in profound cultural, political, and social change. Because the reach and repercussions of social movements can be great, it is easy to overlook how organizations can be the target of and location for social movements. Such activity extends beyond acknowledging that organizations are vehicles for collective change primarily because they serve as venues for resource and member development (Hensman, 2003; McCarthy & Zald, 1977; Minkoff & McCarthy, 2005). Rather, as will be illustrated in this chapter's case study, a micro social movement can occur *within* an organization. How such movements develop is particularly important when considering how low-power actors can successfully engage in organizational change.

All organizations have power structures and political processes, and these dynamics serve as the foundation for understanding movements within organizations (Morrill, Zald, & Rao, 2003; Zald & Berger, 1978). In social movements, organizers engage in strategies that shift power to their constituents or members and that alter political processes so that their side obtains needed resources or secures the hoped-for results. A parallel phenomenon occurs when change agents engage in organizational transformation—they alter power structures and political processes so that the desired change occurs (Hargrave & Van De Ven, 2006; Minkoff & McCarthy, 2005; Morrill & Rudes, 2010; Morrill et al., 2003; Scully & Segal, 2002; Zald & Berger, 1978).

Social movements exhibit an array of strategies and tactics in pursuit of change outcomes including sit-ins, marches, picketing, advocacy, educational efforts, legislative lobbying, and consciousness raising. Even with such variation, social movements tend to follow similar developmental cycles: recognizing grievances, framing issues, mobilizing participants, engaging in action, solidifying gains, contending with opposition, and maintaining movement work (Gupta, 2009; Hargrave & Van De Ven, 2006; McAdam, Tarrow, & Tilly, 2001; Snow & Soule, 2010). Organizational change also tends to follow these stages from identifying concerns to gathering support, executing a change plan, and solidifying the transformation (Hyde, 2012).

Finally, because social movements target arenas of power, they also engender resistance and backlash and, in some cases, serve as catalysts for counter movements. So too in organizational transformation efforts, and insights from social movements can be used to understand the causes and consequences of dissidence, resistance, and suppression (McAdam et al., 2001; Phillips, Lawrence, & Hardy, 2000; Zald & Useem, 1987). Organizational change agents can use lessons as to how social movement activists contend with oppositional forces in their own strategic planning.

This case study focuses on the emergence of a micro movement within a human service agency. Specifically, this micro movement takes the form of a bureaucratic insurgency, the goal of which is to "change some aspect of organizational functioning" (Zald & Berger, 1978, p. 837). Zald and Berger further note that an insurgency "resembles a coup in that for much of its duration it may be conspiratorial. It resembles some mass movements in that its goals are limited to change in specific aspects of the organization. . . . [B]ureaucratic insurgency in corporate organizations is an attempt by members to implement goals, programs, or policy choices which have been explicitly denied . . . by the legitimate authority of the focal organization. The activity of the insurgents therefore takes place outside the conventional channels of politics of the organization" (1978, p. 838).

This approach to organizational change focuses on activism that begins on the inside and then becomes external to the organization or the organization's location of authority in order to challenge aspects of the status quo (Hargrave & Van De Ven, 2006; Scully & Segal, 2002). Indeed, external support is crucial to its success. Intraorganizational change agents typically hold dual or split allegiances—to the organization, and to a change ideology or vision—that can result in organizational conflict as well as personal dissonance (Courpasson, Dany, & Clegg, 2012; Gutierrez, Howard-Grenville, & Scully, 2010; Kretschmer, 2009; Morrill & Rudes, 2010).

Outcomes of insurgencies depend not only on the strategic capabilities of the activists, but also on the responses of organizational elites who are the targets of the movement. Outcomes range from failure because of suppression by elites, continuance of activism via external means but no recognition by organizational elites, partial recognition by elites such that some of the movement's goals are adopted and an activist enclave remains to promote other objectives, or complete incorporation because of full adoption of movement demands by organizational elites (Morrill et al., 2003; Zald & Berger, 1978). For this type of movement to experience success, the organizers need to operate without garnering the attention of elites for as long as possible. This is especially true for the intraorganizational change agents who are low-power actors, since they are particularly vulnerable to actions by organizational elites if their activities are deemed to be threatening (Courpasson et al., 2012; Kretschmer, 2009).

THE CASE

Background

This case focuses on a critical juncture in the development of a domestic violence organization. It is told from the perspective of Emily, a newly minted MSW with a concentration in community organizing. The setting is "Sanctuary House," an organization that primarily provides shelter and support services for women leaving domestic violence situations. Founded in the early 1980s by a group of women, many of whom were veterans of the radical feminist movement of the prior decade and some of whom were themselves survivors of sexual violence, Sanctuary House had as its mission, "To work with, and on behalf of, women as they rebuild their lives free from domestic violence and to dismantle the causes of domestic violence through advocacy, education and action." Its early years reflected a woman-centered and empowerment approach to eliminating violence, and the organization was viewed as a vital part of the community's activist, progressive network.

As is often the case with agencies born of social movements, Sanctuary House gradually lost its activist edge. This loss was primarily a result of the need to secure adequate funding, which in effect prioritized services over political activities. While the mission remained unchanged, the staff and programs increasingly reflected professional approaches to addressing the problem of domestic violence. Women seeking assistance were referred to as clients, and were expected to participate in various therapeutic and self-help programs such as substance abuse counseling sessions. These developments in Sanctuary House mirrored an overall trend in the movement to end violence against women (Lehrner & Allen, 2009; Macy, Giattina, Parish, & Crosby, 2010; Maier, 2011).

Sanctuary House grew in size and scope, mostly due to the addition of services. The organization became more bureaucratic in structure (depicted in figure 7.1). New service staff were hired primarily for their

FIGURE 7.1. Organizational Chart for Sanctuary House

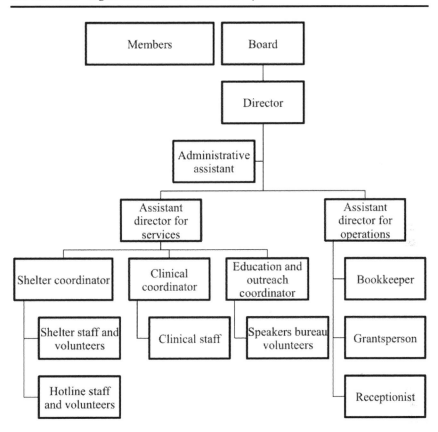

counseling skills and professional training, rather than for their knowledge of or experience with violence against women. Resources were directed to a new shelter facility and to administrative positions that supported financial operations, and decreasingly to legislative advocacy. Education programs focused on how to avoid violence, but not on its underlying societal causes. The organization's community networks tended toward criminal justice and mental health institutions, and away from activist, specifically feminist, groups. In short, the organization that Emily joined resembled a traditional client service agency that happened to work with victims of domestic violence rather than a feminist organization that sought to end violence against women by empowering survivors and addressing the root causes of violence.

Emily had been looking forward to working at Sanctuary House for quite some time and recently had been hired as the organization's education and outreach coordinator (a new position funded by a special foundation grant). She believed that this job would allow her to make good on her commitment to women's empowerment and provide opportunities to use her social work macro skills. After three months in the position, however, Emily questioned whether she had made the right decision in accepting the job.

Initially, Emily thought that her discomfort with the organization was a matter of unrealistic expectations on her part. Two encounters, however, began to challenge this perspective. First, during a social event she shared with friends some of her frustrations. Other women, who had long-term ties to the area's women's movement, overheard these conversations and joined in with some history as well as their own disappointments with how Sanctuary House had developed. Specifically, these women felt that the organization's director and board had cut ties with the feminist movement in order to pursue more financial security. The problem, they suggested, was that Sanctuary House had sacrificed its political identity and credibility, and that this was a concern to feminists throughout the area. Second, Emily began to make connections with some of the veteran staff members still working at the organization. They too reminisced about the virtually abandoned empowerment model and, more specifically, the lack of survivors on staff who could serve as role models for women seeking assistance. These women also pointed to the current director and board as the primary instigators of a service model that placed financial security over political mission. Through these conversations, Emily began to understand that there were pockets of support both inside and outside the organization for the original vision and approaches.

While Emily continued to dialogue with these allies, she also attended her first board of directors meeting and personally observed what she had been told. Board members demonstrated scant interest in mission or vision; indeed, most had little knowledge of the challenges with which domestic violence survivors contended. Much of the meeting focused on fiscal reporting and planning, on evaluating current clinical services, and on bolstering ties with law enforcement. For example, in the interest of financial efficiency several board members thought that services should be denied to women who returned repeatedly to their abusers. They were unmoved by the well-founded assertion that women typically make several failed attempts before effectively breaking away from abuse, and that support at each step was critical to building momentum. While Emily understood that the fiscal concerns needed to be addressed, she was stunned at the disregard for the very issues that the organization was supposed to be about.

Emily knew that in any nonprofit organization the board of directors should represent the voice of the community. Emily and her allies believed that the Sanctuary House board was missing the vital voices of the feminist movement in general, and survivors of partner violence in particular. Furthermore, these women reasoned that a shift in the board's membership, and consequently perspective, would help reset the priorities of the organization. The question became, "How can we bring about this change?"

The Change Effort

Timing is often critical in any change effort. In this case, elections for the board were scheduled for the annual membership meeting in six weeks, with fifteen of the twenty-one positions open. The board's nominating committee already had readied a slate of candidates that included many incumbents; the five new nominees were from human services, law enforcement, and a local business. In past years, the nominating committee's slate ran unopposed. Thus, the membership meeting, which usually was sparsely attended, was mostly an exercise in providing a final stamp of approval. The organization's by-laws, however, had a provision that any member (an individual, other than staff, who provided voluntary or financial support) could be nominated from the floor at the meeting. Emily saw this provision as an avenue for changing the makeup of the board.

Emily convened a meeting with individuals who supported more-explicit attention to feminist values and practices. While most of these women were outside the organization, a select few were disgruntled Sanctuary House staff, mostly veteran workers in the shelter. Through a series of meetings over a two-week period, the group decided that targeting the open board seats and nominating individuals who were more in line with an activist ideology might result in a redirection of the organization. They realized that in order to be successful they would not only need to find willing candidates for the board, but also would need enough supportive members to attend the membership meeting to nominate and vote for them.

With little time (four weeks), and with this organizing needing to be done during nonwork hours, Emily became concerned that it was all simply too much to do. After sharing her worries during an organizing meeting, Beth (a seasoned activist) suggested that the group construct a force field analysis in order to determine whether their goal was feasible, and then prioritize exactly what had to happen and when (see figure 7.2).

The explicit change goal was to "assemble a board of directors that is sympathetic to and willing to promote feminist and empowerment values and actions throughout the organization by nominating and voting for supportive members." Note that the force field analysis weighs more heavily to the restraining forces. In particular, key leaders in the form of the board president, most board members, and the director were likely to oppose the change effort. Usually, leadership needs to endorse organizational change for it to have a chance for success. The insurgency model, however, is designed to circumvent oppositional leadership as the mobilization activities occur outside of the organization. Thus, the strength of outside networks is greatly enhanced as a driving force for change.

FIGURE 7.2. Force Field Analysis for Sanctuary House Change Plan

---

Change Goal:

To assemble a board of directors that is sympathetic to and willing to promote feminist and empowerment values and actions throughout the organization by nominating and voting for supportive members

---

Critical Actors:

Members who could nominate and vote for new board members

Facilitating Actors:

1. Emily

2. Beth

Potential Allies:

1. Some current organizational members

2. Some community folks who could become members

3. Some sympathetic staff

4. Some survivors of violence

5. Feminist organizations in the community

Driving Forces for Change:	*Restraining Forces for Change:*
1. Commitment of the organizing group	1. Short time frame
2. Historical roots of the organization, including its mission statement	2. Opposition from board president and most current board members
3. By-law provision to nominate board members at the membership meeting	3. Opposition from Sanctuary House director
4. Experience of some organizing group members with recruitment and mobilization	4. Finding a sufficient number of sympathetic individuals willing to run for the board
5. Access to networks of feminist activists and sympathizers	5. Recent history that contributed to the inertia or disengagement of current members and that could be difficult to overcome
	6. Job risk for Emily and other staff involved in the change effort
	7. Relative newness of Emily

The force field exercise revealed that tapping into the various networks of the group's members was going to be essential. If they could get sympathetic individuals interested in being active members and in serving on the board of directors, then there was a good chance they could win enough seats to redirect the focus and practices of Sanctuary House. After considerable discussion, the group agreed to the following strategy:

1. Get a list of current members and try to identify those who are sympathetic with the campaign (as it was now being called).
2. Contact those members, explain the campaign, and get them to commit to attending the board meeting.
3. Using the group's political and social networks, recruit new members who would also attend the membership meeting.
4. Identify individuals either from the sympathetic member list or political networks who might be board candidates.
5. Contact possible candidates and discuss their interest in running for the board.
6. Assign a member to nominate and present the "credentials" of each candidate at the membership meeting.

At the conclusion of this long but productive meeting, group members had a clear sense of what needed to be done and who was going to do it. They divided into two teams—one to recruit new members from various networks (headed by Beth) and the other to contact the current members seen as sympathetic to get them engaged and if possible encourage them to run for the board. The explicit change goal of this effort (mentioned above) would inform the broader transformation goal: "Take Sanctuary House back to its empowerment and feminist roots so that those values fully informed the practices and procedures of the organization."

Over the next two and a half weeks, the two teams engaged in intensive outreach to their targeted groups. With just a week to go before the membership meeting, they had signed up seventy-five new members, twelve individuals (including three who identified themselves as survivors of domestic violence) had agreed to be nominated for the board, and a sizeable number of current members had agreed to attend the meeting. Perhaps more important, organizing members reported considerable interest and enthusiasm in their conversations. One theme that emerged was that community people, who were sympathetic to Sanctuary House but had felt marginalized by its apparent focus, were excited to be reengaged. This activation of latent community support would be necessary if the organizing group won the board elections.

The organization's fundraiser noted this spike in membership, though she attributed it to Emily's expansion of community-based educational programs. Otherwise, the activities of the teams went unnoticed by the organization's elites. All organizing meetings occurred during nonwork hours, and Emily was careful to not discuss these activities with even supportive coworkers while on the job. She did, however, use her community programs to promote membership in Sanctuary House.

This lack of awareness by organizational elites came to an abrupt end as the sign-in immediately prior to the annual membership meeting began. As the large meeting room of the Unitarian Church began to fill, the board president, several board members, and the director began to wonder what was going on. There were mostly new faces, and a lot of them. There was also a palpable energy in the room that had not been present at other meetings. The board president called the meeting to order as close to the designated start time as she possibly could. Beth (the spokesperson for the change group) challenged this, noting that there were many members who had arrived on time but who were still waiting to register. After a fifteen-minute delay, and in front of a packed room, the board president again called the meeting to order, and gave a brief (and, some observed, nervous) welcome. She then asked that the nominating committee chair provide a report and offer the slate for board member elections.

The nominating committee chair presented the slate and then asked for a motion that these individuals, as a group, be approved for three-year board terms. Before that could happen, however, Beth called for a point of order. She stated that, according to the by-laws, there needed to be the opportunity for members to nominate board candidates from the floor. Almost as one, the nominating committee chair and the board president realized what had happened. At first, they claimed that any new nominees should have been cleared by the board's committee, but reluctantly they conceded that Beth was correct and opened the floor for nominations. One by one, twelve members stood up, and each nominated an individual for an open board position. In turn, those twelve nominees briefly shared their qualifications, including their desire to use empowerment and feminist values, for the board.

The meeting was now at a crossroads. There was the slate of fifteen individuals put forth by the nominating committee that represented the status quo and a set of twelve individuals essentially running against that status quo but not as a slate. The by-laws did not address this situation, and no one at the meeting could remember a contested board election. After much discussion during which several incumbent board members accused Beth of using "ambush tactics" and orchestrating a "hostile takeover," a decision was reached to have the twenty-seven nominees run as individuals. The top fifteen vote getters would join the board. Each member wrote on a piece of paper his or her fifteen choices. Ballots were collected and then the wait began. There was an awkward, strained silence in the room.

After thirty minutes, the nominating committee chair posted the results. All twelve individuals nominated through the efforts of the change group had been elected, with the other three slots going to two incumbents and one newcomer. Members burst into enthusiastic applause. Chastened, the nominating committee chair and board president congratulated the winners. Because the meeting had gone on for such a long time, the president then called for a motion to end the meeting, which was rapidly given and seconded.

Emily could not fully comprehend what had happened. She had done so much networking behind the scenes to make this moment possible, but was hesitant to celebrate too visibly since she did not want to jeopardize her job. Nonetheless, she joined Beth in thanking those members who had supported their vision and congratulated the newly elected board members, including those who were part of the board slate. She also knew that now the difficult work of transforming the board, and hopefully the organization, had begun.

CONCLUSION

This insurgency achieved its initial goal of getting change supporters and allies elected to most of the open board positions. The micro movement also recruited a number of new, sympathetic members and reengaged some of the existing membership. In this sense, the insurgency was successful and this success stemmed primarily from the use of existing external networks to garner the necessary support and commitments. A second critical factor was that the organizational elites did not understand what was occurring and thus could not suppress the insurgency. This is probably an indication of just how disconnected the elites were from community-based political or activist networks. The tight timeline of the insurgency also facilitated the "under-the-radar" work of the change agents.

But as with many organizational insurgencies, this change effort had a narrow scope. As Emily realized, the more difficult work of transforming the board so that it actively embraced and promoted the original feminist values would take much more time. The board was now split, with just a slight majority favoring the feminist and empowerment ideals of the change agents. Thus, this insurgency signifies incremental change in the organization (Gupta, 2009). For the insurgency to have a lasting impact, the organizing that occurred prior to the membership meeting now needed to serve as a foundation for continued change.

In this way, one type of micro movement becomes the springboard for the next. This parallels cycles in large-scale social movements, in which either one strategic phase is the groundwork for the next, or a movement facilitates the emergence of a related collective action (Gupta, 2009; McAdam et al., 2001). Other examples of social movements in organizations include the coup d'état, in which a change in executive leadership is the goal, and the mass movement, in which the aim is the expression of collective grievances by line staff with the hope of redress (Zald & Berger, 1978). Of course, subsequent organizational change need not follow a specific type of movement, but rather could initiate another cycle of identifying and framing the issue(s), mobilizing for action, responding to opposition, and stabilizing the change effort (Hyde, 2012).

The purpose of this chapter was to suggest how insights from the social movement literature can inform our understanding of organizational change from below. While the organizational change described here was relatively modest, it nonetheless served as an important first step in a longer-term transformation process. In addition to the actual change, this case also suggests how the vision, analysis, and skills of a young social worker can serve to reenergize an organization.

DISCUSSION QUESTIONS

1. This change effort follows the movement model of an insurgency, but Emily was not wedded to a particular strategy or set of tactics. What mix of strategies and tactics were evident in this change process? (See chapters 3 and 4 for ideas.)
2. Emily was careful to engage in the organizing effort during nonwork hours. Why might she have felt the need to do so? If she had decided to do some of this organizing on the job, what factors should she have taken into account?
3. This case is an example of using existing organizational components as leverage for change. What are these components? In human service organizations, what characteristics could serve as springboards for change?
4. The change in the board of directors signified a first step toward achieving the broader goal of returning Sanctuary House to its activist roots. What might the next steps be in this process? Given those steps, what would a force field analysis for this next phase look like?
5. Sanctuary House reflected a common trend in service organizations with a social movement foundation—increased focus on client-oriented programs in order to secure funding. If the change plan at Sanctuary House continues, how can this funding issue be addressed? Would returning to its activist roots threaten the acquisition of resources?

REFERENCES

Courpasson, D., Dany, F., & Clegg, S. (2012). Resisters at work: Generating productive resistance in the workplace. *Organization Science, 23*(3), 801–819.

Gupta, D. (2009). The power of incremental outcomes. *Mobilization, 14*(4), 417–432.

Gutierrez, B., Howard-Grenville, J., & Scully, M. (2010). The faithful rise up: Split identification and an unlikely change effort. *Academy of Management Journal, 53*(4), 673–699.

Hargrave, T., & Van De Ven, M. (2006). A collective action model of institutional innovation. *Academy of Management Review, 31*(4), 864–888.

Hensman, M. (2003). Movement organizations: A metaphor for strategic actors in institutional fields. *Organization Studies, 24*, 355–380.

Hyde, C. (2012). Organizational change rationales: Exploring reasons for multicultural development in human service agencies. *Administration in Social Work, 36*(5), 436–456.

Kretschmer, K. (2009). Contested loyalties: Dissident identity organizations, institutions, and social movements. *Sociological Perspectives, 52*(4), 433–454.

Lehrner, A., & Allen, N. (2009). Still a movement after all these years? Current tensions in the domestic violence movement. *Violence Against Women, 15,* 656–677.

Macy, R. J., Giattina, M., Parish, S., & Crosby, C. (2010). Domestic violence and sexual assault services: Historical concerns and contemporary challenges. *Journal of Interpersonal Violence, 25*(1), 3–32.

Maier, S. (2011). "We belong to them": The costs of funding for rape crisis centers. *Violence Against Women, 17*(11), 1383–1408.

McAdam, D., Tarrow, S., & Tilly, C. (2001). *Dynamics of contention.* New York: Cambridge University Press.

McCarthy, J., & Zald, M. (1977). Resource and social movements: A partial theory. *American Journal of Sociology, 82,* 1212–1241.

Minkoff, D., & McCarthy, J. (2005). Reinvigorating the study of organizational processes in social movements. *Mobilization, 10*(2), 289–308.

Morrill, C., & Rudes, D. (2010). Conflict resolution in organizations. *Annual Review of Law and the Social Sciences, 6,* 627–651.

Morrill, C., Zald, M., & Rao, H. (2003). Covert political conflict in organizations: Challenges from below. *Annual Review of Sociology, 29,* 391–415.

Phillips, N., Lawrence, T., & Hardy, C. (2000). Inter-organizational collaboration and the dynamics of institutional fields. *Journal of Management Studies, 37,* 23–43.

Scully, M., & Segal, A. (2002). Passion with an umbrella: Grassroots activists in the workplace. *Social Structure and Organizations Revisited, 19,* 125–168.

Snow, D., & Soule, S. (2010). *A primer on social movements.* New York: W. W. Norton & Company.

Zald, M., & Berger, M. (1978). Social movements in organizations: Coup d'état, insurgency, and mass movements. *The American Journal of Sociology, 83*(4), 823–861.

Zald, M., & Useem, B. (1987). Movement and countermovement interaction: Mobilization, tactics, and state involvement. In M. Zald & J. McCarthy (Eds.), *Social movements in an organizational society* (pp. 247–272). New Brunswick, NJ: Transaction Books.

8

Rebecca's Place

Women Experiencing Homelessness Changing Organizational Structure and Attitudes about Them

Helen P. Hartnett

INTRODUCTION

Shelter is an important temporary resource for people who experience homelessness. Unfortunately, it has become one of the predominant responses and often the only available service in many communities. Little has been published about the role of shelter as a solution to homelessness; more has been published that questions it as an effective response to this social problem (Burt, 2001; Hartnett & Harding, 2005; Hopper, 1990).

Those who critically evaluate shelter have demonstrated that it may inhibit people's ability to secure income, housing, and social supports (Burt, 2001; de Costa Nunez, 1994; Hartnett & Harding, 2005; Hopper, 1990; Veness, 1994). For women, the reality of shelter may exacerbate a power-poor position and reduce a sense of personal power. Literature related to women who experience homelessness is most often tied to differing perspectives on social problems, whether they are framed as residual (individual) or institutional (societal) conditions (Gorman, 2010). Therefore, scholars have documented personal or individual reasons that women seek shelter including domestic violence, failed relationships, substance use, and mental illness (Barge & Norr, 1991; McChesney, 1995). In contrast, others state structural reasons including poverty, unemployment, housing costs, and women's position in society as contributing factors (Burt, 2001; Veness, 1994). Additionally, the individual reasons for seeking shelter represent power-poor positions of women, particularly the lack of resources to leave violent relationships or maintain mental or physical health. Regardless of one's perspective (residual or institutional), all of these factors are most closely tied to poverty or lack of sufficient income. This chapter describes an example of service provision that attempted to minimize an individual perspective, and instead maximize the power of women to challenge the structures that strip power from them, whether intentionally or unintentionally.

Thus, this chapter focuses on addressing poverty and access to income as an integral component of the provision of shelter to women as a response to the social problem of homelessness. Examining the organizational structure and culture of shelter reveals that women who experience homelessness often are stripped of personal power, being told when to wake, when to sleep, bathe, and so forth (Hartnett & Postmus, 2010). This results in staff as guards and the women in shelter as the guarded. This relationship contributes to a dance of power within the facility and can result in negative outcomes not only for the people served, but also for social service staff whose role becomes that of watcher rather than helper. The case described below emphasizes a developmental approach to solving social problems, including people most affected in the process through empowerment and advocacy (Gorman, 2010).

Force field analysis provides an avenue to examine how power is distributed in any attempt of organizational change. Force field analysis allows the social worker to develop a strategy to shift the balance of power (Brager & Holloway, 1993). By examining where power lies and what forces promote or impede change social workers can create a path to change. Ultimately, it is the responsibility of the social work profession to honor and value the worth of every human and to respect self-determination (National Association of Social Workers [NASW], 1999).

The case presented here is an example of women taking charge of shelter services. It uses force field analysis to examine potential shifts in power and demonstrates how women who experienced homelessness and women staff members were able to determine the organizational structure, policies, and climate of a new shelter. It speaks to how social work organizations can be influenced from the bottom up and the ultimate outcomes for all involved. It also attempts to consider how social service organizations contribute to participant responses. Unlike a trickle-down democratic process, these organizations attempted to trickle up and through (Crook, 2002).

THE CASE

Background

I was an MSW student at a Midwest university. I pleaded with my field advisor to have a field placement at a local shelter serving people who experienced homelessness. Although my advisor met my request with trepidation, the graduate social work program agreed. The program's reservations consisted of concerns about the chaos in the environment, my safety, and my ability to learn with this population. I completed the foundation year placement during one summer working thirty-two hours a week. I remained in that setting for my advanced year placement as an administrative student. I met amazing people and was drawn to those who struggle to find housing and employment while living in less-than-desirable conditions. I learned the concept of resilience by watching it every day.

I focused my master's thesis on the experiences of women in a shelter that served 125 men and 35 women. My thesis revealed what the literature had demonstrated: women were stripped of power within the facility. Also, the women did not self-identify as "homeless" but rather believed that they were making important choices to leave violent relationships, get off the streets, get into recovery, and find employment and housing. Conversely, the female staff described the women as "homeless" and spoke of how the women were irresponsible and needed to "fix themselves." This was in direct contrast to the women's perspectives. They wanted opportunities and discussed long histories of power-poor positions. In addition, the shelter environment often recreated these positions; the women spoke of their experiences of sexual violence and intimidation in the shelter (Hartnett, 1992).

I decided that something needed to change for these women, and developed a strategy to attempt to create a new facility and move the women. Hence, the shelter became the target of change. The initial goal was to remove the women from the shelter that also housed men. The focus was to change the location of shelter for single women. An initial secondary goal was to help the women gain a sense of power and control over their lives. This secondary goal became primary as the change process proceeded.

In order to accomplish the change of organizational location and policies, I considered all of the powerful and important people who would be part of the process. Using a force field analysis (figure 8.1) allowed me to consider both driving and restraining forces and also identified the actors in the process. I will discuss each group within the context of the case. As will become clear, some of the actors' roles changed often based on actions they took and their participation in the process.

Process of Putting the Pieces Together

I first shared the results of my research with the executive director to assess her reaction and determine her level of support for change. The executive director (a critical actor) was concerned about how women were treated and agreed that something needed to change. Hence, I became a facilitating actor who would help drive the process of change. I then approached the women in the shelter and spoke about the results of my research in order to gauge their impressions. Although somewhat apprehensive, they supported a client-centered change in organizational structure and process. At this point, it was clear that support from the ground up was in place, which motivated me to strategize with the executive director and the women about a possible course of action.

FIGURE 8.1. Force Field Analysis for the Women's Housing Program

Change Goal:

To create a housing program that values the contributions of women experiencing homelessness in its design, maintenance, and management

Critical Actors:

1. Director of the Community Shelter Board

2. Executive director of the shelter

3. Executive director of the Housing Corporation

4. State funders

Facilitating Actors:

1. Nonprofit Housing Corporation Director

2. Student intern

Potential Allies:

1. Other service providers

2. Women experiencing homelessness

3. Community members

Driving Forces for Change:	*Restraining Forces for Change:*
1. The shelter director supports creating a new and separate facility. (Amenable, Potent, Consistent, A Working Force)	1. Creating a new program would be costly. (Potent and Consistent, A Framing Force)
2. The intern and social worker support this goal and have credibility within the shelter and with funders. (Amenable, Potent, Consistent, A Working Force)	2. The community has little desire for new neighborhood programs. (Consistent, A Framing Force)
3. A new program can improve women's success in finding housing, thus it would be more effective and a better use of public dollars. (Potent and Consistent, A Framing Force)	3. Other service providers feel threatened. (Amenable but not Consistent, An Unpredictable Force)
4. Women who experience homelessness desire to have a different environment and be successful. (Amenable, but not Consistent, An Unpredictable Force)	

The initial plan was to develop an executive summary and press release to begin to influence the critical actors who might seek to maintain the status quo. These included state funders and the director of the community shelter board, a communitywide funding agency. Potential allies, who also needed to be influenced, included service providers and community members. We created and distributed the executive summary using local media and state venues. People took notice. Private high-status donors who supported local shelters were appalled by what they understood the women were experiencing. Their pleas inspired the local director of the community shelter board, and a meeting was scheduled.

The community shelter board director was somewhat skeptical about the proposed change, knowing that this would mean the creation of a new shelter that would translate into more expenditures. I believed that if the director gave some monetary support state funds might become available, thus making it possible to secure other sources of money through status as a community housing development organization (CHDO). Hence, the author and the women in the shelter decided to create a new organization (a CHDO) that would qualify for housing trust funds from the state. As one compromise, the executive director provided one year of salary support to plan the effort. The other compromise was reducing the number of beds at the current shelter, reducing the need for monetary support. The executive director agreed to that reduction. A CHDO was formed with a group of women as the board of directors. A woman experiencing homelessness chose the name—Together Home—and we incorporated the CHDO. The board of directors consisted of service providers of housing programs for women, and women who were either currently or previously experiencing homelessness. Thus, ultimate decision making was in the hands of a variety of women, elevating them to high power status.

A meeting was scheduled with state funders and the women in the shelter were able to provide direct testimony to the need for such a program. With other money on the table, the state knew that there was support. Still, the location and the actual budget had not been determined. We contacted a local realtor who gave leads to available property and enlisted the women in the shelter to visit many potential places. The first was a former nunnery, with twelve rooms, that the women thought was too small. Several other locations would require too much renovation. One possibility was a small apartment complex, two buildings, named Sunnybrook Farms. This would have been a perfect place, but it was far from public transportation and the price of acquisition was high. Although we rejected this option, the name Sunnybrook Farm became the inspiration for the name for the new program, Rebecca's Place, after the book *Rebecca of Sunnybrook Farm* (Wiggin, 1903). Having a name allowed us to gather more support from the community. We developed additional promotional material outlining the rationale for the program and the needs of a new facility.

What the others and I found interesting was that some of the attitudes and actions of other service providers were the most powerful restraining forces working against this change effort. For example, when we announced the plan at a community meeting with providers, many asked, "Are you going to let the women run the place?" They did not believe in a participant-directed approach and wanted to maintain the status quo of professional administration. I attributed this to both ideological differences and concern for funding control. After all, a new program reduced money available to others. However, the board of directors comprising service providers and women using services stood strong and used their drive and voice to successfully outweigh the power of the others.

We began to consider the challenge of finding a location that was affordable and that we could manage. After all, we were service providers, not housing managers. The executive director suggested that we contact the local nonprofit housing provider to see if there might be a small complex available. This suggested a perfect solution, to have a housing agency provide maintenance, which they do well, while we provide service, which we do well. We located a complex that was 60 percent vacant and were able to sublease three buildings of our own. The women who might stay there were thrilled with the location and thought it would work, with them sharing apartments rather than sleeping in dorms. The executive director helped me contact the executive director of the CHDO and the author and the executive director of the CHDO met to discuss the possibilities. Again, another critical actor was convinced to support the change effort. The CHDO was also willing to make adjustments to the space to create a large common area. We drew up a budget, which allowed us to return to the state to secure the necessary support to move forward.

Prior to opening, we needed to meet with local community and law enforcement personnel who might be potential allies. After learning about the program, most were supportive because the apartments would be staffed 24/7, potentially providing greater safety for the community and the residents of the other buildings. After gaining support, my first task was to hire staff. The author hired Beth as the assistant director. The author and the assistant director hired support staff in a cooperative effort. Importantly, all staff hired visited the shelter where women were housed prior to moving for the author and the assistant director to judge the staff's reactions. Another component of the process was asking the question to all that we interviewed: Why do women experience homelessness? If the answer demonstrated an individual or residual view of homelessness, we did not consider those individuals for employment. This was an additional attempt to create a new organizational structure that would maximize the structural view of homelessness and hopefully give power back to women experiencing homelessness.

The next task was to acquire furniture and the necessary supplies to operate a residential facility. The community was very supportive with donations. As a team building exercise, all staff hired went to retrieve furniture in a rented U-Haul. Once all necessary supplies and equipment had been acquired, all of the women together decided where furniture would be placed. Additionally, the group made all decisions with regard to any artwork or decorations. This is consistent with the Hull House philosophy that people should have control over their environment and that there should be aesthetics in living (Breiland, 1990). This process increased the sense of power and ownership of all staff and residents in the creation of Rebecca's Place. Hence, staff became high-power actors in the process.

Structure and Rules

In order not to replicate the top-down structure of other programs, the women who would stay in the program determined policies and practices. The women decided that we would not have regulations about when to go to bed or wake up, and that women would be allowed to have "nights out." This was particularly important so women could visit family, friends, or significant others for a night out without fear of losing their space. This enabled the women to maintain social support networks. Curfew was set at midnight for safety, but it was flexible, allowing women to work different shifts and thus to maintain employment. As the goal was to help the women find personal power, they were also involved in all administrative aspects of the program. Women signed up for chores, grocery shopping trips, and cooking while also assuming high-power positions of decision making and responsibility.

Other organizational aspects contributed to the culture and climate of Rebecca's Place, including the women's free access to supplies and food. When supplies ran out for the month, they were gone and the women knew this. All women were given two laundry tokens and two bus passes per week, regardless of need. Also, weekly housing meetings were held to discuss process, issues, and changes that might need to occur. These meetings often resulted in changes to policy and practice, but these were determined by the women who called Rebecca's Place home, albeit temporarily. For example, at one meeting the women discussed an issue concerning time spent on the phones (two pay phones had been installed inside). They decided as a group that fifteen minutes was an appropriate time limit for a call. They also devised a system for taking messages and we purchased a message board. Another component of these meetings was the elections of representatives of the program participants to attend staff and board meetings.

Staff struggled for language to use for the women staying at Rebecca's Place. Many had been referred to as clients, consumers, and customers. When the issue was raised at a staff meeting, the representatives stated that they preferred the term "program participants." The women believed that the word "consumer" meant all they did was take and not give back. They wanted a word that implied an active role in the program. From this time on, women were referred to as participants. This is another example of how participants became actors in the organization change process and how their desire to be heard became a driving force.

We All Struggled with a Power Shift

Although the concepts of empowerment and self-determination are part of an important ideology that many of us learn in our social work programs, practicing them was not always easy. We all struggled in varying ways to allow our own power to manifest itself, to share power, and to allow others to lead. The women experiencing homelessness struggled with exercising power and the responsibility of doing so. One example of that struggle occurred when the open house was planned, a big and important community event.

Women staying at Rebecca's Place elected a planning committee and reported to staff what they needed, and who they would like to attend. They asked us to invite several local politicians, many service providers, the police, and members of the local community. They asked for food and a microphone and a stand from which to sing and deliver testimonies. This was their debut and their open house. Staff was to arrive on time and allow the women to guide the process. Staff helped clean and organize the residence. At 4:00 p.m., with the event beginning at 5:30 p.m., no food had been prepared and some of the women who were responsible were not on site. I became anxious and wanted to jump in and do the work. We knew the importance of such events for community and political support, and that they eventually translate into financial support. Also, as a new approach or experiment it was important to put our best foot forward. Beth told me to relax and go to her office and not worry. She stated, "It will be what it will be, but it is theirs." Ultimately, as Beth predicted, the women came through and the community was very impressed. The women took the stage and introduced speakers and guests, and the staff helped. This was a great lesson for all of us. The women learned what they could accomplish and that they were bright and resourceful, and the staff, community, and funders witnessed this accomplishment firsthand. The staff also learned that it is not necessary to control the participants in order for them to thrive.

Another lesson for the women who stayed in Rebecca's Place were the expectations living there placed on them. Many women were not accustomed to having both rights and responsibilities. For some, this was too much and they chose to leave and return to other programs. For others, it took several days and sometimes weeks to understand that they were trusted and responsible for all of our success. Often the lesson came from other women. For example, we did not lock up food and had snacks and supplies available at all times. In the beginning, many women would take a lot, thinking that it might be gone, not realizing that it would be there and that we were all in this together. Often, women would tell newcomers to remember that we all had to make this work and it was not just about them. Hence, women learned that having power was also about sharing it with others, and not just keeping it for themselves.

Outcomes

We all experienced a variety of amazing outcomes from participating in the creation and operation of Rebecca's Place. For the women experiencing homelessness, employment and housing outcomes exceeded other sheltering programs by more than 40 percent, measured by the women obtaining a permanent residence. Sharing apartment spaces allowed women to see that they could rent together, and many moved out together to offset the high costs of rental housing. Additionally, providing participants with laundry tokens and bus passes allowed them to seek employment and receive the services needed independently, helping to build confidence in living alone. Unintentionally, these items also created a barter system within Rebecca's Place. Women traded bus passes for haircuts or extra laundry tokens. Others did laundry together to save on tokens.

We believed that the change in power also translated into ownership of Rebecca's Place and a commitment to the program. One example of an organizational outcome was when the toilet paper ran out for the month. The women knew the budget and also how much was purchased each month. One month we ran out one week early. This was announced at a house meeting, and before we knew it, participants returned their excess toilet paper or purchased it and placed it in the cabinet. We knew then that all of us were invested in the success of the facility and that women were not only using their power, but also understanding the responsibility of it.

On another occasion I was on call for the 12:00–8:00 a.m. shift on Christmas night. I had received a video for Christmas and took it with me along with snacks and soda. Much to my surprise, I was met at the door by five women who had waited to stay up with me and enjoy some movie time. I put in the movie, *Coal Miner's Daughter*, which chronicles the life of country singer Loretta Lynn. The film portrays poverty in Appalachia and the eventual success of the singer. The women were stunned that white people lived in such conditions. Many had not been aware of the coal mining industry or of "holler living." Through the film, we gained awareness of the variety of lives people face and the ways in which people overcome the barriers placed in front of them. This led to a powerful discussion about how society shapes our experiences and the institutional perspective on poverty.

A potent example of commitment was when one of the women relapsed from her crack cocaine addiction. Several women came to get Beth to tell her the woman had relapsed. Beth talked to her, as one of the policies was that program participants needed to be free of substance to help support those who were struggling. The woman became very violent and Beth asked her to leave the building, then called the police. The woman would not leave, and the women staying at Rebecca's Place surrounded Beth to protect her and were able to get the woman to leave. They stated, "You are going to ruin this for all of us." This sentiment was commonly aired and became a driving force for women using their high-power status to look out for each other and Rebecca's Place, keeping each other in check. Thus, staff were able to help rather than to enforce rules.

Importantly, the women of Rebecca's Place changed community and service providers' perceptions of the power of women and organizational change. Many were surprised and delighted by the success of a different approach to change, from the bottom up rather than top down, and some providers began to reconsider their own organizational practices.

Not all outcomes were positive for all of the women participating in the maintenance of Rebecca's Place. For some women, the expectations were too high, and they left. Others could not handle sleeping in apartment rooms rather than in a dormitory. Some commented that not having staff watching them made them feel unsafe. Perhaps this was an outcome of shelter environments they had experienced, which were often characterized by stealing and violence. Whether negative or positive, all are powerful examples of how the organization may influence participant behavior (Crook, 2002).

Some of the staff were also unable to handle an environment that did not give them ultimate power over participants. They struggled with allowing women to choose their paths without constant intervention. Several social work interns had similar responses and were asked to leave.

CONCLUSION

Using the force field analysis proved to be an important tool in creating organizational change. Interestingly, this case demonstrates how sometimes the powerful actors are not those that might be anticipated. It was more difficult to convince staff and other service providers of this approach. Although not all of them were initially supportive of the change efforts (indeed, their sentiments were restraining forces), they ultimately became important participants in facilitating the maintenance of the change. Additionally, some of the women who called Rebecca's Place home, albeit temporarily, were not always eager to embrace a program that asked them to exercise their own personal power to contribute to its success. This suggests that the force field analysis model should also be used as a model for program maintenance as actors' roles and power shifts may change and threaten the initial change effort.

Most importantly, social workers need to remember that power can be mobilized for people when we least expect it. We must believe in the people we work with and value their power to create and maintain change.

DISCUSSION QUESTIONS

1. How do the debates about the causes of homelessness influence solutions?
   a. What might a residual solution include?
   b. What might an institutional solution include?
2. Why is it difficult for social workers to share power with clients? What factors inhibit our ability to do so? (Hint: Think about organization and political factors.)
3. How does using force field analysis allow us to examine organizational structure?
4. How might force field analysis be used to consider how programs are maintained?

REFERENCES

Barge, F., & Norr, K. (1991). Homeless shelter policies for women in an urban environment. *American Journal of Nursing, 23*(3), 145–149.

Brager, G., & Holloway, S. (1993). Assessing the prospects for organizational change: The uses of force field analysis. *Administration in Social Work, 16*(3), 15–28.

Breiland, A. (1990) The Hull House tradition and the contemporary social worker: Was Jane Addams really a social worker? *Social Work, 35,*134–138.

Burt, M. (2001, October). *What will it take to end homelessness?* Washington, DC: Urban Institute.

Crook, W. (2002). Trickle-down bureaucracy: Does the organization affect client responses to programs? *Administration in Social Work, 26*(1), 37–59.

de Costa Nunez, R. (1994). *A shelter is not a home or is it? Lessons from family homelessness in New York City.* New York: Homes for the Homeless.

Gorman, T. (2010). *Promoting community change: Making it happen in the real world* (5th ed.). New York: Brooks/Cole.

Hartnett, H. (1992). The women we call "homeless": The politics of interpretation (Unpublished master's thesis). Ohio State University, Columbus.

Hartnett, H., & Harding, S. (2005). Geography and homelessness: Implications for community practice with people we call homeless. *Journal of Progressive Human Services, 16*(2), 25–46.

Hartnett, H., & Postmus, J. (2010). The function of shelters for women: Assistance or social control? *Journal of Human Behavior in the Social Environment, 20*(2), 289–302.

Hopper, K. (1990). Public shelter as "hybrid institution": Homeless men in historical perspective. *Journal of Social Issues, 46*(4), 13–29.

McChesney, K. (1995). A review of the empirical literature on contemporary urban homeless families. *Social Service Review,* (September), 429–459.

National Association of Social Workers (NASW). (1999). *Code of ethics.* Silver Springs, MD: Author.

Veness, A. (1994). Designer shelters as models and makers of home: New responses to homelessness in urban America. *Urban Geography, 15*(2), 150–167.

Wiggin, K. D. S. (1903). *Rebecca of Sunnybrook Farm.* Boston: Houghton Mifflin Company.

9

Beyond Inclusion Training

Changing Human Service and Public Organizations

June Ying Yee, Helen Wong, and Tanja Schlabitz

INTRODUCTION

Today, many human service and public organizations strive to be accessible to their diverse external customer groups (those individuals or organizations in the community with specific needs) and to promote inclusion and excellent customer service. More attention needs to be paid to the internal workings of the organization to identify factors that either help or hinder them in achieving their intended outcomes. This chapter explores the organizational challenges in meeting the needs of diverse external customer groups and presents an inclusion framework to help identify alternative strategies that respond more effectively to these needs. It illustrates the application of this framework through a case example at the Regional Municipality of Halton, Ontario, Canada; there a Special Projects Team in the Social and Community Services Department successfully implemented an inclusion initiative.

ORGANIZATIONAL CHALLENGES—
WHY ARE THERE TENSIONS AND STRUGGLES?

Many agencies find it difficult to align intended values, goals, and actions to their mission, strategy, processes, and systems. This misalignment creates tensions and contradictions. Typically, service provision has an ideological basis that influences who is or is not entitled to services, and does not

The authors thank the Special Projects Team for their contribution to this article. We would also like to recognize the team members for their commitment to inclusion in both principle and practice.

address the root causes of a problem (Bishop, 2005). The consequences are that organizations will unintentionally create systemic barriers to the services offered while trying to meet external customer needs. Systemic barriers refer to institutional policies, procedures, and practices entrenched in the operation of established institutions that result in the unfair exclusion of social groups, and may include lack of customer service access, or employment and promotional opportunities within an organization (Ontario Healthy Communities Coalition, 2004; Wong & Yee, 2009). Systemic barriers are evident when clusters of external customers are excluded from receiving much-needed services.

Exclusionary practices take place within the organization's core values and normative practices on three levels: individual, organizational, and societal (Yee & Wong, 2009). First, exclusionary practices begin at the individual level with frontline workers or managers in the organization. They can consciously or unconsciously exclude (i.e., deny resources or opportunities) in their day-to-day interactions with external customers. Bishop (2005) asserts that all those who work in an organization should be seen as institutional power-holders, regardless of whether they are frontline workers or senior management. According to Bishop (2005), institutional power-holders in human service and public organizations will inevitably face an equity conflict. This occurs when a staff person fails to understand that people who face some barriers require different supports and resources in order to gain the same access to services as those who do not face the same barriers. The onus is on the institutional power-holder to address this inequity. Institutional power-holders may choose not to see an inequity because they have unknowingly accepted the societal, liberal ideology and unconsciously operate from "an individualistic, or liberal, worldview" (Bishop, 2005, p. 147).

This exclusionary dynamic often occurs because of one's social location (Yee & Wong, 2009). At the individual level, assumptions and biases are usually based on one's social location, which frames one's understanding of an external customer or coworker. Power imbalances attributed to one's social location are deeply rooted within society and the organizations reflect this by granting privileges to some, and not granting them to others.

Those working in human service and public organizations often come from privileged social locations and take for granted that the world is structured according to their own norms and values. Those who lack experience or knowledge in working with differences may be uncritical of the structures within which they work. One's social location can produce gaps in seeing someone else's reality and life experience. If those who are mainly from the dominant culture (white, male, heterosexual, able-bodied) shape the norms and values of the organization, then at an organizational level these norms and values are institutionalized, and reinforced or rationalized by the practices of the organization (Yee & Wong, 2009).

At a societal level, these norms and values often become *unquestionably accepted* as the way things are done in all organizations and institutions (Yee & Wong, 2009). This attitude results in collusion in maintaining the status quo by those within organizations and institutions. In essence, the way of doing things stays the same, despite the fact that it is denying resources and opportunities to marginalized external customer groups. Marginalized groups often have no access to human services due to systemic discrimination. In this chapter, we will discuss the necessity of making inclusion a core organizational value that must be continuously examined and reinforced throughout the organizational change process to prevent the system from reverting to exclusionary practices and coopting those who are working in the organization so that they do not see that they are being exclusionary.

AN INCLUSIONARY APPROACH

Much of the literature suggests that top-down change does not ensure more inclusionary practices in an organization or improve its external customer service (Blanchard, 2010). Such an approach "assumes that those with less power, that is staff, will always comply with the directives of those with greater power" (Wright, 2010b, p. 21). This supposition conveys a lack of insight into how organizational change processes work because it is actually the frontline staff who are uniquely positioned to be responsive to the needs and rights of consumers. Thus, the frontline workers' input is vitally important to inclusionary organizational change.

The challenge for senior management is to recognize that frontline staff may not see the connection between the need for change and how that change is aligned with the values and mission of the organization. They may not see the connection because they are too busy carrying out the day-to-day work of the organization, or they may feel powerless in providing input, or they may not know how to best challenge the internal workings of the system since the system itself is rigid and not open to input from the inside or outside, including from managers, community groups, and external customers. In addition, as low-power actors, staff may fear speaking up due to preconceptions about the real or believed negative consequences of challenging the status quo. Therefore, senior management must work with frontline staff in a way that demonstrates how inclusion is implemented and allows them to provide information and constructive input on improving the internal workings of the organization. Change must come about through collaboration rather than be management driven.

An inclusionary organizational change process is one that enables senior management, middle management, supervisors, frontline workers, and administrative support staff, to buy in to a common and unified mission, strategy, system, and structure (Baulcomb, 2010; Fullan, 1993; Song,

2009). Yet it is difficult for an organization to be actively involved in both getting there (the process) and being there (the outcome), since it may be a challenge to obtain collaboration and consensus among the different stakeholders.

Organizational change processes should move toward a particular value set (Fullan, 1993). At a basic level, if we understand inclusion to mean "a situation that exists when disadvantaged communities and designated group members share power and decision-making at all levels in projects, programs, and institutions" (Henry & Tator, 2006, p. 306), then we can understand that this value set should apply not only to those working in the organization, but also to those who receive services from the organization. To challenge the equity conflict, we need to create outcomes focused on minimizing inequities experienced by various external customer groups. An inclusionary organizational change process looks at how inclusion as a core organizational value in the delivery of client-centered services can be effectively used to promote inclusion and attract diversity in a way that is measurable and accountable both to those working in the organization and to those affected by its decisions (external customers and community).

IMPLEMENTING CHANGE

Since Brager and Holloway's (1978) seminal work on the use of force field analysis in assessment for organizational change, there has been much literature on understanding the various forms of resistance and barriers to implementing real organizational change (Bishop, 2005; Henry & Tator, 2006; Lopes & Thomas, 2006; Wright, 2010a). That literature focuses on inclusion, diversity, and anti-oppression as critical to the organizational change process. The change process also requires a meaningful change in values and accountability from all actors in an organization. Furthermore, an inclusionary organization is one that acknowledges that barriers to creating change do exist in the values of the organization. All organizations can claim that they are inclusive, yet are they really? On a practical level, inclusivity would require "the formation of new organizational structures, the introduction of new cultural norms and value systems, changes in power dynamics, the implementation of new employment systems, substantive changes in services delivered, support for new roles and relationships at all levels of the organization, new patterns and more inclusive styles of leadership and decision making, and the reallocation of resources. Strategic planning, organizational audits and reviews and monitoring and accountability systems are all considered an integral part of the management [of an inclusionary organization]" (Henry & Tator, 2006, p. 322).

We argue that the key barrier to an organizational change process is the power of the decision makers. Specifically, senior management are faced with both the equity conflict and the creation of hierarchical organizational divisions. This barrier prevents low-power actors from communicating openly and working closely with senior management to solve organizational tensions that, at a structural level, are exclusionary.

Structurally, most organizations do not have or allow for the requisite processes, mechanisms, and feedback loops to enable them to work collaboratively toward a common value and mission of the organization. Moreover, organizations continuously benefit from three essential inputs into their internal system: (1) external consultants who have expertise in diversity and inclusion to challenge them on how their internal processes and structures may be producing and reproducing exclusionary effects; (2) customers and external community partner agencies that can show the organization how it is negatively affecting clients' access to needed services; and (3) a logic model with a focused intended outcome on inclusion that is ultimately monitored by input from external customers.

CASE EXAMPLE: REGIONAL MUNICIPALITY OF HALTON, SOCIAL AND COMMUNITY SERVICES DEPARTMENT

The Regional Municipality of Halton in Ontario, Canada, serves more than 450,000 residents in the city of Burlington, the town of Halton Hills, the town of Milton, and the town of Oakville. It has an operating budget of CAD$562 million (Regional Municipality of Halton, Social and Community Services Department, 2006) and provides a wide range of services that include wastewater management, emergency medical services, public health services, and a variety of human services through the Social and Community Services Department. With a commitment to caring and excellence, the department has five key divisions of service delivery: housing, employment and social services (social assistance), children's services, services for seniors, and intervention and business services.

The department carries out its work through a philosophy of client-centered care. From an organizational perspective, to implement a client-centered culture requires an inclusive organizational change process, in which the departmental management team is responsible to lead and be accountable for ensuring that structural changes are made to organizational culture, policies, practices, and services. In addition, the departmental management team needs to create opportunities and support for buy-in, participation, and mutual accountability. This approach is essential, because frontline staff and supervisors, as lower-power actors, are responsible for the implementation of changes to daily practices. Organizational context also refers to understanding the potential opportunities for change, given the specific structure, including the relationships and roles among the different internal stakeholders (Brager & Holloway, 1993).

Key to the department are the Special Projects Team, frontline staff, and external customers. Before any intended outcome can be identified as the first step in the organizational change process, inclusion needs to become the core organizational value in the delivery of client-centered services. The department supports the definition and the understanding that inclusion is a strategic organizational process of eliminating barriers and implementing change based on the acceptance that not all groups have equal access to services and positions of leadership due to societal and systemic barriers such as racism, sexism, ableism, and heterosexism (Ontario Healthy Communities Coalition, 2004). Therefore, the intent of the inclusion initiative is to enhance internal and external customer service, client-centered services, and access to services.[1]

The Special Projects Team

The Special Projects Team in the Regional Municipality of Halton is a unique team composed of special project coordinators, a staff development coordinator, a mental health coordinator, an administrative assistant, and a supervisor. They are accountable to the director of intervention and business services in the department. The team helps facilitate organizational change initiatives that are aligned with both the departmental and corporate strategic plans. Team members work in a highly collaborative way and seek to integrate inclusion in all facets of their practice. They aim to ensure that inclusive participatory decision making is incorporated in the planning, development, and implementation of initiatives.

Figure 9.1 provides a force field analysis for the Halton example. The change goal is the integration of inclusion as a core value in all areas of practice within the Regional Municipality of Halton. The analysis indicates only two working forces; one is a driving force and the other is a restraining force. The working driving force in this case is the presence of organizational champions or ambassadors, who act as a critical collective supporting the change goal. The working restraining force is the anticipated difficulty of translating the value of inclusion to a form of practice at all levels of the agency that holds everyone accountable to the change goal. Identifying these opposing forces helps with strategizing how to achieve the change. For example, one strategy used by the organization was to implement required training for staff on how to practice inclusion on an individual, team, and organizational level. Inclusion training is one example of a strategy that supports the working driving force while mitigating and addressing the working restraining force.

---

[1]Internal customers are those who work at the staff, management, or administrative levels. Their role and responsibilities are to implement the policies, procedures, services, and/or processes of the organization. Often, we do not think about how internal customers work together to change policies, procedures, services, and/or processes. Similarly, we often do not allow external customers to provide input on the internal workings of the organization.

FIGURE 9.1. Force Field Analysis for Region of Halton Inclusion Effort

---

Change Goal:

To integrate inclusion as a core value in all areas of practice within the region of Halton

---

Critical Actors:

1. Chief administrative office
2. Commissioner
3. Social and Community Services directors (department management team)
4. Management teams
5. Special projects team

Facilitating Actors:

1. Front-line and nonmanagement staff
2. Student interns
3. Volunteers

Driving Forces for Change:	*Restraining Forces for Change:*
1. Endorsement from the chief administrative officer (A/U, P/H, C/U)	1. For some, resistance to shifting the way things currently are done (status quo) (A/H, P/H, C/U)
2. Support and commitment from the departmental management team (A/H, P/H, C/U)	2. Difficulties anticipated in translating the value of inclusion to a form of practice at all levels of the agency that holds everyone accountable to the change goal (A/H, P/H, C/H—a working force)
3. The presence of champions or ambassadors in the organization who can act as a critical, collective mass that supports change goal (A/H, P/H, C/H—a working force)	3. Perception by some that the corporation/division was already inclusive (A/U, P/H, C/U)
4. Resources (financial, staffing) allocated to inclusion (A/U, P/H, C/U)	4. Lack of sustainable resources and funding (A/U, P/U, C/U)
5. Having a special projects team dedicated to focusing on the change goal (A/H, P/H, C/U)	5. Recent change in the commissioner and other restructuring (A/U, P/U, C/U)
	6. Lack of established accountability mechanism and thus direction for inclusive organizational change (A/H, P/H, C/U)

Decision:

Proceed with the proposed change goal; seek strategies to address the restraining forces.

Strategy:

Develop an inclusion lens, provide inclusion training, and develop an inclusion framework for accountability to lead to organizational change.

Source: Wong & Yee, 2009.
Key: A = Amenability
     H = High
     P = Potency
     U = Uncertain
     C = Consistency

A force field analysis is useful in assessing the feasibility of the change effort. However, when engaging in inclusion or diversity work, it is best to modify a force field analysis to include a logic model that operates within an overarching inclusion framework. A logic model can be defined as a sequential, reflective analysis of the processes and actions to enact a change goal. Modifying a force field analysis in this way helps to (1) provide a continuous, reflective evaluation to explore whether current or new processes and actions taken at each step positively impact marginalized communities; (2) identify alternative strategies to respond more effectively to excluded groups; (3) explore thoroughly the internal workings of the organization to identify factors that either help or hinder achieving intended outcomes and ensure inclusivity in the change process; (4) allow for a built-in accountability for every positional role within the organization; (5) illustrate continuity between values and goals to the actions, processes, and systems used at each step; and (6) allow for critical self-reflection on how one's actions and decisions impact the intended outcome at each step and acknowledge that inclusivity means a willingness to continually challenge one's own values, assumptions, and practices.

Introducing the Inclusion Framework

An inclusion framework is helpful for organizations. (1) It can be an analytical planning tool that can be used to assess an organization's readiness to ensure inclusion in all facets of service provision. (2) It can help determine which strategies to use at various points in becoming a more inclusionary organization. (3) Finally, it allows for continuous monitoring of progress toward inclusionary organizational change. An inclusion framework should be user friendly: that is, it should be flexible and adaptable so it can be used at different levels of work in the organization, from the micro level (i.e., everyday service delivery) to the macro level (i.e., corporate policy development). Also, the framework should facilitate the observation of measurable outcomes.

Implementing inclusion as a core value in an organization requires the following:

1. a collective vision about the intended outcome to be achieved;
2. the identification of organizational challenges that may hinder achieving the intended outcome;
3. open and authentic discussion of the origins of these challenges and how to address them at a systemic level;
4. the identification of the processes and structures that support the intended outcome known as levers;
5. a conscious awareness and identification of the critical (chief administrative officer, the commissioner, the social and community services director, the divisional management team, and the Special Pro-

jects Team), facilitating (frontline and nonmanagement staff, student interns, and volunteers), and low-power actors, and their role in the organizational change process;

6. identification of effective interventions and strategies to turn challenges into opportunities;

7. the identification of concrete steps that connect individual behaviors to organizational accountability; and

8. indicators (measures of success).

For this case example, these steps are presented in figure 9.2.

The initial actions taken by the department were in response to a report, "Inclusive Cities Canada—Burlington: Voices, Perspectives and Priorities" (Community Development Halton, 2005) that emphasized the importance of inclusion within cities and communities.[2] The Special Projects Team began by developing an inclusion lens tool (Wong & Yee, 2009) to enhance customer service delivery. The tool is a set of self-guided, critically reflective questions to help staff in the delivery of client-centered service. This tool was developed in the context of an organization-wide inclusion planning that involved external and internal environmental scans and strategic development. The department also supplemented the tool with training. These activities, built on previous reflective practice training from the Our People Care™ program (that supports workplace wellness developed by Credit Valley Hospital), set the stage for inclusion work. The Special Project Team predicted that staff who participated in reflective practice training were more readily able to reflect on their own social location, which is a crucial step in helping them identify areas of systemic exclusion. Feedback from those who attended both reflective practice and inclusion training said that they felt motivated and that the skills learned applied to their work.

The Special Projects Team As Effective Change Agent

The Special Projects Team exemplifies how critical actors can be effective change agents within organizations. However, for this change to take place, the organization must have certain processes and structures, known as levers, to support and sustain the change work. It is also important to determine who is responsible for making change happen. Furthermore, senior management must support an environment in which collaboration is demonstrated, be open to being challenged by others, and proactively take actions to address systemic exclusion. For example, the departmental management team championed the work of the Special Projects Team not only by providing tangible resources such as adequate staffing, but also by using

---

[2]Inclusive Cities Canada is a project of five social planning organizations in cities across Canada that has the goal to examine and enhance social inclusion in communities.

FIGURE 9.2. The Inclusion Framework of the Halton Region

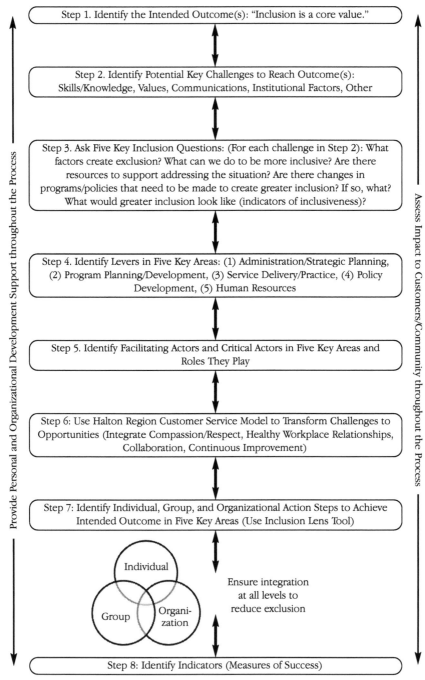

Provide Personal and Organizational Development Support throughout the Process

Assess Impact to Customers/Community throughout the Process

Step 1. Identify the Intended Outcome(s): "Inclusion is a core value."

Step 2. Identify Potential Key Challenges to Reach Outcome(s): Skills/Knowledge, Values, Communications, Institutional Factors, Other

Step 3. Ask Five Key Inclusion Questions: (For each challenge in Step 2): What factors create exclusion? What can we do to be more inclusive? Are there resources to support addressing the situation? Are there changes in programs/policies that need to be made to create greater inclusion? If so, what? What would greater inclusion look like (indicators of inclusiveness)?

Step 4. Identify Levers in Five Key Areas: (1) Administration/Strategic Planning, (2) Program Planning/Development, (3) Service Delivery/Practice, (4) Policy Development, (5) Human Resources

Step 5. Identify Facilitating Actors and Critical Actors in Five Key Areas and Roles They Play

Step 6: Use Halton Region Customer Service Model to Transform Challenges to Opportunities (Integrate Compassion/Respect, Healthy Workplace Relationships, Collaboration, Continuous Improvement)

Step 7: Identify Individual, Group, and Organizational Action Steps to Achieve Intended Outcome in Five Key Areas (Use Inclusion Lens Tool)

Individual

Group

Organization

Ensure integration at all levels to reduce exclusion

Step 8: Identify Indicators (Measures of Success)

the team's work across divisions, throughout the corporation and with the external community, to inform strategic and advocacy work. The departmental management team also invested time to experience the pilot sessions of the inclusion lens training module (Yee & Wong, 2009).

From an inclusionary perspective, the departmental management team supports the work of the Special Projects Team by understanding that it works directly with internal and external customers and thus can most accurately identify external customers' needs to help inform organizational decision making. The Special Projects Team was uniquely positioned within the organization to cross over departments and to work directly with the external community. The team understood where corporate, community, senior management, and staff were situated and built on their strengths to generate change.

Organizational Change Effort and Outcome

The Inclusion Framework developed and implemented by the Special Projects Team is presented below. Each of the eight steps is detailed. The reader should refer to figure 9.2 for an overview of the entire framework.

Step 1: Identify the Intended Consequences. This is an essential step in any organizational change process because it lays the foundation for actions and strategies to achieve the outcome. As a first step, this also reminds everyone that during each subsequent step of an inclusionary organizational change process, it is important to continuously and critically reflect on how one's actions and decisions can affect the intended outcome. During this process, change agents may discover factors that result in the modifying of the intended outcomes. Modifications should always be checked from an inclusionary perspective, that is, to determine whether the revised intended outcome effectively addresses systemic barriers to reduce inequities for marginalized communities. Otherwise, exclusionary practices may return.

Before identifying the intended outcome, the Special Projects Team assessed the readiness of the internal and external environment in the development of an inclusion strategy, vision, and intended outcome. The Special Projects Team members acknowledged that they are not experts in defining any particular issue, but rather saw themselves as convenors or connectors that link people, information, and resources to facilitate the development of inclusion strategies.

Initially, the corporation had conducted research (Regional Municipality of Halton, 2010) on the changing demographics of the region. These research findings helped the Special Projects Team situate its inclusion work within broader community needs.

The vision for inclusion at an organization-wide level was set by the corporation through a commitment statement. Signed in April 2009 by the regional chair and chief administrative officer, this commitment statement stated that the Regional Municipality of Halton welcomes, respects, and values diversity and provides services in a way that meets needs of the customer (Regional Municipality of Halton, 2009). The role of the Special Projects Team was to help carry out this commitment and create linkages within the department between the various interests of the stakeholders, to move forward a joint vision of inclusion. Before achieving such a broad outcome, the team recognized the need to model the inclusion initiative as a successful project within the department. They envisioned that its success would cause a ripple effect for wider, systemic change. The team worked to link the corporate strategic inclusion vision to the departmental inclusion goals, and reinforced this vision by supporting existing processes and structures that captured pivotal opportunities to embrace inclusion as a core value.

Step 2: Identify Potential Key Challenges to Reach Outcome(s). In an inclusionary organizational change environment, the focus is not only on the outcome, but also on the process. When interactions among organizational members are increased, changes in decision making regarding organizational practices, processes, policies, procedures, and rules become more democraticized. This, in turn, can have a positive impact on client engagement. It is important to openly invite debate and contention, and to create an environment that explores all issues and challenges from multiple perspectives. This process promotes authentic dialogue, collaborative problem solving, and role modeling to others so a safe and open communication process can emerge. Identifying potential key challenges is an important step to developing subsequent strategies and actions. Key challenges evolve from the organizational context, meaning that some challenges may be unique to the dynamics within the organization. However, common factors can stand in the way of organizational change. For example, skills and knowledge that reflect the value of inclusion may not be fully understood within the context of the organization.

Developing collaborative relationships was a key inclusive strategy of the Special Projects Team that helped identify organizational challenges. The team was aware that all perspectives are relevant in shaping an inclusionary organization. They tried to anticipate challenges by using what they learned from prior departmental and community change initiatives. To determine the scope of challenges to inclusion, the Special Projects Team spoke directly with external customers and internal and external stakeholders. The respondents were asked to define inclusion and identify barriers that could stand in the way of embedding inclusive practices. They also asked respondents to identify the strengths within the department so the team could continue supporting those behaviors and actions that were structurally inclusionary within the organization. Recognizing that external customers may feel freer to talk with those who are external to the region, the team recruited consultants (two of this chapter's authors) who had expertise in inclusive organizational change. Conversations between those consultants and the team helped shape the design of the training and the development of the inclusion lens (Wong & Yee, 2009).

Below are some of the challenges discussed in the consultations and interviews that became matters for agency members to address:

Skills/Knowledge: There was a consensus that the entire agency needed to develop a collective organizational understanding of what inclusion means in practice.

Values: In order for the entire department to systemically operate from an inclusion approach, it would take a paradigm shift in values on the part of all organizational members. However, inclusion was seen as a value that made work more meaningful for agency members.

Communication: An inclusionary organization must promote open, transparent, and strong lines of communication by implementing a feedback loop that incorporates feedback from management to staff, staff to external customers, and customers to external partners.

Institutional Factors: Resources, leadership, and strategic directions should be increasingly aligned and operated from an inclusion approach.

Step 3: Ask Five Key Inclusion Questions for Each Challenge. Now that the challenges have been identified, the next step involves asking the key inclusion questions and discussing issues openly to explore solutions at practice, program, and policy levels to bring about systemic change. Table 9.1 outlines the five key inclusion questions and their significance.

The Special Projects Team designed the five main inclusion questions so that agency members could engage in a deeper discussion and (a) identify

TABLE 9.1. Key Inclusion Questions for Step 3

Key Inclusion Questions	*What the Question Answers*
a. Are there factors creating exclusion? If so, what are they?	This identifies what is creating the exclusion.
b. What can we do to be more inclusive?	This identifies strategies or ways (the how to) to address exclusion.
c. Are there supports and resources I/we require to support me/us in addressing the situation?	This identifies the supports and resources that the organization, team, or individual would need to provide to address exclusion.
d. Are there changes in programs/ policies that need to be made to create greater inclusion? If so, what changes are required?	This identifies changes at an organizational level to ensure that there is no exclusion.
e. What would greater inclusion look like? (What are indicators of inclusiveness?)	This identifies observably and measurably what being inclusive would look like in organizational practice.

the root (underlying) cause of the challenges; (b) develop the necessary strategies to address it; (c) identify the supports and resources required at an organizational, team, or individual level; (d) discuss what changes need to occur; and (e) develop indicators to know if the challenges have been addressed. These questions were designed to be reflective so that agency staff could examine the structural, systemic causes of exclusion. From an inclusion perspective, it is important not only to identify and name the systemic roots of exclusion, but also to take action. The steps of expanding the conversation to explore solutions and developing monitoring and accountability mechanisms promote organizational change.

Steps 4 and 5: Identify Levers in Five Key Areas and Identify Facilitating Actors and Critical Actors. Levers are the processes and structures within the organization that set the conditions to achieve the intended outcome. The role of the Special Projects Team is to help identify what levers within their organization support the outcome of inclusion as a core value. To ensure that the values of inclusion have an organization-wide impact and change, the Special Projects Team identified levers in each of the key areas of operation of the department or organization (see figure 9.3 and table 9.2). It is necessary for the change agents to link the levers to a position or team within the organization where accountability rests to ensure that the goals are met.

FIGURE 9.3. The Inclusion Framework: Steps 4 and 5

Step 4: Identify Levers in Five Key Areas

Administration and Strategic Planning	Program Planning and Development	Service Delivery and Practice	Policy Development	Human Resources

Step 5: Identify facilitating actors and critical actors in five key areas and roles they play.

- Facilitating actors: Members whose approval, disapproval, or neutrality has a decisive impact on critical actors
- Critical actors: Members who have the power to adopt or reject the desired change, i.e., special projects team

Who?	Role?

TABLE 9.2. Key Areas of Operation, Levers, and Actors for the Inclusion Framework

Key Areas of Operation	Identify Levers	Who Are Critical Actors? Who Are Facilitating Actors? (Step 5)
Administration and planning	Example: Provide resources and support for inclusion initiative by senior management.	
Program planning and development	Example: Ensure external input is defined and used in all change management or program development designs.	
Service delivery and practice	Example: Ensure community agencies and external customers have input into program planning in order to remove service and access barriers.	
Policy development	Example: Consider inclusion questions in policy development.	
Human resources	Example: Ensure questions that assess knowledge of inclusion are part of interview process for management and leadership positions.	

To identify the processes and structures necessary for an inclusive organization, the Special Projects Team used the key strategy of building engagement and awareness to promote collaboration and buy-in for the inclusion initiative. For example, the team maintained a connection to external community partners who participated throughout the initiative. The team informed the city of Burlington, the Halton Multicultural Council, the Halton Diversity Advisory Committee, the Inclusion Reference Group, and client reference groups of the progress of the initiative at each pivotal stage.

The communication strategy established by the Special Projects Team was key to the organization connecting with the various stakeholders. The vehicles included a blog, newsletters, e-mail, phone calls, in-person updates, presentations, and progress reports. This strategy kept inclusion on the regular agenda and in the minds of stakeholders. The team recognized that maintaining awareness of the progress of the inclusion project would increase the likelihood that the needed support and resources are in place, and inclusive actions are carried out by stakeholders.

Identifying critical and facilitating actors is crucial to the success of any organizational change initiative (Brager & Holloway, 1993). This provides the opportunity to identify inclusion ambassadors as facilitating actors. Ambassadors advocate for inclusion and help build engagement and momentum toward the intended organizational change. Ambassadors continuously strive to challenge any forms of systemic exclusion. They are also able to take direction and leadership from groups who are excluded (Lopes & Thomas, 2006) to ensure that the community's needs are heard and met. It is equally important to identify who may be neutral or who has not bought into the values of inclusion, and why. For example, some managers may be neutral or may not be open to structural inclusion because they assume that change may incur cost, resources, or time. It is important to understand why certain people are not engaged in order to find ways to address their fears or concerns.

Pivotal to operating from an inclusion framework is ensuring that the values of inclusion respond to the needs of customers. Thus the Special Projects Team continuously sought ways to involve and incorporate feedback from external customers at every opportunity in decision-making processes. It was important to acknowledge that all critical, facilitating, and low-power actors within an inclusive organization have the potential power to address systemic and structural exclusion in their work. Thus, critical and facilitating actors must be mindful of ensuring that external customers' voices are represented and that discussions regarding this inclusion of voices occurs in their teams.

Step 6: Use Regional Municipality of Halton Customer Service Model to Transform Challenges to Opportunities. The move from getting there (steps 1–5) to being there (steps 6–8) as an organization involves identifying innovative methods and new approaches to deal with identified challenges that shift the status quo from individual inclusive practices to a systemwide inclusive organization. Understanding that maintaining the status quo can perpetuate the exclusion of certain groups means that change is vital to be able to continuously create more-inclusive and more-comprehensive approaches to provision of client-centered services. The Special Projects Team recognized that addressing organizational challenges requires creative solutions developed in collaboration with stakeholders. In conjunction with the internal and external community partners, the team developed an innovative comprehensive departmental customer service model that promotes the four core components when providing client-centered external and internal customer service: (a) compassion and respect, (b) healthy workplace relationships, (c) collaboration, and (d) continuous improvement. To ensure that inclusion is a systemwide core value, the departmental customer service model integrated components within key areas of operation: administration and strategic planning; program planning and development; service delivery and practice; policy development; and human resources. Examples of the integration of these four components in client-centered service included having client input into all aspects of project planning and implementation, inclusion lens training, reflective practice training, and evaluation.

Step 7: Identify Individual, Group, and Organizational Action Steps to Achieve Intended Outcome in Five Key Areas. It is important to identify the individual and related group and organizational action steps within each of the five key operating areas that integrate the departmental customer service model. It is necessary to link individual actions and behaviors to group and organizational accountability for sustainability and to ensure that actual changes have occurred at the organization-wide level. As illustrated in figure 9.2 (between Steps 7 and 8), integration needs to occur on all three levels within human resources:

1. Individual: Staff members can describe ways in which they have provided inclusive external customer service.

2. Group: Teams can articulate how they provide inclusive external customer service at divisional meetings.

3. Organizational: Staff members can demonstrate inclusive external customer service. This level is part of the performance review process.

Participatory decision making is another inclusionary strategy used by the Special Projects Team to facilitate collective ownership of intended core values, vision (Chapman & Fullan, 2007), and outcomes. The Special Projects Team structured participatory decision-making opportunities by encouraging teams to work through the inclusion framework by developing individual, group, and organizational action steps within inclusion training. First, the inclusion training provided a day of team building around inclusion. Second, it allowed for an open discussion about the challenges and ability to implement inclusion. Third, it required participants to identify the levers and processes to address the challenges. Fourth, it provided opportunities for the participants to develop action strategies to support inclusion in their teams. Song (2009) notes, "Successful planned change occurs when the organizational members 'own' or 'buy into' the process and outcome of organizational change" (p. 201). In other words, training is effective when staff members participate in and take ownership of the initiative that promotes greater accountability in the development and planning of inclusion as a core value.

The Special Project Team actively sought and facilitated many kinds of different inclusive opportunities, while remaining mindful of the intended outcome. For example, staff participated in workshops on the availability of interpreter services throughout the region in order to be more responsive to customers with language barriers. Another example in which the Regional Municipality of Halton created greater accountability was by revising the corporate annual performance plan for nonunion staff. These plans incorporated the measure of inclusion as an optional core competency. As mentioned earlier, the Special Projects Team worked in collaboration with external consultants to develop an inclusion tool (Wong & Yee, 2009). This tool was a set of self-guided questions focused on inclusion in six different areas of service provision: (a) being self-aware, (b) communicating, (c) engaging community, (d) addressing barriers, (e) embracing diversity, and (f) providing excellent customer service. The tool helped staff critically reflect on and challenge their values, assumptions, and biases in their practice and then to determine whether they and their teams were integrating the values of inclusion at an organizational level. Challenging assumptions meant questioning whether those values were a part of the dominant norm that reinforces the status quo and perpetuates exclusionary practices. Challenging assumptions also allowed agency members to seek alternative strategies that result in systemic inclusion and organizational change.

The inclusion tool is a strategic mechanism that (1) reinforces the message that inclusion is an important organizational value and an expected standard of practice for everyone, beyond simply attending inclusion training; (2) provides a set of questions to identify challenges and create strategies toward inclusive organizational change in every aspect of work at the organization; (3) is tangible, concrete, and can be used by any staff in any organization; (4) can be used for evaluative purposes; and (5) keeps the conversation going and therefore supports the sustainability of the inclusion initiative.

Step 8: Identify Indicators (Measures of Success). Once the action steps were determined, staff within each of the key operating areas must determine whether the actions meet the intended outcomes. Indicators are concrete and measurable and can be qualitative or quantitative. For example, an indicator may be that staff share and discuss issues of structural inclusion that affect external customers in their weekly team meetings, and then develop strategies to address these issues. The Special Projects Team explored ways to identify indicators that measure both the process and the outcome of the inclusion initiative. The team recognized that the change process was equally, if not more, valuable than solely focusing on actions, because inclusionary organizational change required an internal shift in values and attitudes along with behaviors. For example, they measured whether staff felt increased confidence in the resources and supports available to them to do inclusion work.

Two Other Important Elements in the Halton Inclusion Framework

The last two elements of the framework focus on processes that are incorporated at each of the eight steps (discussed above). These elements are (a) to provide personal and organizational support throughout the organizational change and logic model process, and (b) to assess the impact on clients and external customers and the community throughout the process. These components are crucial in enabling all staff members to continuously reflect on their work and to be able to complete each step of the framework.

Providing personal and organizational support is an important, though often overlooked, part of the organizational change process. Many organizations are aware that they need training and provide it to some degree, but rarely spend the time to reflect on how this type of training will relate directly to intended outcomes, goals, actions, and behavioral shifts. Training opportunities should be assessed according to the relevance of the intended outcome and to the beneficial impact for clients.

The Special Projects Team linked planning and training to organizational change initiatives. In essence, training is a strategic vehicle that builds on the needs of internal agency members and clients and the vision and outcome the organization seeks to achieve. For example, as part of the curriculum in the two-day inclusion training, the team asked participants to discuss challenges to implementing the inclusion approach and what kinds of supports they might need to address these challenges.

The organization has derived many ongoing achievements from the inclusion training and the use of the inclusion lens tool. There are more staff members identified as ambassadors. Children's Services, a division within the department, has a newly formed inclusion reference group. New partnerships are being developed and staff members at all levels of the organization are discussing inclusion in case management and planning, policy development and evaluation. An inclusion perspective was used to aid in the development of an accessible employment resource center and in the recruitment and hiring of more-diverse work teams from the community. Most recently, the inclusion lens tool supported the Coordinated Intervention Services team in its review of existing practices, processes, and policies in providing emergency shelter for newcomer families. They want to enhance their partnership with a local settlement agency to promote long-term sustainability of newcomer families in Halton.

The most essential component of the inclusion framework is to assess the impact on clients and the community at each step. It is important because as one works through the steps, each intentional action and strategic decision should have a positive effect on external customers and the community. It is important to make central the needs of external customers as the driving force of all actions and strategies. Taking such an approach ultimately results in the essence of client-centered service. The Special Projects Team takes every opportunity to role model and to challenge themselves and their colleagues with the following question: "What is the impact of our decisions on clients and customers and how are they involved in the decision-making process?" This question opens the discussion to the kinds of strategies needed to ensure that external customers are a part of the decision-making process. Such questions set up the expectation that inclusion is integrated in providing client-centered services.

This approach has had broad ripple effects and helped to increase inclusion strategies and actions across the department and corporation. Several regional department heads asked the Special Projects Team to assist in the following strategies within the corporation: (1) conduct a review of external customer surveys through an inclusion lens; (2) conduct a review of corporate policies through an inclusion lens; (3) help integrate the inclusion lens in a public engagement strategy; (4) help integrate the value of inclusion in the departmental customer service model; (5) help integrate inclusion in the results-based accountability methodology to measure impacts on external customer service; (6) help develop inclusion as a core competency in corporate annual performance management. Such examples provide clear evidence that inclusion is becoming recognized as an essential core value at a systemwide level.

Human service and public organizations struggle to be more inclusive of their most marginalized populations, including those who face barriers related to gender, race, class, sexual orientation, and ability. We argue for the need not only to make inclusion a core value of any organizational change process, but also to ensure that organizational change processes are accompanied by a logic model. Aside from having inclusion as a core value, holding the intentional goal of creating outcomes that are targeted and focused on meeting the needs of the most marginalized external customers is key to creating an inclusionary organization. Providing excellent external customer service is not easy, but it can be accomplished once organizations have taken a hard look at their internal institutional processes, mechanisms, feedback loops, and, especially, the barriers and obstacles that prevent internal customers from being able to effectively work toward the intended outcome of inclusion as a core value.

CONCLUSION

The Regional Municipality of Halton is a governmental institution that provides human services as part of its broad range of public services. The region as a whole has taken steps to implement an organizational change process that focuses on the intended outcome of adopting inclusion as a core value. In particular, the Department of Community and Social Services achieved early successes in adopting inclusion as a core value. This momentum sets the foundation for the development of a critical mass of champions or ambassadors for inclusion who ultimately will transform the organizational culture toward greater inclusion. These shifts will ultimately ensure the sustainability of the change, in which inclusionary practices are no longer an option, but a necessity.

DISCUSSION QUESTIONS

1. Why is understanding one's social location important to implementing inclusionary practices and processes?
2. How can this framework help facilitate inclusion as a core organizational value?
3. What organizational change strategies can be implemented to integrate inclusion as a core value within human service agencies?

REFERENCES

Baulcomb, J. (2010). Management of change through force field analysis. *Journal of Nursing Management, 11*(4), 275–280.

Bishop, A. (2005). *Beyond token change: Breaking the cycle of oppression in institutions.* Halifax, Canada: Fernwood Publishing.

Blanchard, K. (2010). Mastering the art of change: Ken Blanchard offers some strategies for successfully leading change. *Training Journal,* 44–47.

Brager, G., & Holloway, S. (1978). *Changing human service organizations: Politics and practice.* New York: Free Press.

Brager, G., & Holloway, S. (1993). Assessing prospects for organizational change. *Administration in Social Work, 16*(3), 15–28.

Chapman, C., & Fullan, M. (2007). Collaboration and partnership for equitable improvement: Towards a networked learning system? *School Leadership and Management, 27*(3), 207–211.

Community Development Halton. (2005). *Inclusive cities Canada-Burlington: Community voices, perspectives and priorities.* Retrieved from http://www.cdhalton.ca/pdf/icc/ICC_Burlington_Full_Report.pdf

Fullan, M. (1993). *Change forces: Probing the depths of educational reform.* London: Falmer Press.

Henry, F., & Tator, C. (2006). *The colour of democracy: Racism in Canadian society* (3rd ed.). Toronto: Harcourt Press.

Lopes, T., & Thomas, B. (2006). *Dancing on live embers: Challenging racism in organizations.* Toronto: Between the Lines.

Ontario Healthy Communities Coalition. (2004). *Inclusive community organizations.* Toronto: Ontario Health Communities Coalition.

Regional Municipality of Halton. (2009). *Commitment statement.* Unpublished document prepared by the Regional Municipality of Halton, Oakville, Canada.

Regional Municipality of Halton. (2010). *2007–2010 Strategic plan.* Retrieved from http://www.stopthequarry.ca/documents/Halton%20Region%202007_PPW_Plan.pdf

Regional Municipality of Halton, Social & Community Services Department. (2006). *Halton region budget and business plan.* Retrieved from http://webaps.halton.ca/search.cfm?q1=community+services+department&I5=Search

Song, Y. (2009). The leadership effectiveness in the process of planned organizational change. *Public Organizational Review, 9*(3), 199–212. DOI: 10.1007/s11115-009-0075-x

Wong, H., & Yee, J. (2009). *Inclusion lens tool: Inclusion lens training.* Oakville, Canada: Regional Municipality of Halton.

Wright, S. (2010a). Dealing with resistance: Pushing through change is bound to meet with opposition, but there are ways to win over the sceptics. *Nursing Standard, 24*(3), 18–20.

Wright, S. (2010b). Taking charge of transformation. *Nursing Standard, 24*(3), 20–22.

Yee, J., & Wong, H. (2009). *Inclusion training material: Session 1.* Oakville, Canada: Regional Municipality of Halton.

10

A Transforming Grassroots Organizing Tale

If You Can't Walk, You Can't Ride

Nancy Ayer

INTRODUCTION

In this chapter, I tell the story of a grassroots organizing campaign that changed the perception of people with disabilities, changed the lives of the activists with disabilities, and changed a community. This chapter provides an account of a five-year community change effort, as well as a discussion of the theoretical underpinnings, and a description of the formal and informal organizational and community structures we encountered and utilized. We used a force field analysis to assess and identify our allies, obstacles, strategies, and the tactics which proved to be successful.

THE CASE

Some Background

The story began with a small not-for-profit organization that was formed in Maine to provide support for people with disabilities—the Southern Maine Association for Handicapped Persons (SMAHP). This organization is made up of people with disabilities and their allies who recognized the many obstacles facing people with disabilities. The organization's mission was to find ways to support people with disabilities and work to supplement the programs and services that existed in the community. The group primarily collected donated items such as walkers, wheelchairs, and other adaptive equipment that individuals in the community needed but did not have the resources to acquire themselves. The organization also recognized the limited transportation opportunities for people with disabilities, so they organized a volunteer transportation program, providing rides for individuals in the community.

The only formal city or county transportation service that was available at that time was a paratransit system. This city-run transportation system provided transportation only to medical appointments and only for people with disabilities. It was the only game in town, and people with disabilities who needed to attend a medical appointment had no other choices unless they had their own accessible vehicle. The paratransit system was overloaded with requests. It did provide curb to curb services, but much of the time riders would wait literally hours to be picked up and transported to their appointment, and then wait hours to be picked up to return home. A typical thirty-minute medical appointment usually consumed at least four to six hours of a patient's time. On many occasions, the initial pick up did not happen and the riders would miss their medical appointments and have to reschedule.

The volunteer transportation system organized by the SMAHP became quite popular. However, it made only a small dent in the problems that many people with mobility impairments faced going from one place to another. Soon this program was overwhelmed with more requests than they could handle. In addition, the volunteer program was unable to assist people who used motorized wheelchairs because typically persons with the mobility impairment did not have the ability to transfer from their wheelchair to the vehicle or, if they did have the ability to transfer, the volunteer could not transport the motorized wheelchair due to its weight. In these cases, patients used a push wheelchair, but that completely removed the person's independence, because a volunteer needed to push them wherever they needed to go.

The organization's members realized that the lack of accessible transportation was a systemic issue that they needed to address by changing the overall system rather than simply by adding more services. After considerable discussion among the board of directors and the membership, the SMAHP made a very significant change in their mission and focus.

The SMAHP became the Maine Association of Handicapped Persons (MAHP) and stopped all service provision in 1981. MAHP established a new mission of changing the public perception of people with disabilities and promoting equal rights for all people with disabilities. We moved from being a regional, southern Maine service program to being a statewide advocacy organization, and expanded our membership to include people with all types of disabilities as well as allies, friends, and family members who were not currently people with disabilities. The decision to significantly expand the composition of the membership was wise and thoughtful. We knew that many of our allies who were not disabled wanted to live in a community that provided equal rights and opportunities to all its members. Many of our "temporarily able-bodied members," as we referred to ourselves, understood that any one of us can become a person with a disability at any time and many of us had friends or family members who experienced enormous limitations. This is a good example of the principle of self-interest. We were helping volunteers and members, and the public to understand that our effort to rehabilitate the community and increase accessibility was in everyone's best interest.

In the early 1980s, uniting all people with disabilities was a somewhat radical idea; most people with disabilities were accustomed to working in isolated groups that were identified by their disability and service provision. Organizations and support groups for people with sight impairments, people who were deaf or who had hearing impairments, people with intellectual disabilities, and people who were psychiatrically labeled were separated from each other, and thus lacked awareness of their commonalities.

Although collective empowerment was an exciting, effective new strategy in the disability rights movement at that time, it required community building within the disability community. We were initially surprised at the level of discriminatory attitudes each group of people with disabilities had for each other. In hindsight, this is not so surprising as the lack of interaction and exposure to one another is a significant negative outcome of segregating people by disability. It was very important for us to understand and address these attitudes as we focused on the goal of our new organization to promote equal rights for people with disabilities. We saw the opportunity to create accessible transportation as an effective vehicle to create more opportunities for the public to interact with people with disabilities, which we believed would begin to change the public perception of people with disabilities. It also had the potential for cross-disability organizing.

Our initial grassroots strategy was to go where people with disabilities lived, which was primarily in subsidized housing for the elderly and disabled. We went to all the subsidized housing facilities in Greater Portland and began a dialogue with the residents with disabilities. The meetings were small, somewhat informal and fun, which are essential ingredients needed to build a membership organization and recruit volunteers. We always brought snacks and held an open forum where we talked about the types of opportunities and activities people were interested in having more access to. The list was always very similar from one group to the next: classes at the local universities, volunteer opportunities, part-time jobs, entertainment, dining out, and developing lives that included more social activities. The major barrier was transportation. The paratransit system would provide transportation only for medical appointments.

An organizer must pay very close attention to what is happening in the community when developing a grassroots organizing campaign. In our case, at approximately the same time that we were organizing groups of people with disabilities in subsidized housing facilities, we learned that the city of

South Portland was about to purchase a new fleet of buses for its public transportation system. This information had been in the news for months. The public transportation system, called Metro, was a tri-city bus system that was unionized and that included Greater Portland including the cities of South Portland, Portland, and Westbrook. South Portland decided to leave the Metro system and develop its own, nonunion bus system, which was unwelcome news to the unionized bus drivers. Predictably, the bus drivers who drove for South Portland lost their jobs with Metro and had to go to work for its new, nonunion bus system.

With the new fleet of buses about to be purchased for South Portland, it was clear to the organizers and members of the MAHP that this was the time to move forward and work toward accessible public transportation. The energy in our organization began to gain momentum as the group started to think of the possibilities of moving independently throughout their community and moving forward with their personal goals.

Once our board of directors accepted the goal of gaining access to public transportation, we began to gather more data from people within the disabled community, and to research successful accessible public transportation systems in other states. We sought out areas of the country that were the most similar to Maine with regard to weather. Seattle was a leader in this respect with a well-developed disability rights organization and a great deal of research regarding equipment such as lifts and tie downs (to prevent wheelchairs moving around on the bus).

Another important distinction we made during the transformation of the SMAHP to the MAHP was to define our work of promoting equal rights and opportunities for people with disabilities as a civil rights issue. We named our public transportation campaign Project Access. MAHP used this opportunity to educate the public that accessible public transportation was an equal rights issue and a civil rights issue, and not a help the handicapped issue. Citizens with mobility impairments paid taxes yet could not use the public transportation system.

From an organizing perspective, identifying disability rights as a civil rights issue presents some interesting opportunities and dilemmas. On the one hand, members of the public, those who do not have anyone in their life who is mobility impaired, are unlikely to think about how people who use wheelchairs get around the community. As a campaign, Project Access provided us with an opportunity to educate the public about the need for accessible public transportation, curb cuts, and accessible public buildings, including schools, post offices, courthouses, and public housing. This new information was helpful in making the public more aware of unnecessary obstacles in the environment. This promoted a shift in thinking about rehabilitating the community rather than just thinking about rehabilitating the individual person with a disability.

It was important for community members to keep in mind that anyone can become a person with a disability at any time. This is not the case, for example, with regard to a person's race. This awareness can make people uncomfortable. The fear that most people have—"What if I become a person with a disability?"—can be turned into a positive force to organize around and, as in our case, can help build the organization. With the understanding that, "I may need this someday, or one of my friends or family members may need a community that is accessible to people with disabilities," self-interest could be reinforced and used to mobilize the community and build the organization. This represented a major paradigm shift for the community.

We were a small grassroots organization with a low budget. We understood that we would need to make news and use the media to move forward on all of our goals:

- *building* the organization,
- *teaching* the public that equal rights for people with disabilities is a civil rights issue that is in everyone's interest,
- *teaching* the public that accessible public transportation is a right of all community residents and taxpayers, and
- *chipping away* at the negative public perception of people with disabilities.

As we moved forward with our agenda, the public became increasingly aware of their commonalities with people with disabilities.

Force Field Analysis

We conducted a force field analysis (see Brager & Holloway, 1978), the results of which are presented in figure 10.1. After completing our assessment, we determined that we had a reasonably strong possibility of being successful with our community change effort. If we had concluded that this community change effort was not feasible because the driving forces were too weak or the restraining forces were too strong, we would have regrouped and determined what we needed to do to make this community change effort more feasible. For example, we might have needed to strengthen and increase the numbers of citizens with disabilities who were ready to become activists or we might have needed to work on our state human rights law to include people with disabilities as a protected class. Also, had the city already purchased a new fleet of buses prior to our organizing effort, we would have needed to rethink our community change effort and develop different change goals.

After completing our force field analysis, we determined that we had potential allies in the media, the transit union, and the public at large. We then had the data necessary to determine that a collaborative level strategy

FIGURE 10.1. Force Field Analysis for the Project Access Campaign

---

Change Goals:

1. Make public transportation accessible to people with disabilities in South Portland, Maine, and then go statewide.

2. Change the public perception of people with disabilities within the disability community and among the public.

3. Build the Maine Association of Handicapped Persons.

Critical Actors:

1. Maine Supreme Court

2. Maine Superior Court

3. Maine Human Rights Commission

4. South Portland City Council

Facilitating Actors:

1. South Portland's city manager and legal counsel
2. The transit union
3. The media

Driving Forces for Change:	*Restraining Forces for Change:*
1. Pressure from citizens with disabilities (W)	1. Discriminatory attitudes toward citizens with disabilities (W)
2. Pressure from the transit union (W)	2. Limited funds for grassroots organizing (F)
3. Community support (W)	3. Considerable paradigm shift for the public regarding their perception of citizens with disabilities (U)
4. The media (W)	
5. The Maine Human Rights Act (F)	
6. The need for ethical, moral, and financially responsible action (F)	
7. The fact that the city was going to purchase a new bus fleet (F)	

Key: (W) Working: Potentially usable forces in achieving the change goal(s).
(F) Framing: Forces that are consistent, stable, and predictable.
(U) Unpredictable: Forces whose behavior is unknown to you or cannot be predicted.

and its tactics were appropriate. We believed our goal was rational, economical, and ethically and morally responsible.

Collaborative Level Strategy and Tactics Begin

When the city announced it was in the process of purchasing a new public bus fleet, something that happens only every twenty years, we understood that it was the time to act. Let the collaboration begin!

We determined that we needed to educate the media. This was a critical step because the media, for the most part, was entrenched in a status quo perspective, viewing people with disabilities as dependent and sick people who lacked any hope of education, employment, or relationships. The status quo perspective was that people with disabilities were perceived as helpless and were to be pitied. We presented the Project Access campaign to representatives from the media, including editorial boards and news directors at television and radio stations. We explained how and why the SMAHP became the MAHP and discussed why the rights of citizens with disabilities was a civil rights issue. We hoped these efforts would pay off in the future and help us meet our goals of educating the public in order to change their perception of people with disabilities and so help us build the organization. We needed the media to understand the civil rights perspective of our work.

We also met with the transit union leadership and many bus drivers during the collaborative phase of our community change effort. We wanted to present our requests and have them hear directly from mobility-impaired people how the paratransit system was broken and useless. The transit union and drivers were on our side almost from day one. Since the city of South Portland decided to not permit the workers in their new bus system to unionize, all the bus drivers, mechanics, and other public transit employees who wanted to keep their jobs had to quit the union. As you can imagine, the formerly unionized transit workers experienced the city of South Portland's position as being extremely negative. Losing their union resulted in the loss of the power of collective bargaining.

When developing your community change effort, it is essential to begin at the most collaborative level possible and make those efforts as public as possible. Even if you suspect that your organizing efforts will need to move into the more conflictual campaign level, it is important that all parties have an understanding of the issues as a result of previous collaborative tactics. This facilitates the organizational actors being willing to return to the collaborative level after any escalation of tactics. The collaborative level is a good starting place to make your issue known to the public and to recruit more supporters through education and mild persuasion regarding a rational suggestion for change. If and when the organizational actors you are attempting to collaborate with (in this case, the city of South Portland) do not appear to be cooperative or rational, that situation can serve to strengthen your cause and help build your organization.

With appropriate notice to the media, the leadership from the MAHP and South Portland citizens with disabilities began meeting with the leadership of the city of South Portland. We explained our goal for South Portland to purchase an accessible new bus fleet. For several months, we met with many levels of decision makers in the city government, beginning with the city manager, and asked for his support and direction. We attended those meetings prepared with a great deal of data related to cost effectiveness and the gains for citizens with disabilities and the city of South Portland as a whole. We educated ourselves on the relevant technology and presented the city with information on well-run, accessible, public bus systems in cities with similar weather as the northeast. We kept the media abreast all the way, and as the story grew and tensions mounted, the media became more interested and involved. We became news, and created numerous opportunities to get our message out to the public.

Sadly, but not surprisingly, we were faced with almost solid rejection. The city officials considered our request as "out of the question." They (able-bodied administrators) touted the paratransit system that was "curb-to-curb service" (but only to medical appointments) as a much better system for "the handicapped."

Moving into Campaign-Level Strategy and Tactics

At this point, we understood we were moving into the campaign level, but still hoped and had the goal of moving back to a collaborative level in the future. We continued to meet with the city manager, the mayor, the transportation committee, and the city council.

At each meeting we organized or were invited to we continued to talk with the press and send out press releases to all the media outlets. As the meetings continued, MAHP and the city of South Portland became increasingly far apart in resolving the issue of accessible transportation. We were now firmly planted in a campaign-level strategy. The media had picked up on our Project Access campaign and we were being covered on the television news and radio and newspaper articles; in addition, we were the topic of editorials. As we moved forward with our goal of educating the community, some members of the public began thinking about these issues for the first time. We intentionally made this a public dialogue and debate.

Heading to Contest Strategy and Tactics

We were "blessed" with some very offensive and polarizing comments made at a city council meeting. The three local television stations, the newspapers, and the radio stations were recording comments made at the meeting. We had managed to get Project Access on the agenda. We filled the room with more than fifty people with disabilities who witnessed disparaging remarks made about people with disabilities in reference to our demands for accessible public transportation. The media aired these offensive comments that shocked the community and moved the public closer to our position. This resulted in increased membership, donations, letters to the editor, and individuals calling to volunteer. It was a heartwarming response that galvanized us and gave the campaign a needed push.

When disparaging comments were made at the South Portland city council meeting about people with disabilities, who were taxpayers and citizens, we realized we had clearly entered into an even more conflictual contest level strategy and tactics. The city of South Portland's legal counsel mistakenly determined we had no legal standing because South Portland did not accept any federal funds. The only federal protection in place banning discrimination against people with disabilities was a regulation in Section 504 of the Rehabilitation Act (1973) that required programs and municipalities to make their programs and services accessible to people with disabilities if they accepted federal funds. The Americans with Disabilities Act (1990) was years away from enactment.

However, the MAHP chose to use the Maine Human Rights Act (1971) because people with disabilities are included as a protected class under this legislation. We read the law and learned that people with disabilities in Maine were not to be discriminated against in places of public accommodation, on land, air, and sea. We filed a complaint with the Maine Human Rights Commission (MHRC), again using the media to keep the public informed. We won the case and were quite relieved that we were finally moving forward. However, soon after the MHRC's decision, the city of South Portland announced that it would not accept or follow this decision and if we wanted the MHRC action implemented, we would have to take the city to the Maine Superior Court. This was another unpopular decision witnessed by the community: their city refused to follow the Maine Human Right's Commission's decision.

Although we knew we were moving ahead to the next appeal level, the Maine Superior Court, our time was running out to stop the ordering of the inaccessible bus fleet. We could not get an injunction to stop the city from ordering the buses. The city proceeded to order an entire fleet of buses that were not accessible. The new bus line was scheduled to come online and be promoted to the greater Portland community on a very cold January 3, 1983. The MAHP's Project Access campaign did not want the introduction of this new fleet of inaccessible buses to receive any favorable press. On the contrary, we saw this as another opportunity to educate the public. After running this tactic by our attorney to make sure it was legal, we contacted the city of South Portland and told them we were doing a public education campaign and inquired whether they had any signage left to sell on their new buses for the first month of service. More good luck: they did have signage left to sell on all the front and backs of all the buses! We said, "Great, we will buy all that advertising for the first month of the new bus fleet." And so we did. Each new bus had on the front and the back a large sign that said, "IF YOU CAN'T WALK YOU CAN'T RIDE." Next to that slogan was a large wheelchair-accessible symbol with a red circle and line through it. The other side of the sign read, "SUPPORT ACCESS FOR ALL," "The Maine Association of Handicapped Persons," and our phone number. This was another very successful tactic, requiring the city of South Portland to advertise their discriminatory decision for the first month of its new bus fleet. It prepared the community for the upcoming Maine Superior Court case and again, educated the public and initiated people calling us to join the organization and make donations to our cause.

The MAHP took the case to the Maine Superior Court only to learn that the courthouse was not wheelchair accessible. The Maine Superior Court was in violation of Section 504 of the Rehabilitation Act because it neglected to make its programs or services accessible to people with disabilities. Nevertheless, the MAHP's case was heard in the Maine Superior Courthouse. More than thirty people who were mobility impaired, including our attorney, were carried into the courthouse daily to watch or engage in the court proceedings. While our Superior Court case was proceeding, the MAHP filed and won a complaint against the U.S. Department of Justice for the Maine Superior Courthouse not being accessible to people with disabilities. This victory resulted in a consent decree that required every courthouse in Maine to become wheelchair accessible. This was big news, and the media covered it extensively, attracting even more people to join our Project Access campaign.

The Maine Superior Court decided in favor of the MAHP. We won our case against the city of South Portland. We were ecstatic, only to learn that the city of South Portland decided almost immediately to appeal the case to the Maine Supreme Court, which still was not accessible. Given that the Department of Justice complaint was in place, the Maine Supreme Court moved its proceedings to Portland City Hall Council Chambers, an accessible location. This was apparently the first and only time the Maine Supreme Court moved its venue to address a legal case. The proceedings lasted five days. At this point, our Project Access campaign had grown into a major, ongoing news story that was well covered by the media.

The Maine Supreme Court decided on behalf of the MAHP and ordered the city of South Portland to retrofit its entire new bus fleet and wrote into the judgment a requirement for the city of South Portland to use the MAHP as trainers for the bus drivers and new riders. This clause in the judgment was critical: since the MAHP had done its homework, we had learned of communities with similar resistance that knowingly purchased equipment that would not hold up and failed to provide much in the way of training for drivers and riders. Of course these systems failed and the ridership of people with disabilities in these communities was minimal.

Outcomes

The transit system became our ally, which resulted in securing the best equipment on the market, providing well-organized training events for new riders and well-trained drivers who were sincerely invested in providing quality accessible public transportation. I believe this occurred largely because we invited the transit union and nonunion personnel to join our Project Access campaign from the very beginning of our grassroots activities. This resulted in a heavily used accessible public transportation system with no accidents. This system has been in place for almost twenty-five years. The MAHP's work resulted in the following gains:

- This effort changed the lives of thousands of people with disabilities who now have access to education, social lives, employment, volunteering, and a degree of spontaneity in their lives.
- We moved forward in changing the perception of people with disabilities within the disabled community. Through increased interaction and exposure, the public perception has also improved.
- We increased the membership of the MAHP statewide disability rights organization.
- We played a significant role in a social movement, challenged the public's perception of people with disabilities, and secured equal access to public transportation for people with disabilities in Maine.

THEORIES AND PRINCIPLES

Let's review the theoretical underpinnings and principles that directed this organizing effort. The principle of parsimony was a very important theoretical underpinning of this community change effort. Parsimony is often referred to as the principle of least contest. According to Brager and Holloway (1978), "The principle of parsimony is most important when the practitioner requires a third party support for his change effort. He must appear reasonable and responsible to that party, or at least be able to present an effective public case to explain whatever 'unreasonableness' is required. 'Jumping the process'—that is, violating the protocol that prescribes that mild actions precede extreme ones—can endanger a good cause" (p. 141).

I believe our awareness and skillful use of this principle was vital to the success of this community change effort. We understood it was essential to involve the public. The principle of least contest served our community change effort well in regards to educating and winning the support of the community to make public transportation accessible to all community members.

Our community change effort was modeled after Saul Alinsky's teachings about direct action organizing. The Midwest Academy succinctly spells out the fundamental elements of direct action organizing as follows: "The essence of Direct Action Organizing is that it focuses on building organizations to be sustainable and be around for the long-haul. This is done by focusing on the power of individuals to improve their own lives and act collectively to win victories for themselves and their communities by altering the relations of power" (Discover the Networks, 2010). Furthermore, principles of this approach encompass the following:

- Alter the relations of power between people, the government, and other institutions by building strong permanent local, state, national and international organizations;
- Win concrete improvements in people's lives;
- Make people aware of their own power (by winning victories). (Habitat International Coalition, 2011, paras. 3–5)

As a social worker, working in the role of community organizer, it was incredibly powerful to see, feel, and be a part of building an organization, witnessing how collective empowerment works, and witnessing the lives of individual people with disabilities evolve with hope for their future. These people had never considered themselves to have the opportunity to be independent, able to move freely about the community, get an education, become employed, enjoy some spontaneity in their lives, and become full participating community members.

It is important to keep in mind that the assessment, strategy, tactic development, and implementation in this community change effort was community based; however, all of these interventions are easily transferable to making changes within organizations. Organizational change is almost always necessary when we think critically and discover ways to improve or increase resources and services.

As outlined in our professional code of ethics, social workers have an ethical responsibility to the broader society. We are required to engage in social and political action to ensure that all people have equal access to the resources, employment, services, and opportunities to meet our clients' basic human needs to develop fully. We are required to promote the general welfare of society from local to global levels and to promote the development of people, their communities, and their environments. We are required to facilitate informed participation by the public in shaping social policies and institutions (paraphrased from Standard 6 of the *Code of Ethics of the National Association of Social Workers,* Social Workers' Ethical Responsibilities to the Broader Society, Section 6.04 P.26, 27, National Association of Social Workers [NASW], 2008).

CONCLUSION

I conclude this chapter with an excerpt from Saul Alinsky's *Rules For Radicals* (1971), in which he discussed the ideal elements of an organizer: "Curiosity, irreverence, imagination, sense of humor, a free and open mind, an acceptance of the relativity of values and of the uncertainty of life, all inevitably fuse into the kind of person whose greatest joy is creation. The organizer . . . finds his/her goal in creation of power for others to use" (pp. 79–80).

Community organizing is a social work role, yet Alinsky's discussion of the ideal elements of an organizer also describes the ideal elements of a social worker regardless of role. When I think about all the roles we play as social workers, I realize we need to have a compulsive curiosity that knows no limits and in some circumstances combine this with irreverence. We use imagination: imagination is the inevitable partner of irreverence and curiosity. We must maintain a good sense of humor and a free and open mind. Social workers must have confidence in their ability to do what they believe must be done. Finally, I think social workers would agree that we are constantly creating the new out of the old.

I hope the principles in this chapter will resonate with you and empower you to acknowledge the elements of the ideal social worker and community organizer.

DISCUSSION QUESTIONS

1. How do the tactics used in this case support the principles of direct action organizing?
2. What are the levels of practice, from micro to macro, as well as some of the accompanying unanticipated gains?
3. What are two possible additional tactics at the collaborative, campaign, and contest levels that incorporate the principles of direct action organizing?

REFERENCES

Alinsky, S. (1971). *Rules for radicals: A pragmatic primer for realistic radicals*. New York: Vintage.

Americans with Disabilities Act. P. L. 101-336. (1990). http://www2.ed.gov/about/offices/list/ocr/docs/hq9805.html

Brager, G., & Holloway, S. (1978). *Changing human service organizations: Politics and practice*. New York: Free Press.

Discover the Networks. (2010). Heather Booth. Retrieved from http://www.discoverthenetworks.org/printindividualProfile.asp?indid=1641

Habitat International Coalition. (2011). Organizing: Fundamental principles of direct action organizing. Retrieved from http://www.hic-net.org/articles.php?pid=2161

Maine Human Rights Act. c. 501, §1. (1971). http://www.mainelegislature.org/legis/statutes/5/title5sec4551.html

National Association of Social Workers (NASW). (2008). *Code of ethics of the NASW*. Washington, DC: Author.

Rehabilitation Act. P. L. 93–112, 87, Stat. 355. (1973). http://www2.ed.gov/policy/speced/reg/narrative.html

11

Overcoming Organizational Obstacles to Forming Empowerment Groups

A Consumer Advisory Board for Homeless Clients

Marcia B. Cohen

INTRODUCTION

The term "empowerment" is currently in vogue in social work, indicating a renewed interest in practice approaches that seek to increase client control over the social and organizational environment. Although the term may be relatively new, the goal of client empowerment is steeped in the social work tradition, particularly in the origins of social group work. Toseland and Rivas (1984) contrasted the diagnosis and treatment focus of the Charity Organization Societies with the focus of the settlement houses, which "offered groups as an opportunity for citizens to join together to share their views, to gain mutual support, and to exercise the power derived from their association for social change" (p. 40). Group work, as practiced by the settlement house workers, emphasized the use of groups to promote education, peer group association, and community change.

In the 1930s, 1940s, and 1950s, as group work was influenced by the professionalization movement in social work, interest gradually shifted to more remedial and psychotherapeutic group approaches (Brown, 1991; Toseland & Rivas, 1984). As group services began to be offered in more clinically oriented settings, the influence of psychoanalytic theory on group practice became stronger. Increasingly, group work was focused on diagnosis and treatment more than on education, socialization, and social change (Alissi, 1980).

The pendulum swung back again during the turbulent decade of the 1960s, when social work rediscovered its historic link to social reform (Fisher, 1987). Group work educators such as Papell and Rothman (1966) and Wiener (1964) articulated and refined the social goals model of group work that emphasized participatory democracy, cultural diversity, and social change. The 1960s also saw the emergence of the social action model of community organization practice. Although it differed in methodology and the size of the target systems, community organization's social action model and group work's social goals model both emphasized the redistribution of power to disenfranchised community or group members.

Since the 1960s, the social change perspective in social work has largely been overshadowed by remedial approaches emphasizing pathology and individual change. Whereas the mutual aid focus of group work's reciprocal model (Gitterman & Shulman, 1986; Schwartz, 1961) represents a departure from this trend, its primary emphasis is on interpersonal growth rather than on social change.

Practitioners working with oppressed client groups have recently begun to develop empowerment-oriented practice approaches that emphasize the shifting of power and resources to consumers of services (Breton, 1988; Cohen, 1989; Cox, 1988; Parsons, 1988; Solomon, 1985). The groups described by these authors represent creative extensions of the reciprocal model in which increased power and control, along with mutual aid, are primary goals. The empowerment intervention strategies used by these groups were described by Cox (1988) as those methodological approaches that mobilize consumers of services, their families, and their communities toward (a) self-care and (b) authentic involvement in the creation of a better environment. The transfer to clients of knowledge and skills necessary for accomplishing these tasks through the use of group work strategies is an essential component of such interventions (Cox, 1988).

Cox (1988) stressed the importance of the "personal as political" and viewed the focus of group activity as covering a continuum from private issues to public troubles (Schwartz, 1974). From this perspective, a social action group can enhance the physical and mental health of individual participants, and a group focused on self-care can evolve into a potent force for social change (Cohen, 1988; Cox & Longres, 1981).

The literature reflects a growing interest in empowerment-oriented groups for homeless clients (Berman-Rossi & Cohen, 1988; Breton, 1988; Glasser & Suroviak, 1988; Lee, 1986). The groups described by these authors are rich and varied: a dinner preparation group in a transitional residence, a health issues group in a women's drop-in center, an activities group in a women's shelter, and an educational group in a soup kitchen. These groups span the private troubles–public issues continuum, but all integrate some elements of self-care, self-help, mutual aid, and social change. As Breton (1988) pointed out, "It may be that if group workers ally themselves to oppressed populations, they will simply have to abandon the luxury of forever dichotomizing between 'social action groups' and other types of groups. All their work will have to involve a struggle for a more just society, and in their work, they will need to apply the skills of 'social action group work.' Furthermore, the struggle for a more just society cannot take place exclusively within the confines of the small group—it must transcend it and involve action in and on the environing social system" (p. 59).

Further development is needed of empowerment-oriented group approaches that transcend the dichotomy between individual and social change. Issues of group formation will require particular attention because groups that seek to intervene in the distribution of power are likely to encounter daunting organizational barriers.

This chapter discusses efforts to develop an empowerment-oriented consumer advisory board (CAB) in a New England agency serving homeless and low-income clients. The social services component of the agency provides information, referral, housing assistance, case management, and support group services under the direction of a casework supervisor. A breakfast soup kitchen is staffed by volunteers and supervised by the executive director. The objective of the CAB was to increase the influence of clients in agency and community decision making. This chapter analyzes obstacles to group formation, and explores strategies for overcoming organizational resistance to social action–oriented empowerment groups.

FORMATION OF A CONSUMER ADVISORY BOARD

The CAB was initiated several years ago when members of the agency's program committee identified a need for consumers to have a voice in formulating agency policy. A related goal was to provide clients with opportunities to develop organizational change skills including issue identification, priority setting, strategy formulation, and negotiation. Although social action–oriented goals were primary, there was an expectation that the CAB would promote mutual aid among its members.

The program committee (that was appointed by the board of directors) comprised agency social workers and board members, several of whom were social work faculty at local universities. Two of the social work faculty members proposed the CAB. They both had been involved with the agency for several years, had expertise in the field of homelessness, and had conducted an extensive research project involving agency clients. The CAB proposal came from individuals who were well respected in the agency. The educators saw the CAB as a logical extension of the agency's commitment to client empowerment, as articulated in its mission statement.

Staff members on the program committee agreed with the CAB concept but voiced fears about stirring up client anger at the agency. When the CAB proponents attempted to reassure staff that anger would more likely be directed at city officials and landlords than at the agency, staff expressed concern about the possibility of jeopardizing the agency's relationships with these external systems. Despite the misgivings, the program committee unanimously approved the CAB, and the board of directors gave its formal sanction.

The program committee held a series of planning meetings, and the group formation process began. Although the committee retained the overall responsibility for implementing the group, it selected two group facilitators: one of the faculty members who proposed the CAB, and an undergraduate social work student doing her field placement at the agency.

Staff and students approached clients and invited them to a preliminary meeting to discuss the CAB. Signs giving the date and time of the meeting were prominently displayed. Eleven consumers attended the preliminary meeting, along with the two group facilitators and several staff members. One of the group facilitators made an opening statement clarifying group purpose: "Most poor and homeless people have little power or control over many aspects of their lives, including the services they receive. This agency wants to develop a consumer advisory board in order to make sure your voices are heard. . . . The CAB would consist of representatives of agency consumers, people who come here for breakfast or for help with social services. The purpose of the CAB would be for consumers to be able to comment on agency services, recommend new services and programs that might be offered here, and identify issues of concern to homeless and poor people in this city" (from personal notes kept by facilitator).

The group facilitators group members to identify some of the issues they would like to see the CAB address. Consumers responded enthusiastically by raising a number of problems within the agency and suggesting a variety of solutions.

Staff discomfort with this process soon became evident. When several group members raised the problem of overcrowding in the agency reception area, one staff member became visibly annoyed. She stated that there was no point in discussing this matter because nothing could be done about it. Group members raised several other issues, ranging from a request for more fresh fruit at breakfast to the growing difficulties in obtaining housing assistance from the city. The group facilitators indicated that these were just the kind of issues that the CAB, once formed, would be able to address. They further stated that although they could not promise that every change suggested would be made, everything brought up in the CAB would at least be heard.

The group facilitators invited group members to a second preliminary meeting several weeks later and to attend the first CAB membership meeting the following month. The group facilitators ended the meeting by reiterating the importance of the CAB as a vehicle for client input into decision making. Several group members indicated an interest in serving on the CAB, but others expressed frustration that the meeting had been "all talk and no action."

One of the group facilitators recorded the following observations after this meeting: "The meeting was well attended, eleven members. It was a good group, very diverse in terms of age and gender and very verbal. The group raised a lot of important issues and made some creative suggestions. Sara seemed very threatened by the discussion, however. Sara seemed particularly defensive. Maybe the agency isn't really ready for client input. I think we ended up giving clients a very mixed message, 'we want to organize a CAB to give you a voice but we don't really want to hear what you have to say'" (from personal notes kept by facilitator).

The second preliminary meeting was attended by six consumers and was similar to the first in terms of issues raised and staff response. The third meeting had only two consumers in attendance. The group facilitator recorded the following comments after the third meeting: "Only Gina and Billy came to today's meeting, which was supposed to be the first CAB member meeting. It was very disappointing. Several others said they would come but they haven't been around for a few days and may have forgotten. I'm also not sure if staff reminded everyone although Cora did put up some signs" (from personal notes kept by facilitator). The agency cancelled the fourth scheduled meeting, and put the group on hold until after the summer because of the apparent lack of interest. This decision, made in March, surprised the group facilitators and the consumers.

Developing a group with the explicit goal of increasing client influence initially seemed a fairly simple task in view of the agency's philosophical orientation. In practice, however, it proved quite difficult. It is one thing for an agency to be deeply committed to the abstract goal of client empowerment and quite another for agency staff to actively support the formation of a group that seeks to shift power to clients and, by implication, away from themselves. Even fostering the empowerment of clients in relationship to community resource systems felt problematic to staff who had worked hard to develop amicable relationships with these external systems.

ORGANIZATIONAL RESISTANCE

What went wrong? It appears that organizational resistance severely hampered efforts to organize the CAB. Although the group's purpose was firmly rooted in the agency's mission and formal agency sanction was readily forthcoming, staff never really embraced the CAB concept. Satisfied with the agency's overt endorsement, proponents of the CAB failed to reach out and address underlying fears about the group. Shulman (1984) cautioned, "A common mistake is for a worker to decide on the need for a group and then to set about 'selling' colleagues on the idea. Rather than presenting their own views on the need for it and inviting feedback and discussion, workers may set about trying to influence their colleagues, creating the illusion that they are involving others in the process" (p. 179).

The faculty members, in proposing the CAB, would have done well to heed Shulman's warning. They needed to tune into staff concerns about the CAB and to reach for negative feelings while fully involving staff in the planning effort. The staff envisioned the CAB as a militant group that might bring the wrath of powerful community leaders down on the agency. The faculty members made it clear that they viewed these fears as groundless, but staff knew that they would have to pick up the pieces if the professors were wrong. An honest discussion of the potential pitfalls and potential gains of an activist client group might have enabled agency personnel to join with the faculty members in a more wholehearted endorsement of the CAB. This process would have modeled an ability to elicit and respond to negative reactions, a skill that staff would need in their subsequent interactions with potential CAB members.

The CAB proponents, overly confident about the outcome of their efforts, did not conduct an organizational analysis (Northen, 1988). In particular, they failed to assess the potential effect of the agency's lack of experience with groups as well as its limited resources in staff time, funds, and space. In the absence of an organizational analysis and without full staff involvement in the planning process, genuine agency sanction remained elusive. That social work educators knowledgeable about the principles of group formation skipped this crucial step speaks to the dangers of overconfidence.

A parallel process was evident. The faculty members on the program committee asked for input from staff in planning the CAB but failed to really hear and respond to staff concerns. Staff members at the CAB meetings acknowledged the goal of increasing client input but were unable to hear what clients had to say. Staff members' difficulty hearing the clients seemed to stem from their fear of criticism directed at the agency. The faculty members were similarly uncomfortable with criticism of their CAB proposal. They expected the staff's philosophical adherence to the goal of empowerment to override the staff's fears.

A COMMUNITY ORGANIZING PERSPECTIVE ON RECRUITMENT

Failure to obtain full agency sanction was not the only barrier to the formation of the CAB, however. The nature of the client group to be recruited posed additional obstacles to the organizing process. Members of a low-income client population living a precarious day-to-day existence in shelters, on the street, doubled up with friends, or in furnished rooms find it difficult to plan to attend a meeting. Scheduling CAB meetings several weeks apart may have had the effect of reducing momentum and limiting attendance.

Although posting signs and announcing the CAB meetings were appropriate recruitment tactics, additional organizing strategies were needed. Staff compiled a list of potential recruits for the CAB, but no one had clear responsibility for contacting specific individuals, and there was little follow-up. Moreover, because client attendance at the agency was often sporadic, locating the organizing efforts solely on site meant that some potential recruits were not informed about meetings. To be effective with this client population, outreach efforts needed to be better planned and more systematic.

Kurland's (1978) planning model outlines a systematic approach to recruitment in which the following questions are addressed: Who will take responsibility for pregroup contact? When will contact occur? Where will the group be located? How will group members be prepared for the first meeting? In the CAB example, these questions would have generated a plan in which specific individuals were responsible for pregroup contacts with clients to maximize consumer awareness of upcoming CAB meetings. Kurland's planning model dovetails well with a grassroots community-organizing approach (Cohen, 1988; Haggstrom, 1987; Staples, 1984). Consumer boards are central to the tradition of community organizing, and reflective of social group work history (Brown, 1991; Burke, 1983).

Ideally, efforts to recruit CAB members would have included going to the shelters, rooming houses, and other locales frequented by members of the local homeless community. Because this homeless population is a well-developed community group with strong social networks and distinct social cliques (Cohen & Wagner, 1992), an effective organizing strategy should have included identifying and reaching out to indigenous leaders in each of the homeless community's subgroups and mobilizing these individuals to promote participation in the CAB (Alinsky, 1971; Sherry & Lipschultz, 1984; Staples, 1984).

The community organizing literature also suggests that recruits be involved in events that will provide them with tangible successful outcomes (Sherry & Lipschultz, 1984; Staples, 1984). Although a strategy of beginning with small, preliminary meetings and building up to a larger, general meeting can be effective (Sherry & Lipschultz, 1984), organizing events are far more likely to be successful if they offer immediate, concrete gains (Alinsky, 1971). If early CAB meetings had resulted in fresh fruit at breakfast or an invitation to consumers to discuss overcrowding with the program committee, attendance at subsequent meetings might have increased. In the absence of any such tangible outcomes, participants had reason to believe that the proposed CAB would indeed be all talk and no action.

ORGANIZATIONAL CHANGE ANALYSIS

Could the CAB proponents have anticipated some of the organizational obstacles encountered and been better prepared to overcome them? The literature on organizational change, an important part of the social work knowledge base, suggests that the answer is "yes."

The agency discussed in this article was small, with staff drawn almost exclusively from the social work discipline. It operated with few codified rules and an informal and relatively flat decision-making structure. Using the terminology of the organizational change literature, this agency structure was one of low complexity, low formalization, and low centralization (Brager & Holloway, 1978; Germain & Gitterman, 1980).

Brager and Holloway (1978) suggested that receptivity to organizational change is maximized when organizational structures are characterized by high complexity, low formalization, and low centralization. The agency in the case example meets two of these criteria, suggesting that change can be effected in this setting but might require the employment of indirect influence. Germain and Gitterman (1980) referred to the simultaneous existence of strong support and strong opposition to a proposed change effort as a "blinking red and yellow light," in which outcome cannot be predicted and a low-key approach is indicated.

Further information on staff composition is necessary for a comprehensive organizational analysis. Although the agency is the region's primary provider of services to the homeless population and serves a large client population, it operates with few paid staff. The four paid positions are executive director, casework supervisor, case manager, and dayroom aide. During the school year, six bachelor of social work and two master of social work student interns function as integral members of the social services staff.

During the period in which the group facilitators attempted to organize the CAB, the executive director position was vacant. The position remained unfilled for five months, creating considerable duress for a staff that was already stretched quite thin. The casework supervisor assumed many of the director's responsibilities during this period in addition to her own supervisory and direct practice roles. Had an executive director been in place, he or she would have been in an optimum position to provide needed leadership for the CAB. As it was, the casework supervisor, who might have supported the CAB under different circumstances, was stressed and overloaded.

FORCE FIELD ANALYSIS

A force field analysis (Brager & Holloway, 1978; Lewin, 1951) reveals several forces restraining the CAB initiative. The CAB, which would inevitably create additional work, was proposed at a time when the agency was severely short staffed. Moreover, individuals who, though well respected by staff, were peripheral to the organizational system made the proposal. The CAB proposal also raised the specter of client anger at a time when staff felt particularly overburdened.

Another restraining force was that neither of the two group facilitators was fully within the agency system. One was a student, a relatively low-power actor who was at the agency only two days a week. The other was a faculty member who was infrequently on site. Organizing efforts were inevitably relegated to staff who had neither the time nor the energy to devote to them and for whom the CAB was not a priority.

A final restraining force was the fear, expressed by staff, that client empowerment within the larger community would "get the agency into trouble." Brager and Holloway (1978) pointed out the importance of assessing economic and political forces that can restrain or propel a change effort. This agency had multiple funding sources, including local grants. Agency staff feared that municipal funding might be threatened if local officials came under attack by the CAB.

Driving forces for the CAB initiative included the strong client service ideology of the agency and its explicit commitment to the empowerment of homeless people as articulated in its mission statement. Another driving force was the influential position of the faculty members in relation to staff, most of whom were their former students. This, combined with their membership on the board of directors, afforded the faculty members considerable legitimacy. A third driving force was the diverse nature of the agency's funding. To the extent that municipal funding might have been jeopardized by an activist CAB, the existence of multiple funding streams would have protected the agency from serious economic sanctions by the city government.

INTERVENTION TACTICS

Brager and Holloway (1978) and Patti and Resnick (1972) described a continuum of interventive modes or tactics in organizational change. These tactics range from those characterized by cooperation to those entailing conflict. The three primary interventive modes are collaborative tactics (cooperative), campaign tactics, and contest tactics (conflictual). The basic criterion in selecting a change tactic is the degree of commonality of or divergence between the goals of the change agent and those of the change actor. Where many of the goals are commonly shared, collaborative tactics are generally the most appropriate.

The agency staff in this example ascribed to the goals of client empowerment and client service embodied by the CAB. Although they may have been ambivalent about the operationalizing of these goals, particularly at a time of acute stress in the organization, this perception of goal commonality was the most important factor guiding choice of tactics (Brager & Holloway, 1978). In the CAB situation, the perception was one of common adherences to empowerment goals and a client service ideology. A collaborative approach to this organizational change effort, which would depend on securing the active support of the casework supervisor, was indicated. If collaborative tactics had proved unsuccessful, a campaign approach, in which consumer demand for a CAB was generated, would have been a logical next step.

GROUP FORMATION STRATEGY

The strategy implied by this organizational change analysis can be readily synthesized with the approach suggested by the group work and community organization literature. The author of this chapter formulated an eight-step group formation strategy based on the preceding analysis:

1. The CAB organizing effort was planned so that it did not coincide with the temporary vacancy in the executive director position.
2. Organizational resistance was identified and fully addressed.
3. Staff were actively involved in the process of group planning under the leadership of the executive director.
4. Sufficient staff and students were assigned to the CAB project so that intensive outreach efforts could be sustained.
5. At least one group facilitator was a full-time staff member.
6. Indigenous leaders in the client community were involved in recruitment efforts.
7. Initial CAB meetings resulted in concrete gains for consumers.
8. The particular characteristics of the client group were considered in determining the temporal aspects of group meetings.

This group formation strategy depended heavily on obtaining genuine agency sanction. Because client organizing is a labor-intensive process requiring deployment of agency resources, organizational support must be more than tacit. Although this group formation strategy would take longer to implement, it was far more likely to be effective than the approach that was actually taken.

CONCLUSION

The worsening social problems of the 1980s and 1990s point to a need for empowerment group models that emphasize social change. CABs and similar vehicles for increasing client power in human service organizations represent one such model. The notion of consumer participation in agencies serving low-income clientele is hardly new. It does, however, need to be revived and refined. Groups aimed at increasing client power are likely to encounter organizational resistance, particularly when clients are members of a stigmatized group. Creative approaches drawn from a range of social work methods are needed to overcome organizational obstacles to social action–oriented empowerment groups.

This examination of an unsuccessful attempt to organize a CAB points to a group formation strategy that incorporates practice knowledge from the literature on group work, community organization, and organizational change. Although this strategy will not be applicable to all empowerment groups or all agency settings, the approach to strategy formulation through an integration of knowledge from different traditions within social work should be useful in many contexts.

The challenges facing social workers in the twenty-first century will be considerable. Social workers will not be able to meet them if they continue to compartmentalize knowledge. By building on practice wisdom from previous generations and from different segments within the profession, social work practitioners can continue to expand their knowledge base and prepare themselves for the future. Empowerment-oriented group approaches that integrate mutual aid and social action represent an important direction in social work knowledge building.

POSTSCRIPT

A year after the fledgling CAB was put on hold, a group consisting of the author and several staff members successfully organized a consumer-directed action group at the agency. They carefully followed the eight-step group formation strategy, and avoided the pitfalls encountered in the original organizing effort. Although the group has chosen not to call itself a CAB, its goals and activities are very similar to those originally envisioned (Cohen, 1994).

DISCUSSION QUESTIONS

1. What were the major errors made by the change agents in this case example?
2. This chapter's conclusion suggests that integrated practice wisdom drawn from the group work, community organization, and organizational change practice literatures is necessary to overcoming organizational obstacles to social action–oriented empowerment groups. What are some of the advantages of this type of integrated, multitiered approach?
3. According to the postscript, a year after the events described in this chapter occurred a consumer-directed action group was successfully organized at the agency. How do you account for this successful outcome, in view of the earlier difficulties encountered by the change agents?

REFERENCES

Alinsky, S. (1971). *Rules for radicals*. New York: Random House.

Alissi, A. (1980). Social group work: Commitments and perspectives. In A. Alissi (Ed.), *Perspectives on social group work practice* (pp. 5–29). New York: Free Press.

Berman-Rossi, I., & Cohen, M. (1988). Group development and shared decision-making: Working with homeless mentally ill women. *Social Work with Groups, 11*(4), 63–78.

Brager, G., & Holloway, S. (1978). *Changing human service organizations: Politics and practice*. New York: Free Press.

Breton, M. (1988). The need for mutual aid groups in a drop-in for homeless women: The Sistering case. *Social Work with Groups, 11*(4), 47–61.

Brown, L. (1991). *Groups for growth and change*. New York: Longman.

Burke, E. (1983). Citizen participation: Characteristics and strategies. In R. M. Kramer & H. Specht (Eds.), *Readings in community organization practice* (pp. 105–127). Englewood Cliffs, NJ: Prentice Hall.

Cohen, M. (1988). Tenant organizing with mentally ill, formerly homeless women. *Catalyst: A Socialist Journal of the Social Services, 6*(2), 33–37.

Cohen, M. (1989). Social work practice with homeless mentally ill people: Engaging the client. *Social Work, 34*, 505–509.

Cohen, M. (1994). Who wants to chair the meeting? Group development and leadership patterns in a community action group of homeless people. *Social Work with Groups, 17*(1/2), 81–87.

Cohen, M., & Wagner, D. (1992). Acting on their own behalf: Affiliation and political mobilization among homeless people. *Journal of Sociology and Social Welfare, 19*(4), 21–40.

Cox, E. (1988). Empowerment of the low-income elderly through group work. *Social Work with Groups, 11*(4), 111–125.

Cox, E., & Longres, J. (1981, March). Critical practice—curriculum implications. Paper presented at the Annual Program Meeting of the Council on Social Work Education, Louisville, KY.

Fisher, R. (1987). Community organizing in historical perspective: A topology. In F. Cox, J. Erlich, & J. Tropman (Eds.), *Strategies of community organizing* (pp. 398–404). Itasca, IL: F. E. Peacock.

Germain, C., & Gitterman, A. (1980). *The life model of social work practice*. New York: Columbia University Press.

Gitterman, A., & Shulman, L. (1986). *Mutual aid groups and the life cycle*. Itasca, IL: F. E. Peacock.

Glasser, I., & Suroviak, J. (1988). Social group work in a soup kitchen: Mobilizing the strengths of the guests. *Social Work with Groups, 11*(4), 95–109.

Haggstrom, W. (1987). The tactics of organization building. In F. Cox, J. Erlich, & J. Tropman (Eds.), *Strategies of community organizing* (pp. 405–422). Itasca, IL: F. E. Peacock.

Kurland, R. (1978). Planning: The neglected component of group development, *Social Work with Groups, 1*(2), 173–178.

Lee, J. (1986). No place to go: Homeless women. In A. Gitterman & L. Shulman (Eds.), *Mutual aid groups and the life cycle* (pp. 245–263). Itasca, IL: F. E. Peacock.

Lewin, K. (1951). *Field theory in social science.* New York: Harper & Row.

Northen, H. (1988). *Social work with groups.* New York: Columbia University Press.

Papell, C., & Rothman, B. (1966). Social group work models: Possession and heritage. *Education for Social Work, 2*(2).

Parsons, R. (1988). Empowerment for role alternatives for low-income minority girls: A group work approach. *Social Work with Groups, 11*(4), 27–45.

Patti, R., & Resnick, H. (1972). Changing the agency from within. *Social Work, 17,* 48–57.

Schwartz, W. (1961). The social worker in the group. In W. Schwartz (Ed.), *The social welfare forum.* New York: Columbia University Press.

Schwartz, W. (1974). Private troubles and public issues: One social work job or two? In R. Klenck & R. Ryan (Eds.), *The practice of social work* (pp. 82–101). Belmont, CA: Wadsworth.

Sherry, S., & Lipschultz, C. (1984). Consumer education as community activator. In F. Cox, J. Erlich, J. Rothman, & J. Tropman (Eds.), *Tactics and techniques of community practice* (pp. 209–222). Itasca, IL: F.E. Peacock.

Shulman, L. (1984). *The skills of helping individuals and groups.* Itasca, IL: F. E. Peacock.

Solomon, B. (1985). How do we really empower families? New strategies for social work practitioners. *Family Resource Coalition, 3,* 2–3.

Staples, L. (1984). *Roots to power: A manual for grassroots organizing.* New York: Praeger.

Toseland, R., & Rivas, R. (1984). *An introduction to group work practice.* New York: Macmillan.

Wiener, H. (1964). Social change and social group work practice. *Social Work, 9,* 106–112.

Part III

The Student as Change Agent

The three chapters that comprise part III are based on organizational change papers written by foundation year practice students in an MSW program in response to a course assignment (Cohen, 2013). The assignment is presented here as a resource for students and educators.

ORGANIZATIONAL CHANGE ASSIGNMENT

Students will identify an organizational problem in their field settings. Students will propose an organizational change project to address this problem and develop an appropriate change strategy. Although implementation of the change effort is not required, students are strongly encouraged to attempt implementation where feasible. At a minimum, students should undertake some preliminary steps toward the change goal (data collection, force field analysis, and strategy planning).

The change focus should be on unmet or inadequately met client needs. These might include inaccessibility in agency location, hours of service, or physical environment, lack of responsiveness to the needs of oppressed client populations, lack of sensitivity to issues of cultural diversity, and lack of client self-determination within organizational practices. The proposed change should be one in which some organizational resistance can be anticipated. The following outline should provide some guidance.

1. Description of the organizational context, including its formal and informal structure and agency culture.

2. Identification of the organizational problem or issue to be addressed. Be specific and include the information that led you to identify this particular problem. What indications do you have that others (clients, coworkers) share your perception of the situation? What additional information will you need to collect to determine the feasibility of your change goal?

3. Discussion of data collection. What data have you been able to collect? Be specific regarding what research you have done, whom you have spoken to, and how people reacted. Do you have enough data to develop a change strategy? What information still needs to be gathered and how will you obtain it?

4. Assess the organizational environment using a force field analysis. Identify the critical and facilitating actors and any allies you may have developed to support your change effort. Discuss the driving and restraining forces in your organizational environment, including which are working forces, which are framing forces, and which are unpredictable. On what criteria do you base this categorization?

5. Determine appropriate strategy and tactics. Based on the data collected, the degree of issue consensus and parity of power, and your force field analysis, would you select a collaboration, campaign, or contest strategy, or some combination of these? What criteria led you to choose that particular strategy? How does the principle of least contest fit with this decision? What specific tactics might you employ and why? How much resistance did you or would you anticipate, and from whom? Have you been able to implement your change goal? If not, do you think you may have planted a seed for future change?

The three chapters that follow encompass organizational change efforts in various stages of completion. They include the following settings: a middle school where bullying was identified as a problem, a homeless resource center where steps were undertaken to assist clients in obtaining housing, and a multicultural center where the need for language-appropriate materials to be used within the school setting was identified. These chapters reflect many of the concepts discussed in part I, in particular, empowerment, advocacy, and community. The chapters are presented here to be useful to students and educators as they explore the processes and complexities of bringing about organizational change as low-power actors.

REFERENCE

Cohen, M. B. (2013). Syllabus. Social Work Practice II. University of New England School of Social Work, Portland, ME.

12

Bullying

Organizational Change in a Middle School

Jeremy Brown

INTRODUCTION

This chapter focuses on my efforts to create a clear and consistent intervention program for bullying and other forms of harassment at Somerset Middle School (SMS), where I completed my internship as a social work master's student. There are more than eight hundred children at the school, which serves grades six through eight. Though there is little ethnic diversity at SMS, as is also the case in the region, there is clearly a broad range of abilities, both academic and social.

I worked in the Student Advocacy office at SMS with two other social workers and three guidance counselors. We served and advocated for all students in the school, although the majority of the students we worked with either had learning disabilities or difficulties with social interaction in school.

The formal structure of the school is a hierarchy, with all of the lead teachers reporting to the principal and assistant principal. The Student Advocacy office also reported to the special education director who is above the principal, organizationally. Interestingly, there was no formal description regarding the relationship between the teachers and the social workers and guidance counselors, because they are part of separate organizational systems. The power structure of the school positioned the social workers and guidance counselors under the teachers and the administration. This was evidenced by the lack of cooperation granted to SMS's social workers and guidance counselors when confronting issues involving students. In these situations, the social workers generally acquiesced. However, the teachers often deferred to the social workers when they could not handle the students.

The culture of SMS in general was that of an educational institution designed to foster learning and, to a lesser extent, to encourage civic responsibility. It is located in a relatively affluent town, which affects the school culture. The financial disparity among SMS students is fairly obvious, as manifested by differences in physical appearance and material posses-sions. As is common in our culture, social class was rarely discussed at SMS.

In terms of student behavior, there were a couple of points of interest. First, it appeared that few teachers were trained to perceive and respond to student behaviors as an adaptation of systemic dysfunction in their lives at school and in their homes. I spoke with a graduate of the local university's education program who confirmed that this particular program provided no training for prospective teachers regarding this kind of student behavior. Consequently, teachers seldom, in my judgment, knew how to understand problematic behaviors as indicators for sensitive and systemic attention.

Another aspect of the SMS culture were the relationships between the teachers and administration, and between the parents and guardians. In a sense, the informal structure of the school included the parents and guardians, who could wield informal power within the school. Parents and guardians were capable of demanding or refusing services that students needed. Furthermore, when a child experienced social or other difficulties at SMS, parents could and did threaten the administrators into taking imme-diate action to rectify the matter.

THE PROBLEM FOR CHANGE

During the fall semester, a parent brought to my attention the behavior of a male student I worked with; he had been bullying a girl in his class. Although I had yet to spend a lot of time with this boy, I had experienced him as gen-tle and kind; he was on the autism spectrum, and was a little "quirky" in a way that I found endearing. When I questioned this boy about what was going on, he not only admitted to teasing this female student, but also exclaimed that he could no longer tolerate being the victim of bullying him-self. I had suspected this might be the case. He and I talked about how he wanted me to handle the situation without his name being used and I sug-gested that I speak with some of his teachers about what was going on with the two other male students in his class who were bullying him.

Later that day at a team meeting with his teachers, I mentioned this stu-dent's concerns and requested that I speak with his teachers about the stu-dents who were bullying him. In response, the lead teacher stated that she would have to take this matter to the principal to deal with. When I spoke up about the concerns of the student and his request for how the situation would be handled, the lead teacher asserted that taking the matter to the principal *was* the way these situations are handled. I received no support from the other teachers; my pleas for the team to acknowledge the student's request were ignored. I not only felt deflated as a social work intern, but also felt defeated as this student's advocate. I had failed to uphold his request. What then transpired was that all three boys involved were taken to the prin-cipal's office where the principal met with them together. All three boys denied that anything had ever occurred or been problematic. My student explained afterward to the author that he did not feel safe speaking openly about the bullying with the other boys present.

I knew that this kind of intervention, basically an attempt at conflict resolution, would not work. I feared that it would make matters worse and, at the very least, would be ineffective in stopping specific bullying behaviors. In this sense, putting victims at risk of further victimization is a social injustice. It is for this reason that I decided to focus my organizational change efforts on creating a clear and consistent intervention plan to combat bullying, based on research-based evidence and the voices of students and teachers. I had discovered through conversations with others in the SMS Student Advocacy office that there was no consistent intervention plan for bullying other than the protocol that the lead teacher takes any students involved to the principal's office. The actions taken from that point on are inconsistent and, as was evidenced by my student's experience, insensitive, unjust, and capable of exacerbating the harassment.

ORGANIZATIONAL STRUCTURE AND THE INTERN AS A CHANGE AGENT

One of the issues that I have with the organizational structure of the school is that there is no formal description regarding the degree of parity between teachers and social workers. This lack of clarity implies that SMS is functionally operating with two distinct professional endeavors. Gitterman and Germain (2008) aptly point out, "When an agency is characterized by divergent professional orientations, clients may be held hostage to competitive interests, struggles, and discrepant practices" (p. 479). This made it doubly difficult for me as an intern to determine what might be considered appropriate intraorganizational behavior and expectations of the other staff with whom I work. Moreover, in the case of a school, the social work staff was functioning within a host agency setting, which meant that the educational functions of the organization would inevitably carry more weight than the social work functions. The consequence of this was that I had the position of lowest stature with regard to the formal, organizational chain of command.

In terms of the informal organizational structure, I had a somewhat different sense of where I stood with regard to the teachers, guidance counselors, social workers, and administration. I realized that having knowledge about teachers' and students' behaviors within the school atmosphere granted me a slightly elevated status in the eyes of some staff. I could take advantage of this to some extent, but when it came to affecting formal organizational change, I realized that I still needed more power than I had as an intern.

It was from this unclear, formally disempowered, and weak position as an intern that I decided to try to speak out about what I perceived as a social injustice. This change effort was born out of my awareness of the frequency of bullying and harassment and the manner in which it is addressed at SMS. In order to develop the basis for support for my organizational change, I began by looking at policies on the local and state levels. I discovered a significant disparity between the school district's policy on bullying and harassment and the relevant state law. The Maine State Act to Amend the Laws Governing the Student Code of Conduct states, "The board of directors of each school district shall adopt and implement a policy prohibiting bullying and harassment of all students. The policy shall, at a minimum, include or provide for all of the following. . . . Develop process by which to evaluate on an ongoing basis improved school climate as it relates to bullying and harassment; Develop a process for discussing the harassment, intimidation or bullying policy with pupil; Monitoring and *evaluation of the policy's effectiveness on an annual basis*" (Maine State Act to Amend the Laws Governing the Student Code of Conduct, 2005; emphasis added).

In contrast, the school district policy stated that there should be "*periodic evaluation* of bullying prevention, intervention and training efforts in . . . [the district] schools and reporting to the Board upon request" (Scarborough Public Schools, 2006; emphasis added).

As I began to talk with staff about possible organizational change to better address the problems of bullying at SMS, I began to realize two important points. The first was that I recognized who my allies were and from whom I was already anticipating resistance to change. The other was that the information on policies that I was collecting would be useful for me if I found a collaborative strategy ineffective. Given the nature of my change goal and my perception of contest strategies, I wanted to avoid using and manipulating positional power (Patti & Resnick, 1972) as a tool for change, if at all possible. However, I remained aware of the paradoxical need to increase my own power as perceived by others in order for this change to be successful. Essentially, I did not want to "bully" the administration into changing their protocol but instead wanted to clearly demonstrate that there was a real need for change that was necessary and possible. I then realized it would be more difficult to refute my claims or dismiss them as opinions if they were supported by empirical evidence. To this end, I determined that I would need to do a literature review and create a tool for evaluating SMS's current bullying and harassment policies in order to find evidence to support my change goal of creating a clear and consistent antibullying intervention policy for the school.

LITERATURE REVIEW

I began by reviewing the literature on bullying and bullying interventions. My plan was to create a questionnaire to give to the students, teachers, and administration to identify any differences between these groups in terms of perceived prevalence of bullying at SMS. My sense was that there was a difference, and that reporting, given the current method of handling bullying, did not accurately represent the extent of bullying that actually occurred. Furthermore, there was currently no record keeping of bullying incidences and intervention strategies used, nor were there any annual evaluations conducted to assess the efficacy of said intervention strategies as mandated by state law. I essentially conducted two literature reviews. One was focused primarily on research examining effective antibullying strategies in schools. The other review was more specifically focused on determining what questions would be appropriate for a survey of SMS. Though the two reviews overlapped, the primary literature review also was intended to test the validity of the concerns that I had with SMS's current protocol, such as lack of record keeping and conflict resolution-style interventions.

In 1970, Dan Olweus, a Swedish professor of psychology, conducted what was the first large-scale empirical study of bullying and its victims. A leading authority on bullying and intervention research, Olweus has conducted many influential studies on the effects of bullying and the success of different strategies, including his own systematic approach (Olweus Bullying Prevention Program, 2003). The Olweus Bullying Prevention Program points to the necessity of a systematic approach to prevention within schools. Although there is considerable research validating the effectiveness of the Olweus Bullying Prevention Program, I did not believe that it would be a good use of my time advocating for the adoption of this program in view of anticipated budgetary constraints resulting from the harsh economic climate. In looking at the literature for this particular program, however, I was able to gather key elements of a successful prevention and intervention program that were especially relevant for my organization. According to the Olweus Bullying Prevention Program literature, a successful program is one that does not use conflict resolution between the students who were bullying and the students being targeted; instead, such a program addresses these two groups separately. Furthermore, an effective program contains confidential reporting to record victimization and the details of incidents (Olweus Bullying Prevention Program, 2007).

Much of the remaining literature reviewed concurred with that of the Olweus program. I found a consensus in the literature that the most effective approach to prevention and intervention is to address the school as a culture and system (Espelage & Swearer, 2003; Finger, Craven, Marsh, & Parada, n.d.). Furthermore, Olweus suggested creating a team to assess and operate as an antibullying and harassment task force (Olweus Bullying Prevention Program, 2007). To this end, a number of sources discussed the importance of gathering data from students and school staff to evaluate the atmosphere and extent of bullying (Baldry & Farrington, 2004; Bosworth, Espelage, & Simon, 1999).

DATA GATHERING

The literature review helped to confirm my perceptions and ultimately gave me courage to pursue my change goal of developing a clear and consistent intervention program to combat bullying and harassment at SMS. That said, I wanted to reinforce my proposal further and believed the best way to do this would be to generate data specific to SMS students. Of course, conducting a survey would require the approval of the principal. I discussed this with the staff in my office, and they agreed that the best course of action would be to present a complete draft of a survey to the principal. This way I would be demonstrating the effort that I was already willing to make toward this change.

Essentially, my plan at this point was to work on this change in stages. First, I would design a survey and seek the school's approval to gather data. Second, I would gather data using the survey. Third, I would use the supporting data to further my organizational change goal. Ultimately, I realized that even if SMS accepted nothing more than the results of the survey, I would have succeeded in bringing a greater awareness of the current problem of bullying and other forms of harassment at SMS. Furthermore, I would have helped SMS comply with state law by producing an evaluation tool that could be utilized annually.

The single most important piece of information that I gathered from my literature review on surveys regarded the use of language. It was pointed out that participants are less apt to accurately represent themselves in a survey when they know that the act of bullying is not acceptable (Espelage & Swearer, 2003). I was determined to not use the word "bully" in the student survey but rather to refer to specific behaviors that constitute bullying activity (Bosworth et al., 1999). Furthermore, even though I used the word "bully" in the survey for staff, I made a pointed effort to refer to "students bullying" and "students being targeted." The reason for this particular wording was an effort to use language that is temporal rather than finite. Rather than identify children as bullies or targets, I wanted to identify their behavior and what were hopefully their temporary roles within this dynamic.

Also important for me to consider in this survey were questions regarding social class, race, religion, heterosexism, and homophobia. It was challenging for me to phrase some of these concepts in a clear and concise manner. I discovered that including examples of words or terms that illustrated the concept was most helpful. For example, I used the term "white trash" to illustrate what I meant by comments regarding socioeconomic class. This term was not intended as derogatory but rather as an example of a social class descriptor. Interestingly, I found that when I mentioned to the staff in the Student Advocacy office my intention to include a question on social class, I needed to explain what I meant. This only affirmed my belief of the need to include a topic that was unclear even to the professionals in this environment.

From this point, armed with data from my literature review, I began talking about how to implement the changes that I saw as necessary. I first talked with the lead guidance counselor for the Student Advocacy office about my three-stage plan, and subsequently spoke with my two social work field instructors. Overall, people's responses were positive and encouraging. I also spoke with several teachers and auxiliary specialists, who were also enthusiastic and encouraging. In talking with the lead guidance counselor, I found out that there had been a survey on bullying conducted three years prior by a part-time guidance counselor. Unfortunately, it was difficult for me to obtain the data that had been collected. When I did finally get the information, I asked that the part-time guidance counselor and I meet with the lead guidance counselor to talk about my survey, which at that point I had drafted. I learned in this meeting that SMS had not supported much of the change that had been proposed three years ago. The part-time guidance counselor stated that she had experienced resistance from the teachers in regard to combining antibullying and social justice material into their curricula. I later found out from one of my field instructors that the SMS administration rotated the subjects that teachers teach every two or three years (with the exception of the specialists who teach art, music, and physical education) in an effort to keep their curricula fresh. This certainly helped me to appreciate even more why teachers would be resistant to the added work of including material about bullying and social justice into their curricula.

FORCE FIELD ANALYSIS

It was roughly at this point in my change process that I conducted my force field analysis. Figure 12.1 delineates my change goal and the various roles and forces that made up this change effort.

Figure 12.1 comprises three parts. The first of these, the change goal, is clearly identified. The goal for this effort is to create a clear and consistent intervention program for bullying and harassment at SMS. The second part lists the roles that various people at SMS hold with regard to influencing the change goal. At the top tier are the critical actors whose roles were crucial to the outcome of the change efforts. The critical actors at SMS included the principal and assistant principal, who had the formal power and authority to bring this change proposal to fruition. The second tier consisted of facilitating actors who wielded less power than the critical actors, but who were individuals capable of influencing the critical actors. In this case, the facilitating actors were the lead teachers, lead guidance counselor, and the two social workers (who were also my field instructors) in the Student Advocacy office. The lowest tier consisted of potential allies who, despite their relative lack of formal power within the agency, could be resources in support of the change effort. These allies included some teachers at SMS, auxiliary specialists such as speech therapists and occupational therapists, part-time guidance counselors within the Student Advocacy office, the students and their families, and

FIGURE 12.1. Force Field Analysis for Anti-Bullying Intervention

---

Change Goal:

Create a clear and consistent intervention program for bullying and harassment

---

Critical Actors:

1. Principal

2. Assistant principal

Facilitating Actors:

1. Lead teachers (including lead guidance counselor)

2. Social workers (my two field instructors)

Potential Allies:

1. Some teachers

2. Speech therapist

3. Guidance counselors

4. Students and their families

5. Student peer helpers

Driving Forces for Change:	*Restraining Forces for Change:*
1. Students' concerns/Working force— A, P, C	1. Critical actors might object/ Unpredictable force—A, P
2. Parents' concerns/Working force— A, P, C	2. Lack of resources and funding/ Framing force—P, C
3. Teachers' concerns/Working force— A, P, C	3. Denial of problem/Unpredictable force—A, P
4. Guidance counselors/Social workers' concerns/Working force—A, P, C	4. Negative publicity/Unpredictable force—A, P
5. History, visibility, and existing research/Working Force—A, P, C	5. Overwhelming workload for teachers and staff/Framing force—P, C
6. State law/Working force—A, P, C	6. Organizational resistance to change/Framing force—P, C
7. Lack of bullying records kept at SMS/Working force—A, P, C	7. Students and/or family opposition/Working force—A, P, C
8. Possibility for positive public relations/Unpredictable force (needs more research)—A, P	8. Lack of information/Working force— A, P, C

Key: Working force—High in amenability, potency, and consistency (A, P, C)

Framing force—High in potency and consistency (P and C)

Unpredictable force—Low in consistency or uncertain in amenability, potency, or consistency

the Peer Helpers, a student group at SMS that promoted social justice and social responsibility within the school. I later discovered that the computer specialists were also allies because they were, unbeknownst to me, simultaneously working on a survey to evaluate students' safety on the internet.

Once these actors have been identified, the next step in the force field analysis required brainstorming the possible forces that could have an impact on the organizational change. This step begins with the driving forces, which are characterized as those factors that are beneficial and promote the change. These included concerns of students, parents, teachers, guidance counselors, and social workers; the history, visibility, and existing research on the negative effects of bullying; the state law on bullying and harassment; the lack of records on bullying kept at SMS; and the possibility for positive public relations for SMS. Next were the restraining forces, which are characterized as obstacles to the realization of the change project. These factors included the principal and assistant principal's potential objection to the change effort, the lack of resources and funding, the potential denial of the existence of a problem at SMS, negative publicity for SMS, an overwhelming workload for teachers and staff, general organizational resistance to change, students' or their families' opposition to the change, and the lack of knowledge within the school about the current bullying and harassment problems and their potentially grave consequences.

Once I had identified these forces, I assessed and coded each according to the degree to which I perceived it to be amenable to worker influence, potent with regard to the change goal, and consistent with regard to the change (Brager & Holloway, 1993). I then evaluated each of the driving and restraining forces further based on their particular combination of amenability, potency, and consistency. The result is a description of each force as a working, framing, or unpredictable force in the organizational change process. This was a particularly important step in the force field analysis because it determined the overall feasibility of the change project. If there are, for example, more restraining forces identified as framing than driving forces identified as working, the change effort may not be successful.

My force field analysis suggested that my organizational change plan should be feasible. With the exception of one unpredictable force, the possibility of positive public relations for SMS, all of the driving forces were identified as working. These included the concerns of students, families, teachers, guidance counselors, and social workers; the history, visibility, and existing research in regard to bullying; the state law; and the lack of records on bullying maintained at SMS. The potential for positive public relations was not sufficiently predictable for me to assess whether it had the necessary consistency to identify it as a working force. I would need to obtain more information about this, if possible With regard to the restraining forces, there was more of a range between unpredictable, framing, and working forces. In terms of the restraining forces, those forces identified as working were those where effort can potentially reduce the resistance to attaining the change goal. Those forces identified as framing were obstacles that were unlikely to be reduced, such as a generalized organizational resistance to change. Restraining forces that were assessed as working included the potential of student and family opposition to the change goal as well as a general lack of information about the problem and extent of bullying at SMS. Restraining forces that I assessed as framing included lack of resources, the overwhelming amount of the workload for teachers and staff, and organizational resistance to change. The remaining forces—the potential for critical actors to be opposed to the change goal, the possibility of denial of the bullying problem, and potential of negative publicity—I assessed as unpredictable.

CHANGE TACTICS

Patti and Resnick (1972) describe organizational change processes as consisting of three phases: creating goals, mobilizing resources, and implementing an intervention strategy comprising change tactics. Before conducting the force field analysis, I had anticipated resistance from the critical actors. Knowing that I had discovered a discrepancy between the Somerset School District policy and the state law regarding the frequency of bullying and harassment evaluations, I realized I had potential leverage should the resistance I anticipated manifest itself. However, I also knew that I did not want to initially approach this change in such a manner, and preferred to practice the principle of least contest and begin with collaborative tactics, knowing that I had information regarding the school department's noncompliance with state law to use at the campaign level if necessary. With this in mind, I knew that I would need to produce evidence for my change. Furthermore, it had been three years since anyone had used an evaluation tool to assess the school's bullying and harassment levels. I realized that creating an evaluation tool would benefit the school in meeting compliance with state law, but would also (I hoped) produce results that would support my goal of changing the current bullying and harassment protocol.

I had not anticipated that the principal would be as interested in the survey as she was. In fact, I had been scheduled to present my full draft of the survey at a multidisciplinary team meeting, but was not able to because of other issues that took precedence. I was disappointed and began to wonder if this change effort was going to drag on; I knew that arranging meetings with the principal could be difficult because of her busy schedule. Thus, I was pleasantly surprised to find an email asking me to meet with her early on a Monday morning. One of my field instructors attended the meeting with us.

I had expected that I was going to need to "sell" my survey, but this proved not to be the case. The principal appeared very enthusiastic and urged me to contact the computer specialists who were already devising a survey on internet safety. She said that, rather than have two surveys for students to complete, she wanted them to be combined. I told her about my literature review and she stated that she wanted to read some of my literature, which pleased me because it indicated that she valued empirically based research. We reviewed the student and staff surveys and she made valuable comments about phrasing and requested that we omit certain questions. She requested that the bus drivers not be included as participants for the staff survey, with which I did not agree. I felt very strongly that we should include them, and spoke briefly about my knowledge of the bullying that occurs on buses gathered from the students I met with and cited some literature on the matter. The principal stated that she did not disagree that bullying occurs frequently on buses, but explained that when she has tried to talk with the drivers in the past they have responded as though they were being accused of not doing their job and had become hostile toward her. It appeared to me that this was, in part, a political issue that she was trying to remain diplomatic about, which I could appreciate to an extent. However, I still felt strongly that the survey reflect the experiences of the transportation staff. When I suggested we have someone complete the survey on their behalf, the principal agreed to ask the district transportation supervisor to do so. Though I was not entirely satisfied with the exclusion of the bus drivers from our staff survey, I think this collaborative compromise was very significant in terms of appreciating the unique goals and tasks that both the principal and I were trying to maintain in a manner that was mutually beneficial and respectful.

Even with all of the editing I did on the survey, when it went live on the school's website for students and staff to access, there were problems. For one, I had accidentally included the word "bullying" in one of my response options on the student survey. However, a larger problem was that there were questions listing multiple options, but not the option "none of the above." Fortunately, we were able to fix this problem, but only after some students had already completed the survey. The negative consequence of this was that some of the data were skewed. The positive consequence was that the computer specialists and I have learned to do a test run of our surveys to reduce these overlooked errors in the future, which is certainly valuable. I do not think the data being skewed will reduce their gravity, though it is disappointing that the results may not be a completely accurate representation of students' experiences.

CONCLUSIONS

Despite issues with some of the questions, the survey was successful. The results were compelling and demonstrate what I had suspected about how teachers address bullying issues with students and the degree to which students reported or responded to bullying behavior. Presently, I am working on filtering the results so that I can look at how specific subsets of the student participants responded to certain questions. For example, I can look specifically at how sixth graders who report being bullied on a daily basis responded to questions regarding how they dealt with the behavior; who, if anyone, they told; what the results of reporting the behavior were if they did report it; and whether they have also participated in bullying behavior toward other students this academic year. The value of these results, particularly when they are filtered this way, is that we can gain very specific information about whether SMS's prevention and intervention protocols and programs are effective and for whom.

As of this writing, I have not reached the final part of my plan because I first needed to filter the survey results. I do feel successful about what has been accomplished so far. The survey raised consciousness about bullying throughout the school and there is a commitment on the part of the principal to reevaluate how the principal will respond to bullying at SMS. It remains to be seen whether the change goal of creating a clear and consistent intervention program for bullying and harassment will be realized.

REFERENCES

Baldry, A., & Farrington, D. (2004). Evaluation of an intervention program for the reduction of bullying and victimization in schools. *Aggressive Behavior, 30*, 1–15.

Bosworth, K., Espelage, D., & Simon, T. (1999). Factors associated with bullying behavior in middle school students. *Journal of Early Adolescence, 19*(3), 341–362.

Brager, G., & Holloway, S. (1993). Assessing prospects for organizational change: The uses of force field analysis. *Administration in Social Work, 16*(3/4), 15–28.

Espelage, D., & Swearer, S. (2003). Research on school bullying and victimization: What have we learned and where do we go from here? *School Psychology Review, 32*(3), 365–383.

Finger, L., Craven, R., Marsh, H., & Parada, R. (n.d.). Characteristics of effective anti-bullying interventions: What research says. SELF Research Centre, University of Western Sydney, Australia.

Gitterman, A., & Germain, C. (2008). *The life model of social work practice* (3rd ed.). New York: Columbia University Press.

Maine State Act to Amend the Laws Governing the Student Code of Conduct. (2005). Retrieved from http://www.mainelegislature.org/ros/LOM/lom122nd/8pub301-350/Pub301-350-06.htm#P355_64990

Olweus Bullying Prevention Program. (2003). Brief information about Dan Olweus. Retrieved from http://www.clemson.edu/olweus/history.htm

Olweus Bullying Prevention Program. (2007). Steps to address bullying at your school/tips for school administrators. Retrieved from www.hazelden.org/web/public/document/olweusfacts_steps_at_school.pdf

Patti, R., & Resnick, H. (1972). Changing the agency from within. *Social Work, 17*(7), 48–57.

Scarborough Public Schools. (2006). Bullying. Retrieved from http://www.Scarborough.k12.me.us/

13

Linguistic Liabilities

Refugee Parents' Right to Know in a Language They Understand

Judy Peters

INTRODUCTION

The Multilingual Multicultural Center (MMC) for the North City Public Schools is the central office for language minority children and their families in the school district. MMC provides many supports to the nearly two thousand students it serves. Interpretation (oral) and translation (written) services provided by parent community specialists are a core feature of the center's work. However, the increases in caseload over the past few years have stretched this service thin, resulting in significant gaps between information from the school that English-speaking parents receive and information that parents with limited English proficiency (LEP) receive in their native language, effectively restricting access to parental involvement on the part of LEP parents. This change effort was aimed at offering a comprehensive view of the problem and suggesting a change to improve translation and interpretation services to LEP families.

The Multilingual Center sponsors a mentoring program called Make It Happen. As a social work intern, I mentor two adolescent boys, one born in Egypt to Sudanese parents and one born in Pakistan to a mother from Afghanistan. Determining a method for communicating during the week is part of the requirements for the first session. The boys both enthusiastically gave me their cell phone numbers. Attempting to connect in a mode that was common for preadolescents, I decided to text a reminder to them of our upcoming meetings because many of our meetings have been broken due to snow days or illness.

Strangely, one of the numbers I had been given came back with a reply after my first text: "who dis?" I thought I must have the wrong number, so stopped using it until last week when I decided to try it one more time. Moments later, I received the same reply, which I ignored, but then received a call. I answered the phone, and realized that it was the mother of one of the boys I work with. She of course wanted to know who kept texting her phone, and what it was about. I tried to tell her who I was and not to worry. She said to me that she had, "little English." She seemed so sweet on the phone. I felt terrible about not being able to help her understand, but fortunately I was on my way to the MMC where I knew I could get help. Unfortunately, at the time I thought the boy I was mentoring was from Iraq.

I sat across from the part-time Iraqi interpreter at the MMC office, and asked for her assistance. She was in the middle of helping a couple from Iraq that was registering their son for school, so it was another couple of hours before she was free and able to help. She made the call to the mother, but within moments realized that this mother spoke Dari (a form of Persian spoken in Afghanistan), and not Arabic. I eventually was able to get assistance to identify the one Dari translator who works in the school and e-mail her about the situation, requesting that she make a call to explain. By this time, it was nearly 2:00 and time for me to meet with the boys. Six hours had passed since the initial text, and I knew this mother must be wondering what was going on. I felt helpless.

Resolution came as our Make It Happen meeting began and I found out that this resourceful mother had called the school and had her son come down to the office to explain the situation. Finally, I received an e-mail back from the translator the next day that she also called the mom and would be happy to help if future communication was needed. Discovering that communicating something so simple could take so many hours was a profound lesson for me regarding the reality multilingual families face every day. The challenges of this courageous single Afghani mother raising her children in a culture and language still foreign to her are both the inspiration and the focus of this chapter. I dedicate this chapter to her.

THE SETTING

The Multicultural Multilingual Center of the North City Public Schools consists of a central office of about twenty staff that provides for the specific needs of language minorities for the district. It is a warm, supportive environment for families trying to assimilate to educational culture in northern New England. The North City Public Schools have approximately two thousand English language learning (ELL) students representing sixty languages and about 25 percent of the student body. The MMC office provides services such as school registration, English language testing, interpretation and translation services, summer school, and student mentoring. Keeping up with the needs of a growing multilingual population has caused significant stress on office staff who are clearly devoted to the MMC program and the families they serve. Limitations on their ability to fully meet the demands of the school system are a constant concern. In one case, a single translator is responsible for serving the needs of more than seven hundred students and their families.

The parent community specialists at MMC who provide translation and interpretation services are beloved and counted on by their communities. They tend to offer services far above and beyond the school connection and are known for their integrity, particularly in the area of confidentiality, which is critical because cultural communities within the school district are small. Yet the gaps are significant. The school registration paperwork is not translated into any language other than English. School calendars have been translated into only half a dozen languages, but sixty languages are represented in the district. Teachers frequently send out notices in English only, even permission slips that need to be signed and PTA meeting invitations. This restriction of services to LEP parents provides a considerable obstacle to parents' efforts to understand, support, and advocate for their children's educational experience. This violates a fundamental right of parents to be involved in their children's education and undermines the development of a support system central to students' success at school.

The MMC staff is made up of two directors, three administrators, and a number of other coordinators and specialists. Though the executive director is the primary representative of the agency to the outside, each member of this administrative team appears to have significant influence in his or her individual role. I believe it is noteworthy that many of the staff, including parent community specialists, have been employed in excess of five years. Several staff members have been with the organization since the inception of the agency thirteen years ago. Perhaps even more amazing is the fact that five of the seven continents are represented within this small group that is interwoven with a deep sense of respect and collaboration amidst differing cultures and perspectives.

At MMC, it appears there is a clear awareness of the lack of translation services and the strain it puts on parents. Currently, meetings are being held to discuss the need for increased efficiency and expanding resources. Unease is mounting about unfinished translations piling up on the desks of translators. Though staff members acknowledge the difficulty that this situation presents to parents, there is also a reality of limited resources and anticipated future budget cuts. My hope with this organizational change project is to put a fresh face on the struggles these parents face, the injustice that is occurring, as well as the weight of my ability to put some time and effort into effecting positive change.

THE PROJECT

The Title VI requirements of the U.S. Department of Education's Office of Civil Rights (2000) include a mandate that LEP parents be given school notices and other information in a language they can understand. Furthermore, according to a report by the Northwest Regional Educational Laboratory (NREL; Gomez & Greenough, 2002), Title I and Title III of the No Child Left Behind Act (2001) specifically addresses the need for parents to be not only participants, but also informed and empowered decision makers in their children's education.

The focus of this organizational change project is to research the specifics of this legislation and assess the barriers to compliance specifically as they relate to North City Public Schools. I will review provisions of these laws with respect to basic human rights and the social work code of ethics. Furthermore, this effort will seek to offer suggestions for improving communication between LEP parents and the greater school system by exploring gaps in services as well as demands on parent community specialists who currently serve as the only link for communication between school officials and LEP parents. It may be beneficial to document the number of translation requests that come in, the number of changes made to documents after they are received, the average turnaround time for translation, and the number of untranslated documents sent to LEP parents in one month. I also hope to interview at least one LEP parent one on one to better understand the strain this lack of services places on these parents and their children. Finally, I would like to look at the possibility of any untapped funding sources to support expanded translation services. My hope is to uncover at least one possible solution to support my change goal of improving the school system's translation and interpretation services, thereby increasing communication between the schools and LEP parents.

THE LAWS

As noted above, Title VI requirements of the Department of Education's Office of Civil Rights (2000,) as well as Title I and Title III of the Elementary and Secondary Schools Act, commonly known as No Child Left Behind Act (2001), mandate schools to ensure that LEP parents are uniformly encouraged to participate in their children's education. Districts must reach out to them with school notifications in a language they understand as well as offer ample opportunities for parental involvement (Gomez & Greenough, 2002). The NREL (Gomez & Greenough, 2002) offers further insight into the intent of these directives. It discusses the understanding that parent involvement is predicated on the ability to receive communication from the school about programming, academics, school culture, and other practices in a form that they can interpret. This includes information not only on class content and teacher credentials, but also on how parents can be involved in districtwide policy decisions (Gomez & Greenough, 2002). Title III in particular puts the onus on schools to make efforts to reach out to LEP parents. Section 3302 of Title III requires schools to inform LEP parents how they can "(A) Be involved in the education of the children; and (B) be active participants in assisting their children, (i) to learn English; (ii) to achieve at high levels in core academic subjects; and (iii) to meet the same challenging State academic content and student academic achievement standards as all children are expected to meet" (No Child Left Behind Act, 2001, Title III, Sec. 3302).

The NREL guide suggests that schools reflect on whether parent participation in school governance mirrors the scope of cultures and viewpoints of the district (Gomez & Greenough, 2002). It encourages evaluation of whether minority parents are empowered contributors and decision makers. It implores schools to pay attention to the disenfranchised parent offering opportunities for them to contribute in a meaningful way. Title III further clarifies that the approach to parents should be "based on the most current research that meets the highest professional and technical standards" (No Child Left Behind Act, 2001, Title III, Part A, 1111[d]).

The goals of these educational mandates are consistent with social work's commitment to serve the disenfranchised of society. It specifically supports the values defined in the National Association of Social Worker's (NASW) *Code of Ethics* that maintain the "social justice and dignity and worth of the person" (2008, p. 1). The International Federation of Social Workers/International Association of Schools of Social Work (2004) also confirms the profession's commitment to these codes in their document, *Ethics in Social Work: Statement of Principles* by clearly documenting individual rights to participation, social justice, and self-determination.

THE LITERATURE

Effective parental involvement is paramount to student success. This has been documented by many research studies. Gonzalez-DeHass, Willems, and Doan Holbein (2005) summarize these research findings in their extensive literature review. The numerous studies they discuss seem conclusive; parent involvement has a positive effect on student interest and engagement in school. It helps students to feel capable, self-determined, and integrated, and to realize the importance of the education they are receiving. It also evokes students' feelings of positive self-esteem and well-being.

The work of Arias and Morillo-Campbell (2008) speaks to the barriers many LEP parents face in connecting with schools. These include anti-immigrant sentiment, linguistic isolation, and the potential for a parent's own lack of formal education to create dissonance. LEP parents may feel their cultures are being undervalued. Schools can be overly directive instead of inviting parents to enter into a collaborative partnership. Due to language barriers that impede effective communication with LEP parents, school communities may perceive these parents as disinterested or apathetic about their children's education, when quite the reverse is true. These attitudes have the potential to create a paternalistic and condescending atmosphere within the school system where school communities look down upon marginalized parents. Schools often approach relationships with parents negatively. Arias and Morillo-Campbell (2008) advise instead that schools adopt a strengths-based approach, building on opportunities to incorporate the heritage of these families into the core of their curriculum and educational venues.

DATA COLLECTION

The first step in this change project was to begin quantifying the number of language minority students and families in North City that are affected by the language barriers described above. The MMC had data on the number of families whose home language was other than English, but had not calculated the exact number of students and families actually using interpretation or translation services. With the help of the administrator in charge of data, I was able to look at a spreadsheet that listed each student receiving interpretation services at parent–teacher conferences. There were twenty-four languages listed. The precise number of families was difficult to track in data because students within a family are spread out between the thirteen schools of the district, and because in several cultures represented it is customary to give each child a last name different from the parents' and from each other's last names, making the task of grouping them difficult. The top language groups included Somali at 425 students, Arabic at 137 students, and Spanish at 99 students. Other language groups of more than 50 students were Khmer, Vietnamese, and Acholi. All other languages had fewer than 30 students in each. In some cases, there was only one student requiring interpretation services (i.e., Lingala, Kinymulenge, Champa).

To explore the problem further, I spoke with two colleagues who are social work interns within the North City schools. Both of them described complaints about notes sent home untranslated. In one case, the school regularly sends home notices in English with the phone number of the MMC listed at the bottom to call in the event that the parent or other recipient could not understand the note. While this effort is admirable, it is hardly optimal and surely does not send the welcoming message intended in the legislation discussed above. When questioned about this practice, the administrator for interpretation and translation services said that she was unable to quantify how effective schools are in utilizing translated materials. The office makes every effort to accommodate requests that they receive for translated notices in a reasonable amount of time. Many translated documents are available for schools to use on a central computer drive but enforcement efforts have been minimal and it has been up to the schools to determine how to utilize what is available. Schools vary in their commitment to the effort it takes to ensure that in every case best practices are followed.

As a further attempt at data collection, the author undertook a series of parent interviews. The intent in this process was to discern gaps in effective communication with LEP parents and the implications of those gaps. Terry came to the United States in 2003 from Cambodia. She has two daughters in high school. They all recently became American citizens. Terry is learning English, but it is difficult. I tried at first to ask her questions on my own without the help of an interpreter, but though I believe she understood my questions, she did not have the words to reply. Pirun, a Khmer interpreter, came to help. I asked her three questions. The first question was how education is different here than in Cambodia and if she believed the differences affected her ability to be involved with her children at school. She did not have an answer. I rephrased several different ways and she still could not answer my question. I decided to move on. I asked her if she ever received notices from school that were not translated. She said that she had received one recently about sports, but she could not say how often this happened. I asked her how she manages when she receives a document in English. She said that she has her daughter translate for her. She said that it is becoming difficult, however, because her daughter is losing her Cambodian language as she is immersed in English. This makes communication very difficult between mother and daughter. When I asked her what the schools could do to help, she said that they needed more interpreters. Throughout my conversation with Terry, she seemed uncomfortable with the questions and somewhat reluctant with the answers. It was unclear how much of her reticence was a function of the language barrier or whether there might have been other cultural factors involved.

I asked two other interpreters for help arranging meetings with LEP parents. It was parent–teacher conference time, so to maximize the parents' limited availability it was suggested that I conduct interviews directly after the conferences. However, neither interpreter was comfortable with this option, and told me that conferences were emotionally charged events and that parents would be less than willing to discuss their experiences immediately afterward. Finally, I asked a colleague with a refugee friend who was fairly proficient in English and had several children in the school district if she would be open to an interview. She also declined to meet.

FORCE FIELD ANALYSIS

Brager and Holloway's (1993) discussion of key actors and the forces at work in organizational settings is a useful framework for analyzing the potential barriers to agency change along with the forces that can facilitate change. Once the change goal was identified as improving the school system's translation and interpretation services in order to increase communication between the schools and LEP parents, I was ready to begin my force field analysis, which is presented in figure 13.1.

At the head of the Multilingual Center is a director. This is the one critical actor who has the final word on whether a new initiative is implemented or adopted. There is access to the director, but she is very busy and it can take weeks to schedule an appointment. The program coordinator and coordinator of translation and interpretation services are facilitating actors. They both acknowledge the problem of untranslated documents, but the program coordinator, in particular, has been hesitant to accept suggestions for change from me, a student intern. Her resistance to the change goal could serve to

FIGURE 13.1. Force Field Analysis for the Interpretation Intervention in Schools

Change Goal:

Improving the school system's translation and interpretation services

Critical Actors:

1. Director
2. Program coordinator

Facilitating Actors:

1. Administrator of district data
2. Coordinator of translation staff
3. Translators

Potential Allies:

1. My field supervisor
2. My field advisor
3. Students' families

Driving Forces for Change:	*Restraining Forces for Change:*
1. Concerns expressed by parents	1. Decreased funding
2. Translators unable to meet need	2. Limitations in expanding services
3. Frustration on the part of staff	3. Staff resistance to change
4. Federal legislation	

undermine the chance of agreement from the director. Just recently, however, the coordinator of translation and interpretation services has become
more interested and amenable to new approaches. In the case of the critical
and facilitating actors, their long-standing history with the organization (in
excess of ten years) and their well-formed camaraderie with each other are
both strengths and potential obstacles to change. Allies in the change goal
include the translators, an off-site field supervisor, my field advisor, and families of language minority students.

Federal legislation under the U.S. Department of Education Office of
Civil Rights (2000) and No Child Left Behind Act (2001) provides a framing
driving force in relation to the change goal. Even though these mandates do
not clearly spell out the exact requirements for compliance, they are likely to
be among the most potent driving forces. The inability of the translators to
meet all the needs for translation is another framing, driving force for
change. The frustration of the coordinator of translation and interpretation
services may also be a driving force for change. She appears to be very concerned about the gaps in the system. However, her commitment to work for
change is tempered by the restraining force of any extra time needed to
bring about improved services for parents: she is already highly taxed by an
excessive workload. Hence, this is an unpredictable force. The frustration of

other staff, particularly the translators, is predictable and potent; therefore, it is a working, driving force as is the frustration expressed by some of the more vocal LEP parents.

The restraining forces of inadequate budget and resources are potent framing forces. The public school system is already facing significant cuts over the next year. Plans are in place to eliminate numerous jobs through attrition and potential layoffs. In a heroic show of concern for the organization, the program coordinator has decided to retire to reduce the stress of the organization and free up funds to continue to support the staff currently at the agency. Additionally, a significant restraining force is the limited degree of concern expressed by the parents and students. In nearly seven months of internship, there have only been a few complaints from LEP families about the lack of translated documents.

I identified three possible reasons for this. First, there are parents who are illiterate who access the services of MMC. Their illiteracy may be due to the interruption of education due to war, a lack of public education in their country, or customs that prohibit the education of women. For them, translated documents would serve little purpose.

Second, though the reality of the lack of interpreted documents is of concern, MMC offers more services and more translators and interpreters than most districts in the state. These interpreters are highly respected and valued by their communities, and to criticize their efforts in any way may counter the esteem in which they are held. Additionally, many parents come from cultures where there is much less school-related paperwork than there is in the United States. The volume of notices may signal an expectation toward parent involvement that those from other cultures may believe is unwarranted. Many other cultures, particularly East African nations, have quite different educational norms, where parent involvement mostly requires ensuring that a child arrives at school. In many countries, ongoing interaction in the school system by parents is uncommon.

Third, these LEP parents may simply be unaware that they are entitled to receive translated documents, and therefore have not raised this as a concern. This could be a working force if anyone else from MMC or I informed these parents of their rights in this regard. There is also a potential for a framing, restraining force of racism and anti-immigrant sentiments among the teachers and staff of the district whose compliance in using translated documents is necessary for any change effort.

DETOURS AND ROADBLOCKS

As Patti and Resnick (1972) point out, "Intra organizational change refers to the systematic efforts of practitioners to effect changes in policies or programs from within their agencies, when they have no administrative sanction for these activities. The legitimization for these efforts is derived from the practitioner's ethical obligation to place professional values above organizational allegiance" (p. 48). The authors emphasize the impact of power differentials between the change agent and the target of change. It speaks to the considerable obstacles that can arise, particularly when low-power actors initiate change.

In the case of MMC, while my efforts to pursue the issue of access to school information for LEP parents was never discouraged, there were various roadblocks that came into play. When I first mentioned the directive federal legislation on the matter, staff responded that it was a general recommendation and did not require specific action. They further added that the staff from the Office of Civil Rights had been to visit them, which only served to distract them from serving clients.

My proposal to offer training for parents to access their children's academic records using translation software was contested with the explanation that the software is not sophisticated enough for parents to track student assignments and progress (although I have since discovered in a mentoring session with students that indeed it is). The director twice canceled meetings with me, and my persistent attempts to reschedule have thus far been ineffective. It became clear that the stamina necessary for organizational change to occur would be significant and would require a tireless commitment and a considerable amount of tenacity.

REFRAMING THE CHANGE GOAL

My efforts at persuasion were expended yet after many weeks there were no signs of progress toward my change goal: it seemed as though the change goal might never be realized. It was then that I remembered the words of Brager and Holloway (1993): "[G]oals often have to be partialized, either by reducing their scope or dividing them into an incremental, multi-step process" (p. 97). It became apparent that it might actually be beneficial to begin building on the significant effort that had already been exerted by the agency to meet the considerable need for translated documents, documents that were actually being underutilized. One day, an assistant teacher came to the MMC office for help with translating a permission slip consisting of two pages of information. The office staff instructed that there was already a standard form for all permission slips available, and directed her to the person that could assist her in personalizing the form for her needs. This simple interaction became the inspiration for my identification of a more modest change effort. A successful effort to assist even one school with improving utilization of already existing documents could serve as the gentle collaborative nudge that would illuminate the important role of improving communication with LEP parents. This approach would allow for additional time to explore the efforts and obstacles in the district's current practices and to determine if further resources will need to be mobilized for effective change to be undertaken.

I arranged a meeting with MMC staff to discuss my findings and proposed change of improving utilization of translated forms and documents in one district school that had low compliance. On the day of my meeting, the coordinator of translation was the only staff person available. She seemed interested in my recommendation and offered to put effort into working with the schools to improve the utilization of the documents already available. Our meeting ended with her suggesting a future meeting with the program director and coordinator. My presentation included a list of resources including two grants: the K–12 grant for translation services, and the Refugee School Impact grant. The coordinator of translation offered information on Transact, a service that offers translations of hundreds of school documents in twenty-three languages. I subsequently learned that Babylon, another translation service, was offering their software to all schools free of charge. The coordinator of translation was aware of Transact because it had been used previously in North City, but was unaware of Babylon. She agreed to work closely with the one school that had been identified as being in greatest need for improved translation services.

Conclusions

It has been a long road, yet even with its bends and turns there seems to have been some mileage gained. At new student registration the coordinator said something I had not heard her say previously. She encouraged the newcomers to be sure to ask for translated documents at the schools that their children will attend. I am encouraged and hope we are headed for eventual systemwide improvement in communication between the North City Public School system and LEP parents.

References

Arias, M., & Morillo-Campbell, M. (2008). Promoting ELL parental involvement: Challenges in contested times. Retrieved from http://greatlakescenter.org/docs/Policy_Briefs/Arias_ELL.pdf

Brager, G., & Holloway, S. (1993). Assessing prospects for organizational change: The uses of force field analysis. *Administration in Social Work, 16*(3), 15–28.

Gomez, R., & Greenough, R. (2002). Parental involvement under the new Title I & Title III: From compliance to effective practice. Retrieved from http://www .missouri-pirc.org/school_downloads/Parental_Involvment_Under_the_New_Title_I.pdf

Gonzalez-DeHass, A. R., Willems, P., & Doan Holbein, M. (2005). Examining the relationship between parental involvement and student motivation. *Educational Psychology Review, 17*(2), 99–123.

International Federation of Social Workers/International Association of Schools of Social Work. (2004). *Ethics in social work: Statement of principles*. Retrieved from http://www.ifsw.org

National Association of Social Workers (NASW). (2008). *Code of ethics* (revised). Retrieved from http://www.naswdc.org/pubs/code/code.asp?print=1

No Child Left Behind Act (2001). P.L. 107-110. 107th Congress, Sess. 1. Retrieved from http://www.govtrack.us/congress/bills/107/hr1

Patti, R., & Resnick, H. (1972). Changing the agency from within. *Social Work, 17*(7), 48–57.

U.S. Department of Education, Office of Civil Rights. (2000). The provision of an equal education opportunity to limited-English proficient students: Title VI. Retrieved from http://www2.ed.gov/about/offices/list/ocr/eeolep/index.html

14

Documenting Homelessness

Organizational Change at a Homeless Resource Center

Amy Russell

INTRODUCTION

Providence Street Resource Center (hereafter Providence Street) is a non-profit organization that provides services for people experiencing homelessness in Ocean City, Maine. Since its inception in 1975, Providence Street has expanded in size, number of programs, and number of low-barrier services available in an effort to facilitate client self-empowerment, self-determination, and client resolution of self-identified problems. Over time, Providence Street has adapted to change along with client needs in order to function as a sustainable client-centered organization.

One of the most common service plan goals that case managers and clients agree upon is assistance with securing permanent or semipermanent housing. While some housing programs are tailored to persons with particular characteristics who are experiencing homelessness (e.g., those with physical and psychiatric disabilities), all require that anyone applying for assistance prove his or her homeless status. Homelessness verification can be established relatively easily for those who utilize the shelter system, either through the women's shelter, the "wet shelter" for active alcoholics, or the city shelter for men, because bed nights are documented. It can be much more difficult for those who are unable to tolerate the shelters and who opt to make alternative sleeping arrangements such as camping, sleeping in places not intended for human habitation (e.g., vehicles), or couch-surfing to obtain verification, however. In cases where clients are adamantly opposed to sleeping in the shelters, innovation in systematically documenting instances of overnight homelessness is essential in improving service to clients, especially with regard to the completion and submission of housing applications.

THE ORGANIZATIONAL CONTEXT

The formal organizational structure of Providence Street is hierarchical. A board of directors provides guidance and decision-making power at the top tier of this nonprofit organization. Below the board, an executive director oversees the operation of the assistant director, the director of development and staff, the director of finance and administration and staff, and the director of operations and staff. Furthermore, under the Providence Street umbrella are the Adult Day Shelter, Teen Services, Community Initiatives, Advocacy, The Women's Shelter, Logan Place (a transitional residence), and the food and volunteer programs. Each of these divisions is supported by additional program coordinators, program assistants, supervisors, case managers, student interns, per diem staff, community organizers, housing support staff, and volunteers.

Providence Street serves people experiencing homelessness and people with low incomes in Ocean City through a variety of services including the Adult Day Shelter (which provides a drop-in center, telephones, mail service, showers, laundry, a clothing closet, outreach, and a safe space to congregate), breakfast, a food pantry, emergency food boxes, advocacy, and case management services. Case management within the client–worker relationship often focuses on issues surrounding housing, health care, employment, mental health services, legal assistance, and education. The day shelter is operated by an Adult Day Shelter services coordinator, an administrative program assistant, two social work supervisors, a full-time case management staff, undergraduate and graduate social work interns who maintain their own caseloads, and per diem staff who oversee service delivery within the day shelter and the exterior courtyard.

Within the day shelter, even the informal structure of the organization is somewhat hierarchical, but all staff members work as a team to ensure service delivery and safety for clients. For example, full-time staff, student interns, and per diem staff alike are granted decision-making power regarding maintaining safety. Drug talk and drug dealing, the consumption of alcohol on site, and hate speech are not tolerated; staff can ask clients to leave for the day or for an extended period if they deem it appropriate. Oftentimes, the consequence of being "out" longer than a day is established through consultation with other staff or with supervisors when necessary. Generally, the decision-making power is shared among staff except for certain supervisory duties (e.g., the distribution of limited funds to assist certain client needs). Additionally, social work staff meetings are held twice each week and provide a forum for discussing new and existing clients, staff and agency concerns, presentations from other social service providers in the area, and announcements.

Overall, the organizational culture at Providence Street is healthy and facilitates the actualization of the agency mission. According to Green's schema (1993), the artifacts of the agency culture are demonstrated through staff activity during the breakfast shift, outreach in the day shelter or the courtyard, case management, social work meetings, and the sharing of space during the lunch hour. Additionally, staff are identified by lanyards and identification badges; and share behavioral norms, language, rites (including rites of passage), and agency stories, history, and annual ceremonies. Staff who share agency values of empowerment, self-determination, and advocacy operate the day shelter. The basic assumptions of the agency include the belief that social service and the pursuit of social justice is a worthwhile endeavor, that the population experiencing homelessness is deserving of respect and dignity, and that clients can work toward their own empowerment and self-determination. Overall, the agency culture strives to be client centered and supportive of both clients and staff members.

THE PROBLEM FOR CHANGE

Within my field placement setting of Providence Street, I am currently engaged in case management with two clients experiencing homelessness who want assistance with housing applications but who refuse to stay in the shelters. Both clients have indicated that they cannot tolerate being at the city shelter and feel that their behavior could become violent if they experience extreme anxiety or are provoked. One client avoids entering the day shelter unless absolutely necessary, while the other is able to only minimally tolerate the space. Consequently, both clients have had to make alternative sleeping arrangements that have included sleeping in vehicles, couch surfing, and camping outdoors. The documentation of bed nights slept within a shelter generally provides the most easily produced and legitimized form of homelessness verification for housing applications. While case managers can and do provide letters of support stating that their clients are indeed homeless, these letters require some kind of substantiation.

Since the shelter documentation avenue is not open to all, given the reluctance of many clients to stay in a shelter, I proposed the creation of an interagency form that can be used to document overnight homelessness by the Women's Shelter staff, city shelter staff, and potentially the police force. Such a form is a direct response to one of the previously mentioned clients sleeping in a car outside the men's shelter in an effort to demonstrate his homelessness. Other case managers at Providence Street have encountered similar cases that require creative problem-solving strategies to determine how to best obtain homelessness verification. The proposed organizational change—the addition of an interagency homelessness verification form—could provide documented, individual instances of observed overnight homelessness that could then be tallied and communicated among social service providers, given the appropriate informational releases. Therefore, when situations arise in which clients are unable to utilize the shelters, documentation of homelessness would still be possible and the client's needs would be held as paramount. Ideally, this form could also be used by willing police officers when they encounter people experiencing homelessness through the night. Ultimately, the development of this form should involve input from participating agencies; this may also increase their likelihood of using it and providing administrative suggestions, including how best to ensure interagency communication.

THE PRACTICE OF ORGANIZATIONAL CHANGE

Although much of social work practice operates on the micro and mezzo levels, an understanding of macrolevel organizational change processes is invaluable in effecting change at any level. Inevitably, in our social work careers we will identify unmet client needs, social injustices, and ways to enhance the operation of social service agencies in which we are employed. Education about organizational change, both didactic and applied, can provide the necessary knowledge and skills to lay the foundation for change endeavors within our present field placement settings and in the future.

The organizational change literature extends back to the 1950s when Kurt Lewin (1951) developed field theory, which readily lends itself to force field analysis. Force field analysis is used to assess whether a proposed change within the organization is realistically possible. It provides a template for articulating the change goal, identifying relevant variables that can promote or inhibit change, assessing potential resources, providing a means to codify forces at work, and planning appropriate strategies and change tactics (Brager & Holloway, 1978). I used force field analysis in assessing the feasibility of introducing an interagency homelessness verification form at Providence Street. The preliminary force field analysis was characterized by several working forces in favor of the change, but further analysis and information gathering were needed.

Gitterman and Germain (2008) state that a change agent first needs to identify a problem in order to formulate a change goal. Goals should be as realistic as possible. Additionally, they should be concrete enough to operationalize in measurable ways in order to determine whether the goal has been accomplished once the organizational change has been implemented. While force field analysis assists in assessing the overall feasibility of a change goal, the process itself is dynamic and can provide new insights into the viability of the change goal itself as new information is gathered. For example, although my proposed organizational change goal is to introduce an interagency verification form, my original intention to simultaneously target multiple agencies is unrealistic at present because more time is needed to gather information about each agency. Additionally, this form is meant to benefit clients who do not utilize the overnight shelter system. Thus, identification of appropriate clients and orchestrating situations in which verification, using the form, is possible, will take time. While the change goal remains the same, for pragmatic reasons I have focused the implementation of this form among the police force assigned to the city shelter area and among the shelter staff. Essentially, this step will act as a pilot to see if the form, once introduced, is used and is beneficial to case managers and clients in providing homelessness verification.

For the purpose of this chapter, I will focus on presenting information gathered at Providence Street, the city shelter, and the Ocean City Police Department. An initial step in planning a change goal is to understand the agency on the individual, group, and organizational levels (Brager & Holloway, 1978). Often this begins with delineating the organizational structure, in this case the organizational hierarchy that represents each person's position within the agency. Having begun a comprehensive discussion of the organizational structure of Providence Street earlier in this chapter, I will now focus more specifically on the hierarchy within the Providence Street Adult Day Shelter.

Organizational charts assist in identifying the critical actors (those with power to affect the change goal), facilitating actors (those who can influence or have access to the critical actors), and potential allies. Additionally, these charts help clarify who to contact in gathering information for the force field analysis. Figures 14.1, 14.2, and 14.3 show the organizational hierarchies of Providence Street, the city shelter, and the Ocean City Police Department, respectively.

FIGURE 14.1. Organizational Chart of Providence Street Resource Center

Adult Day Shelter Services Coordinator
⇓
Administrative Program Assistant
⇓
Social Work Supervisors (2)
⇓
Full-Time Caseworkers (8)   Employment Caseworkers (2)
⇓
Undergraduate and Graduate Student Interns (3)
⇓
Per Diem Staff
⇓
Volunteers

FIGURE 14.2. Organizational Chart of the City Shelter

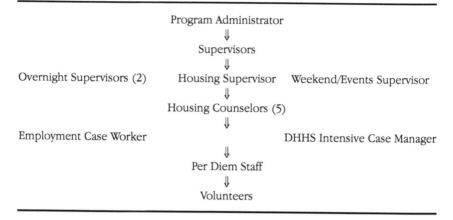

Program Administrator
⇓
Supervisors
⇓
Overnight Supervisors (2)   Housing Supervisor   Weekend/Events Supervisor
⇓
Housing Counselors (5)
⇓
Employment Case Worker   DHHS Intensive Case Manager
⇓
Per Diem Staff
⇓
Volunteers

FIGURE 14.3. Organizational Chart of the Ocean City Police Department

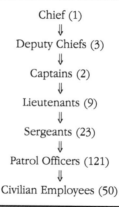

Chief (1)
⇓
Deputy Chiefs (3)
⇓
Captains (2)
⇓
Lieutenants (9)
⇓
Sergeants (23)
⇓
Patrol Officers (121)
⇓
Civilian Employees (50)

The impetus for this organizational change effort was to secure home-lessness verification for clients at Providence Street who do not utilize the overnight shelter system. Initially, another social service provider of one of my clients attempted to advocate for him by asking that city shelter staff keep a record of when this client slept outside the shelter in a vehicle (providing that the client first checked in with desk staff). This strategy was unsuccessful because this provider contacted the Department of Health and Human Services (DHHS) intensive case manager (ICM) who did not know the client directly, was unlikely to encounter him at the shelter, and who was only present at the shelter until mid-evening. Many housing applications require homelessness verification, and further stipulate that verification must be an eyewitness account of someone sleeping in a shelter or other place not intended for human habitation between 12:00 a.m. and 5:00 a.m. I am unaware whether the ICM spoke about this client or his need for homelessness verification with other city shelter staff. My client reported that staff never verified his presence of their own accord or in collaboration with the proposed verification plan.

After contacting the ICM directly and discovering that he is a facilitating actor within my force field analysis, I attempted to contact the overnight supervisors at the city shelter who act as critical actors in that agency. Neither supervisor returned my phone calls. Consequently, I proceeded up the organizational chain of command to direct my energy toward the program administrator. The administrator returned my call and seemed willing to assist in my inquiries. We have since been playing phone tag. Due to the fact that I have not spoken directly to staff other than the ICM, I have been unable to determine if staff is willing to use an interagency homelessness verification form. While I did not approach this subject in a voicemail to the program administrator, I did ask about police presence outside the shelter.

The patrol division at the Ocean City Police Department was the most helpful in explaining the police presence outside the city shelter. As illustrated in the organizational chart (figure 14.3), there are more than 120 patrol officers. Initially, it seemed unrealistic that an interagency form, originating from Providence Street, could gain widespread support and usage from this many officers. Once I learned that there is a regular police presence outside the shelter, I contacted the police department for further information. Currently, there are two officers responsible for responding in the shelter vicinity. However, they are not directly stationed outside the shelter in their patrol cars. These officers cover shifts from 3:00 p.m. to 11:00 p.m., and from 11:00 p.m. to 7:00 a.m. A rotational core of officers is stationed outside the shelter regularly from 6:30 p.m. to 12:30 a.m. This information will enable me to contact a specific set of officers who are familiar with the local population experiencing homelessness in Ocean City and who might be willing to assist in documentation in this geographic area. The Adult Day Shelter services coordinator at Providence Street also suggested that I contact a particular captain within the police force for further assistance.

Overall, Providence Street staff are receptive to the idea of introducing a formalized interagency form that may assist clients in obtaining homelessness verification. The predominant concern is whether other agencies will collaborate in using the form. Figure 14.4 presents the force field analysis thus far. A discussion of the relevant forces will demonstrate how a force field analysis operates to determine if a proposed change goal is feasible.

Organizational change can originate from anywhere in an agency, providing that there is enough support for the change. Brager and Holloway (1993) note that social work practice in the 1970s began to study change efforts prompted by staff and employees who held lower-power positions in

FIGURE 14.4. Force Field Analysis for Interagency Client Verification Project

---

Change Goal:

To develop and introduce an interagency homelessness verification/documentation form for clients who do not utilize the emergency shelter system and who sleep in places not meant for human habitation

---

Critical Actors:

1. Providence Street Adult Day Shelter services coordinator
2. City Shelter program administrator
3. Detective, Ocean City Police Department

Facilitating Actors:

1. Providence Street adult day shelter supervisor #1
2. Providence Street adult day shelter supervisor #2
3. City shelter overnight supervisor #1
4. City shelter overnight supervisor #2
5. City shelter DHHS intensive case manager (ICM)

Potential Allies:

1. Providence Street adult day shelter case workers
2. Providence Street adult day shelter student interns
3. City Shelter housing counselors
4. Clients (who do not utilize the overnight shelter system)
5. Social service agencies (that process housing applications and desire legitimate, quantifiable verification for homelessness status)
6. City Shelter Volunteers

Driving Forces for Change:	*Restraining Forces for Change:*
1. Difficulty verifying personal witness of overnight homelessness experienced by daytime caseworkers and interns (APC = W)	1. Concern and/or resistance toward increased workload (PC = F)
2. Barriers to ensuring housing (APC = W)	2. Negative perceptions of homeless people held by police officers (APC = W)
3. Gaps in system for clients who do not engage in services like overnight emergency shelter (APC? = U)	3. Conflicting philosophies/mission statements among relevant agencies (PC? = F)
4. Similarities in philosophies/mission statements among relevant agencies (APC? = U)	4. Problems with interagency communication (APC? = U)
5. Increase and improvement in interagency communication (APC = W)	5. Denial of a problem (AP = U)
6. Lack of documentation and records (APC = W)	6. Lack of awareness regarding other agencies (APC = W)
	7. Cost of paper and toner to supply forms (PC = F)

Key: A = Amenable force
    W = Working force (High A, P, C)
    P = Potent force
    F = Framing force (High C, Low A)
    C = Consistent force
    U = Unpredictable force (High uncertainty in A, P, or C)

agencies but who desired changes to improve service to clients. Sometimes the professional requirements of an organization can interfere with service delivery; in such cases, organizational change can refocus the agency's work to be more client centered (Gitterman & Germain, 2008). Within field placement settings, interns generally have limited power within the agency. The organizational change effort described in this paper demonstrates a change that was carried out from my low-power position as a graduate student intern. A force field analysis is particularly important in determining whether a given change goal should be attempted. The force field analysis changes as more information is incorporated into it.

The force field analysis in figure 14.4 clearly states what the change goal is, namely to develop and introduce an interagency homelessness verification or documentation form for clients who do not utilize the emergency shelter system and who sleep in places not meant for human habitation. The next two categories identify individuals and groups that have power in relationship to the change goal. These are critical actors and facilitating actors. There are also potential allies from each agency involved, hence a large cast of characters. The identified critical actors are those people who have ultimate decision-making power. This category comprises shelter administrators, coordinators, and high-power police officers. The facilitating actors hold less power than the critical actors, but they are in positions where they can influence these higher-power actors. In this analysis, this category consists of Providence Street and day shelter supervisors and the DHHS ICM. Additionally, while allies may not have power, they can demonstrate support in other meaningful ways, providing strength in numbers. Allies in this change effort include Providence Street case managers and social work interns; other lower-power staff at Providence Street and the city shelter; agencies that process housing applications and desire legitimate, quantifiable homelessness verification; and last, but certainly not least, clients who could potentially benefit from being able to have their homeless status documented.

The next step in conducting a force field analysis involves brainstorming driving forces that can work in favor of the change goal and restraining forces that can work against it. Including others in this process, such as allies or facilitating actors, may bring multiple perspectives and yield a more thorough list of driving and restraining forces. Having more information in the force field analysis can result in a greater understanding of the change process and a more accurate understanding of the feasibility of change.

I identified six driving forces. These were (1) the difficulty for daytime case managers to obtain homelessness verification when verification often requires nighttime eyewitness documentation, (2) stringent verification requirements as a barrier to obtaining housing, (3) gaps in the system for clients on the fringe who do not utilize the overnight shelter system but who are nonetheless homeless, (4) similarities in the philosophical framework and mission statements among potential collaborating agencies, (5) the potential to increase and improve interagency communication, and (6) the general lack of documentation and records regarding homelessness.

The seven potential restraining forces I identified were (1) concern about or resistance by shelter staff and police officers to having an increased workload associated with using the proposed interagency homelessness verification form, (2) negative perceptions of the homeless population on the part of police officers, (3) conflicting philosophical frameworks and mission statements among potential collaborating agencies, (4) problems with interagency communication, (5) denial of the existence of the problem, (6) lack of awareness regarding other social service agencies, and (7) an increase in costs due to the paper and toner required to supply the form within agencies.

Force field analysis conceptualizes these driving and restraining forces as a balance scale in which a disproportionate amount of one or the other creates an environment either open to or opposed to organizational change. Each force is further evaluated on the presence and strength of three attributes: amenability, potency, and consistency (Brager & Holloway, 1978). *Amenability* relates to whether the worker promoting change can influence a force (e.g., whether a driving force can be made more powerful and persuasive or a restraining force can be weakened). *Potency* relates to the degree to which the force will affect the proposed change goal. *Consistency* involves ascertaining the permanency of a force across time. Funding of social service agencies provides a good example of this latter attribute; lack of funding or underfunding of programs can act as a strong, consistent attribute present as a restraining force against change. Referring to figure 14.4, each force is coded for these attributes. The combination of attributes further specifies whether driving and restraining forces are considered to be working, framing, or unpredictable forces in organizational change.

The force field analysis reveals that the proposed change goal to introduce an interagency homelessness verification form is feasible. There are four working, driving forces in favor of the change goal. However, further investigation is needed to understand whether gaps in the system for clients who do not utilize the shelters and the similarities in philosophical frameworks of involved agencies have consistency. Alternatively, opposition to the change goal is demonstrated by two working forces and three framing forces. There are two unpredictable forces (the possibility of issues with interagency communication and the possibility of denying that there is a problem), which need more information. Potentially, these unpredictable forces may be minimized, or eliminated entirely, once more information is gathered. While the force field analysis does not show that the proposed change goal is overwhelmingly feasible, it does indicate that this change has the potential to be accomplished and therefore to benefit clients.

Patti and Resnick (1972) discuss organizational change as phases of creating goals, mobilizing resources, and applying an intervention. After conducting a force field analysis, I am ready to reevaluate the resources available to me to plan how I will introduce an interagency homelessness verification form to Providence Street, the city shelter, and the Ocean City Police Department. The critical and facilitating actors are especially important in this phase because they can provide influence and explicit support for the implementation of this form. In other words, they are potential resources to mobilize. For instance, the Adult Day Shelter service coordinator at Providence Street has offered assistance in reviewing and providing feedback on the proposed form, and I already have initial contact with the program administrator and the ICM at the city shelter regarding difficulty obtaining homelessness verification for particular clients. Captain Messinger at the Ocean City Police Department has a good relationship with Providence Street and may facilitate contact with the regular and rotational officers in the region of the men's shelter, encouraging them to comply with the form. Additionally, the housing counselors at the city shelter may attest to the need for further assistance in providing documentation. While I could not find a mission statement for the city shelter, the mission statements of Providence Street and the Ocean City Police Department are both client oriented.

Providence Street will employ collaborative tactics in implementing the interagency form. The agencies involved, including the subgroup of patrol officers who respond to the city shelter, are all familiar with the homeless population in Ocean City. Both Providence Street and the city shelter actively work to assist in housing clients. Furthermore, the Ocean City Police Department espouses enhancing the quality of life in the city by working with the community to promote a safe environment. There is a high probability that these agencies share goal consensus and will therefore be willing to work together.

Conclusions

Since this organizational change project came about as the result of my difficulties as a case manager in obtaining homelessness verification for my clients seeking housing, the strategy to implement this interagency form will be client centered. Instead of being just another form, filed away and forgotten, there is real potential that this form can gain established use if its benefit to the agencies involved, both in providing services and in promoting social justice, is demonstrated. The introduction of an interagency homelessness verification form is imminent; I hope it will prove useful for clients' agencies and will continue to be used in service delivery.

Epilogue

Several weeks after I completed this assignment, Providence Street approved the Homeless Verification Form (see Appendix 14.1).

REFERENCES

Brager, G., & Holloway, S. (1978). *Changing human service organizations: Politics and practice.* New York: Free Press.

Brager, G., & Holloway, S. (1993). Assessing prospects for organizational change: The uses of force field analysis. *Administration in Social Work, 16*(3/4), 15–28.

Gitterman, A., & Germain, C. (2008). *The life model of social work practice* (3rd ed.). New York: Columbia University Press.

Green, W. (1993). The culture of the non-profit organization. In R. Clifton & A. Dahms (Eds.), *Grassroots organizations: A resource book for directors, staff and volunteers of small, community-based, nonprofit agencies* (2nd ed., pp. 36–46). Long Grove, IL: Waveland Press.

Lewin, K. (1951). *Field theory in social science.* New York: Harper & Row.

Patti, R., & Resnick, H. (1972). Changing the agency from within. *Social Work, 17*(7), 48–57.

APPENDIX 14.1: PROPOSED INTERAGENCY HOMELESSNESS VERIFICATION FORM

Interagency Homelessness Verification Form
Providence Street Resource Center

Client Name:

Date:

Agency Requesting Verification:

Staff Contact Person:

Reason for Request:

Verifying Agency:

Staff Person or Officer (Print):

Staff Person or Officer (Signature):

This serves to verify that _____ resides on the street and was observed sleeping in a place not meant for human habitation overnight.

Narrative:

Contributors

Marcia B. Cohen, PhD, is professor at the University of New England School of Social Work, where she has been on the faculty since 1988. Her areas of scholarship include social movements, homelessness and poverty, mental health, social work practice with groups, and organizational practice. She teaches courses in organizational change, social group work, multilevel practice, and homelessness. Marcia also provides consultation to and serves on the board of several local agencies, including a consumer-run mental health organization. Marcia is a member of the International Association for Social Work with Groups (IASWG), and is cofounder and coeditor of the *Journal of Progressive Human Services: Radical Thought & Praxis*.

Cheryl A. Hyde, PhD, MSW, is associate professor and MSW program director at the Temple University School of Social Work. Her areas of scholarship include community capacity building and civic engagement, multicultural education, feminist theory and practice, organizational transformation, diversity in human service organizations, social movements and social change, socioeconomic power and privilege, and macro practice ethics. Her teaching includes courses on community and policy practice, organizational theory, and societal change. She also facilitates trainings on a variety of topics including human service ethics, working with differences and diversity, creating learning organizations, and supervision. Cheryl serves on several social science and social work journal editorial boards, is on the Sage Advisory Board for Human Services, is former editor of the *Journal of Progressive Human Services*, and is past chair of the Association for Community Organization and Social Administration.

CONTRIBUTORS

Nancy Ayer, MSW, has taught at the University of New England School of Social Work since 1994, prior to which she was a community organizer with a statewide disability rights organization and worked on many local and statewide political campaigns. She received her MSW from West Virginia University in 1976.

Luis Barrios, MSW, is retired. He was formerly director of the Latino Consortium in Chicago.

Jeremy Brown, MSW, is a clinical social worker at the Sebago Education Alliance, a day treatment school that serves multiple districts in southern Maine. Jeremy continues to develop programs and is currently implementing a school-based treatment program using nonelectronic games to teach executive functioning skills to students. He graduated with an MSW degree from the University of New England School of Social Work in 2010.

Edward J. Gumz, PhD, LCSW, is associate professor in the School of Social Work at Loyola University of Chicago. He teaches MSW social policy courses and leadership and development in the social services. His research interests are organizational change, religion and spirituality in social work, and American and international social welfare policy.

Vicky Ha, BSW, is research assistant at the Rush University Medical Center, Chicago.

Helen P. Hartnett, MA, MSW, PhD, is associate professor at West Virginia University, Division of Social Work. She has a record of teaching, research, and service in the areas of homelessness, advocacy and policy practice, community organizing, and the critical evaluation of practice. Her social work practice experience includes a variety of positions in political advocacy, program planning, administration, and research in the area of homelessness.

Nicole Howver is a graduate student pursuing her MSW. She is specializing in child and family welfare. Nicole is interested in working with adolescents in the foster care system and eventually developing a program that helps these juveniles become self-sufficient. Currently she is working in a group facility where she supervises juvenile delinquents and leads them in group discussions.

Jacqueline B. Mondros, DSW, currently serves as dean and professor of the Hunter College School of Social Work. Her research and practice interests are in the study of urban neighborhoods; she has written extensively on community social services, community development, and community organization. In recent years, Jacqueline has focused her scholarship on leadership in human services, and social work education. She is currently working on the implications of social capital for social work.

Judy Peters, MSW, has been employed primarily in medical arenas serving in long-term, acute, and home-care settings. She has a particular interest in working with children and has made this the focus of her studies. Judy received her MSW from the School of Social Work at the University of New England in 2013.

Amy Russell, MSW, continues to work with people experiencing homelessness and issues related to poverty. She is a clinical supervisor and field instructor in Portland, Maine. Amy received her MSW from the University of New England School of Social Work in 2010.

Tanja Schlabitz is director of the Quality and Community Innovation Division within the Halton region's Social and Community Services Department. Tanja has led a number of successful departmental and community initiatives in areas such as housing and homelessness, youth engagement, service coordination, reflective practice, inclusion, and nonprofit sector capacity building. Tanja received a Canadian Public Relations Society Pinnacle award for her work on a communitywide strategy to engage at-risk youth, and the Peter J. Marshall award for her development of a Housing Help Centre model for the Halton region.

Brett Seabury, DSW, is presently emeritus associate professor of social work at the University of Michigan. His academic career has spanned thirty-eight years. He was a member of the Bertha Capen Reynolds Society and later the Social Welfare Action Alliance. Since retirement in 2009, Brett and his wife have raised grass-fed beef, lamb, and natural pork (www.golden fleecefarm.com).

Maria Vidal de Haymes, PhD, is professor in the School of Social Work at Loyola University Chicago, where she teaches social welfare and immigration policy courses. Maria coordinates a migration studies subspecialization and migration-focused international field placements, and is coeditor of the *Journal of Poverty*.

Helen Wong is an organizational development consultant specializing in inclusion and anti-oppression organizational change. She has worked in a variety of fields including settlement, health, and mental health. She is also sessional instructor at Ryerson University. She currently resides near Seattle.

June Ying Yee is associate professor at Ryerson University, School of Social Work, and academic coordinator of the Internationally Educated Social Work Professionals Bridging Program. Her professional and research interests include organizational development, whiteness studies, and antiracism practice.

Index